Legally Speaking

Legally

Speaking

Contemporary
American Culture
and the Law

Helle Porsdam

UNIVERSITY OF MASSACHUSETTS PRESS   Amherst

Copyright © 1999 by
Helle Porsdam
All rights reserved
Printed in the United States of America
LC 98-54186
ISBN 1-55849-207-0 (cloth); 208-9 (pbk.)
Designed by Milenda Nan Ok Lee
Set in Adobe Garamond
Printed and Bound by BookCrafters, Inc.

Library of Congress Cataloging-in-Publication Data

Porsdam, Helle, 1956–
    Legally speaking : contemporary American culture and the law / Helle Porsdam.
        p.   cm.
    Includes bibliographical references and index.
    ISBN 1-55849-207-0 (cloth : alk. paper). — ISBN 1-55849-208-9 (pbk. : alk. paper)
    1. Law—United States.   2. Culture and law.   I. Title.
KF385.P645 1999
349.73—dc21   98-54186
                                                                                CIP

British Library Cataloguing in Publication data are available
This book is published with the support and cooperation of the University of
Massachusetts Boston.

For my parents, Inge and Kjeld Porsdam

Contents

Acknowledgments

I have incurred numerous debts in the course of researching and writing this book. First and foremost, I wish to thank Lewis Sargentich and Alan Trachtenberg. The initial support and continuing encouragement offered by these two mentors, colleagues, and friends meant everything to me—it is not too much to say that without their help I would not have been able to publish this book. Leo Marx deserves thanks too for believing in the book from the very beginning. Venturing as I was into unknown territory, it was invaluable for me to be told that I was on the right track. Thanks also to Jane Marx for taking good care of me and my family during our 1992–93 stay in Boston.

Several Danish and American colleagues read parts of the book and provided me with much-needed advice and information along the way. I wish to thank Marcus Bruce, Dale Carter, David Cowart, Isi Foighel, Mark Gibney, Clara Juncker, Martha Minow, David Nye, Carl Pedersen, Thomas Pettitt, Joel Pfister, Jan Gretlund, Lars Ole Sauerberg, Claus Schatz-Jakobsen, Nils Arne Sørensen, Christen Kold Thomsen, Jens Vedsted-Hansen, and Robert Wells.

Portions of chapters 2, 4, 6, and 9 were previously published in my articles: "In the Age of Lawspeak: Tom Wolfe's *The Bonfire of the Vanities* and American Litigiousness" (*Journal of American Studies* 25.1 [1991]: 39–57); "Law as Soap Opera and Game Show—The Case of *The People's*

Court" (*Journal of Popular Culture* 28.1 [Summer 1994]: 1–15); " 'Embedding Rights Within Relationships'—Gender, Law, and Sara Paretsky" (*American Studies* 39.2 [Fall 1998]); and "Doing What Comes Naturally?—Fish, Posner, and the Law and Literature Enterprise" (*American Quarterly* 44.3 [Sept. 1992]: 494–505). I want to thank the editors of these journals for their help.

Last but not least I wish to use this opportunity to express my thanks to my parents, Inge and Kjeld Porsdam, and to the two men in my life, Matthias Mann and Sebastian Porsdam Mann. It was their love and support that gave me the emotional energy to keep going.

Preface

As a graduate student and teaching assistant in the American studies department at Yale University in the mid-eighties, I used to wonder why so many of the bright young undergraduates in my sections wanted to go to law school after they finished their bachelor's degrees. When I asked them what motivated their interest in pursuing a career in the law, only a few would answer that it had to do with the lucrative salaries and prestige attached to practicing law. For most, the choice of law had something to do either with a wish "to do good" in some general, nonspecified way, or with a wish to defer till some later date any crucial decisions about the future. To these latter, earning a law degree seemed a wise move to make for a young aspiring person in that, rather than predestine you for one particular kind of career, such a degree could get you started on any number of different career paths. With a law degree, there was no telling where you would end up. By going to law school, these students, most of whom were history, English, American studies, or political science majors, told me they would in fact get an extra three years' worth of liberal arts education. This was news to me. None of my friends back home in Denmark who had studied law had ever described their area of study as anything close to general *Bildung*. On the contrary, they considered the law a very specialized, even narrow field of inquiry. If, as a Danish student, you did not exactly know what to do with yourself, you would tend to gravitate in the direction of, say, history, Danish, or political science—certainly *not* in the direction of law.

Here, then, was an interesting cultural difference between Denmark and the United States. The law, as a field of study, a career choice, and a general area of interest, clearly meant something different to Americans than to Danes. The main difference, it became clear to me as I started paying more attention to the ways and workings of American law, lay in people's expectations from the law and lawyers. Whereas in my home country the law is viewed solely as a technical means to achieving a certain end, for Americans the law, in addition to performing such a technical function, also carries a very important symbolic meaning. Unlike Danes, Americans are persuaded that the law, beyond protecting their rights and preserving their liberty, will provide them with truth and meaning—Justice of a higher kind. When a couple of years ago I showed an excerpt from the television show *The People's Court* to my father, a Danish jurist who has been educated in the legal positivist tradition of Danish legal scholar Alf Ross, his reaction was one of stunned silence. Judge Wapner's demeanor and rhetoric reminded him, he then said, more of a priest delivering a sermon to his congregation than a judge handing down a decision. To this day, he also cannot quite believe that what he saw before and during the television show were actually commercials by lawyers and law firms!

It is the role law plays in the formation of American myths and ideologies that is so puzzling to foreigners. American law and American courts have always performed what Kenneth L. Karst calls "a dual constitutional role: not just delimiting the boundaries of individual autonomy and governmental power, but maintaining the institutional base for our nationhood."[1] Much has been thought and written about the law as an instrument of power. From an American studies perspective, however, the role of law in maintaining the American nation and identity is of paramount interest and deserves more careful attention than it has hitherto received.

It is my hope that this book may serve to emphasize the importance of the law to the study of American culture and society. While writing the book, I was struck by the fact that the majority of the people whose work I had been reading and was now quoting were legal scholars. And

---

1. Kenneth L. Karst, *Belonging to America: Equal Citizenship and the Constitution* (New Haven: Yale University Press, 1989), 215.

when, several years ago, I spent a year as a liberal arts fellow at the Harvard Law School, I was surprised at the number of courses taught that focused on the role of law in the formation of American identity and might just as well have been offered in an American studies department. What has only recently begun to register with us in the humanities, it would thus seem, the legal community has been aware of for quite a while: in the discussion of what it means to be an American, the law necessarily forms an important component.

Legally Speaking

Introduction

L aw figures prominently in American culture and society. The current favorite pastime of "lawyer-bashing" testifies to the ambivalence most Americans feel toward lawyers, but when things come to a head it is to jurists, rather than to politicians or even members of the clergy, that Americans turn in their search for answers. All the most important political, social, and cultural discussions are carried out in a legalistic vernacular, aptly termed *rights talk* by Mark Tushnet and Mary Ann Glendon.[1] Regarded by many as the only remaining carrier of the few moral understandings that are still widely shared by an increasingly diverse citizenry, the law has become "the terrain on which Americans are struggling to define what kind of people they are, and what kind of society they wish to bring into being."[2] What in other countries may be seen as merely legal or political-legal expressions and analyses in the United States become the articulation of the ideas and aspirations that define the national identity. Indeed, Sanford Levinson

1. Mary Ann Glendon, *Rights Talk: The Impoverishment of Political Discourse* (New York: Free Press, 1991). Mark Tushnet, "An Essay on Rights," *Texas Law Review* 62.8 (May 1984).

2. Glendon, *Rights Talk,* 3. See also David Ray Papke, "Law in American Culture: An Overview," *Journal of American Culture* 15.1 (1992): 3: "As Americans find and construct meaning in their culture, they are more likely than others to use law, legal premises and legal images to guide them."

has suggested, the United States forms a "faith community," the central sacred text of which is the Constitution. In America, rather than being a *consequence* of national history, constitutional history has *shaped* that history. To be an American means to be a member of the "covenanting community" of the Constitution.[3]

With the Constitution serving as the "constituent agent" of American identity and the central feature of American "civil religion,"[4] it is no wonder that the law has come to make itself felt at virtually every level of American society. "In a nation lacking either an established order or an established church to produce the social cement of legitimate authority, from the beginning Americans turned the rule of law into a 'civil religion'," as Morton J. Horwitz puts it.[5] In contemporary America, it will be argued in this book, the law has come to affect not only people's everyday lives but also their consciousness or mentality, their way of thinking about and formulating social, political, moral, and cultural issues. Historian Jerold S. Auerbach describes the situation in this way:

> By now the predominance of law as a cultural force is beyond dispute. It might be measured by the assertive role of the Supreme Court (whether heroic or villainous is beyond the point); by the hypnotic allure of the courtroom trial as a staple of national melodrama; by the astonishing attractiveness of the legal profession as a career choice. No longer is it possible to reflect seriously about American culture without accounting for the centrality of law in American history and society, and in the mythology of American uniqueness and grandeur.[6]

A number of aspects and facets of contemporary American political and social life testify to this "predominance of law." New statutes and regulations are increasing at exponential rates at all levels of government. The same can be said of reported decisions by courts and administrative agencies. Statutory codes are becoming longer, more complex, and less comprehensible. "Hypernomia" is the name Ralf Dahrendorf

---

3. Sanford Levinson, *Constitutional Faith* (Princeton, N.J.: Princeton University Press, 1988), 95.

4. Ibid., 5, 90.

5. Morton J. Horwitz, *The Transformation of American Law, 1870–1960* (Cambridge, Mass.: Harvard University Press, 1991), 193.

6. Jerold S. Auerbach, *Justice without Law? Resolving Disputes without Lawyers* (New York and Oxford: Oxford University Press, 1983), 115.

has given to this inflation of laws and to the accompanying growth of norms, sanctions, and institutions.[7] Since 1980, the budget of the U.S. Department of Justice has more than quadrupled. In this period as well, the Justice Department's payroll has expanded from 53,400 to nearly 98,000, growing four and a half times faster than federal civilian payrolls as a whole.[8] Likewise, in this century, the number of lawyers has grown twice as fast as the general population. In 1980, 541,000 lawyers were in practice; in 1990, the number was close to 800,000.[9]

> Both in absolute numbers and in proportion to population, American lawyers constitute the largest legal profession in the world. They are also the wealthiest, particularly at the upper extreme but also on average. And they are the most politically powerful, dominating legislatures and executives, both national and state, more strongly than in any other country. Even culturally they are among the most prominent, ranging from mythic figures like Abraham Lincoln to the morally ambiguous but perhaps even better known characters in the mass media, such as the television serial "L.A. Law."[10]

Not everyone would agree with the long-running cliché that Americans are facing a litigation "explosion." Law professor Marc Galanter, for example, has posed a significant challenge to the popular assumption that the United States is going through a litigation crisis.[11] Nor would everyone agree that law functions as the keystone of American civil religion. Lately, there has been an increasing dispute, among political scientists especially, as to whether ordinary Americans are as deferential to judges and courts as particular public figures and scholars have maintained. Thus, Gerald Rosenberg has argued in *The Hollow Hope,* for example, that the Supreme Court played only a minor role in the great civil rights struggles of the 1950s and '60s, and that the importance of

7. Ralf Dahrendorf, *Law and Order,* The Hamlyn Lectures (London: Stevens and Sons, 1985), 146.

8. *Forbes,* Mar. 15, 1993, 91.

9. *The Economist,* Nov. 10, 1990, 28.

10. Richard L. Abel, *American Lawyers* (New York and Oxford: Oxford University Press, 1989), 3.

11. In one of his most influential essays on this issue from 1986, "The Day after the Litigation Explosion," even Galanter admits, however, that "law as a system of symbols has expanded; information about law and its workings is more widely and vividly circulated to more educated and receptive audiences" (*Maryland Law Review* 46.3 [1986]: 38).

Brown v. *Board of Education of Topeka* has been exaggerated by law professors who have a professional stake in overemphasizing the significance of what they professionally study.[12]

While Rosenberg concludes that it was the Civil Rights Act of 1964, not the courts, which put an end to segregation, he hardly takes into consideration the enormous *symbolic* meaning that the *Brown* decision had. Why was it, for example, that the executive and legislative branches did nothing before *Brown* was decided? And what was the impact of the case on African American leaders and the civil rights movement in general?[13] As I see it, *Brown*—and other important Supreme Court opinions—put questions of race and equality on the social agenda, thereby contributing to long-term attitude changes concerning the meaning of American values. If only indirectly, the law influences what Lauren Edelman has called "the normative environment."[14]

In what follows it is precisely the symbolic value of law, the attitudes, ideas, values, and beliefs that people hold about law and the importance they attach to legal decisions, that is of interest. The law provides a kind of "cultural glue,"[15] I shall argue, that binds a diverse nation, serving as a focus of values and aspirations that define the American people. It is not just that the legal dimension of affairs is particularly prominent in the United States, nor just that people turn to the courts more often, on more matters, than elsewhere. Americans turn to the courts with a particular kind of faith, and hope, which survives at a deep level despite all the disappointments and frustrations of the legal process. Deep down, Americans are not just stuck with law, they want to be—all complaints about hypernomia, litigiousness, greedy lawyers, and the adversary system run wild notwithstanding.

If the cultural life of the nation may in any way be considered a reliable gauge, a cursory look at the number of films, television series, and books currently being produced and written suffices to diagnose the United States as a thoroughly law-permeated country. The television

12. Gerald Rosenberg, *The Hollow Hope* (Chicago: University of Chicago Press, 1991).

13. These are questions asked by Stewart Macauley, Lawrence M. Friedman, and John Stookey in *Law and Society: Readings on the Social Study of Law* (New York: Norton, 1995), 589.

14. Lauren Edelman. Quoted in Macauley, Friedman, and Stookey, *Law and Society*, 591.

15. The phrase is Kenneth L. Karst's. See his *Belonging to America: Equal Citizenship and the Constitution* (New Haven, Conn.: Yale University Press, 1989), 29.

series *L.A. Law,* Tom Wolfe's *The Bonfire of the Vanities,* and Scott Turow's *Presumed Innocent*—popular both as novels and as films—are but three examples of cultural products that appealed to the American public in the 1980s. In the 1990s, films such as *A Few Good Men, Philadelphia,* and *The Sweet Hereafter* have reflected American interests in law and lawyers. Books with titles such as *The Lure of the Law: Why People Become Lawyers, and What the Profession Does to Them* and *Lawyers and the American Dream* catch the eye at bookstores all over the country.[16] Up through the 1980s and into the 1990s, one of the ten most popular syndicated television shows was *The People's Court,* presided over by Judge Joseph A. Wapner. Broadcast daily and seen by more than twenty million Americans, this mixture of fact and fiction became so popular that Wapner reached the status of a folk hero. *The People's Court* was revived in 1996. In the new version, which has also become popular, it is former mayor of New York Ed Koch who is the presiding judge. Last but not least, American television viewers have been presented with a new cable offering, the Courtroom Television Network, which broadcasts court cases live. Since Court-TV made its debut in 1991, it has had high daytime ratings, helped along by hotly publicized proceedings such as the William Kennedy Smith rape trial and the O. J. Simpson murder trial.

American commitments to the ideal of law are not new. Since lawyers figured prominently among the founders of the new republic, the country was based on law and on a legal system that centered on litigation. Indeed, with a Declaration of Independence that made not only a moral and political but also a legal case for separation, the Revolution itself was defined in legal terms.[17] In *Rights Talk,* Mary Ann Glendon distin-

16. Richard W. Moll, *The Lure of the Law: Why People Become Lawyers, and What the Profession Does to Them* (New York: Penguin, 1990); Stuart M. Speiser, *Lawyers and the American Dream* (New York: M. Evans, 1993).

17. Cf. the point Robert Ferguson makes in " 'Mysterious Obligation': Jefferson's *Notes on the State of Virginia*" that after having realized that the bulk of the New World remained too remote to allow the use of natural philosophy as the primary structural principle for his *Notes,* Jefferson "turned for relief to the mode of intellectual control he knew best, the law. What does surprise one is the rich implementation of this decision within the structure of *Notes.* The civic tones and disjointed forms of early republican literature take on fresh meaning when we realize that the legal philosophy of the Enlightenment gave Jefferson more than an alternative for discursive method; it also provided an ideal solution to his structural problems. Legal formulation assumed a pattern to incremental knowledge that enabled Jefferson to fuse the organizational needs of *Notes*

guishes two "moments" in the recent history of human rights. "The first of these moments was marked by the late eighteenth-century American and French revolutionary declarations, and the second by the wave of constitution-making and the international human rights movement that emerged in the wake of World War II." At both moments, Glendon tells us, the path taken by the United States was somewhat different from that taken by most European nations. Then, as now, the distinctive traits of the American "rights dialect" were puzzling to foreigners.[18] Thus, to Alexis de Tocqueville, "the judicial organization of the United States is the hardest thing there for a foreigner to understand. He finds judicial authority invoked in almost every political context, and from that he naturally concludes that the judge is one of the most important political powers in the United States."[19]

It is with the second "moment" in the history of human rights, or rather with the effects of this second moment on American society and the American psyche, that this book is concerned. After the Second World War, according to Glendon, "the various streams of ideas about rights that had been agitating Western minds for over two hundred years coalesced into a universal language of rights. In the United States, legal and popular rights discourse intensified in the 1950s and 1960s."[20] Along with an increasing governmental steering of social and economic life, the United States has witnessed in the latter part of the twentieth century a rise in litigation as a way of doing good. By the 1970s, popular writer Walter K. Olson claims in *The Litigation Explosion: What Happened When America Unleashed the Lawsuit,* lawsuits had increasingly come to be described "as litigious persons themselves describe them, as assertions of rights."[21] The aim of this book is to show the extent to which the law has penetrated into and shaped contemporary American culture. The first chapter will be dedicated to an analysis of American exceptionalism and the question of whether or not it still makes sense in today's multicultural environment to talk about one American nation. It

---

to a developmental sense of country" (*American Literature* 52.3 [Nov. 1980], reprinted in Peter S. Onuf, ed., *American Culture 1776–1815,* vol. 12, *The New American Nation, 1775– 1820* [New York and London: Garland Publishing, 1991], 99–100).

18. Glendon, *Rights Talk,* 10.

19. Alexis de Tocqueville, *Democracy in America* (New York: Doubleday, 1969), 99.

20. Glendon, *Rights Talk,* 38.

21. Walter K. Olson, *The Litigation Explosion: What Happened When America Unleashed the Lawsuit* (New York: Dutton, 1991), 4.

will be argued—first in a general and speculative way and then in the context of Melissa Fay Greene's *Praying for Sheetrock* and David L. Kirp, John P. Dwyer, and Larry A. Rosenthal's *Our Town: Race, Housing, and the Soul of Suburbia*—that any discussion about American exceptionalism will have to take into account the role of law and lawyers in American culture and history. It will furthermore be argued that American beliefs in the law as a way to do good, that is, in judicial activism, are rooted in the common law.

Here, as throughout the book, when I talk about the "common law" I do not mean a particular body of legal rules that are different from legislated rules. I mean, rather, a way of looking at law and a way of arguing legally that operate as much in constitutional cases as in areas like torts and contracts. This common-law conception focuses on concrete cases, emphasizes the practical wisdom of judges, understands law to have a moral dimension, and sees law as coming "up" from society to courts, not just "down" from judges to the people. Law so conceived provides a vocabulary that recognizes people's aspirations for rights and justice and provides a forum in which a common discussion may be conducted within a society of diverse groups having no (other) common religion.

Chapters two through eight will concentrate on cultural products—mainly works of literature—in which the law and lawyers play a dominant role. Fairly representative of the contemporary cultural production, these products all display an interesting and telling link between cultural products, analyses of self and society, and the law. Each chapter will focus on a particular aspect or topic concerning law and American culture, which will then be set off, as it were, or illuminated by a cultural text whose thematic contents touch on what has just been discussed. Despite the literary bias evident in my selection of texts, what interests me in this book is less the literary traditions out of which these texts grow as such, but rather the narrative patterns and discursive effects in both literature and popular culture that combine to articulate American commitments to law. Among the texts I have chosen to discuss, furthermore, while the majority belong to American popular culture, there are also a few that may be said to represent the more serious end of the cultural spectrum. Commitment to the ideal of law and faith, despite everything in law's promise, it is important to note, are not just to be found in popular culture; they are also alive and well in more elitist circles.

In chapters two and three, on Tom Wolfe's *The Bonfire of the Vanities* and Scott Turow's *One L, Presumed Innocent, The Burden of Proof,* and *Pleading Guilty,* respectively, the law and the legal system function as a point of departure for a commentary on or criticism of contemporary American society. To both Wolfe and Turow, things are not working out in contemporary America, in large part because the legal system has degenerated into a power-game for greedy and opportunistic lawyers. Everybody is suing everybody else, tipping the pendulum in favor of the pragmatic, "see-you-in-court" level of American law. Lawyers and their clients, Wolfe and Turow admonish, would do well to pay more attention to the quest for truth and justice to which common lawyers of old pledged themselves. In Wolfe's novel, law's promise of unity and reconciliation of differences is merely hinted at in the character of one of the minor players in the Sherman McCoy case, Judge Kovitsky. Within the universe of Turow's "lawyerly" books, on the other hand, it plays a much more prominent role.

Chapter four is an analysis of the original version of the television show *The People's Court.* What made this daily half-hour show so enormously popular with the American public, it will be argued, was not so much the fact that *The People's Court,* to a much larger extent than any of the other shows offered on American television, was "authentic" in that it featured real people and real cases, but rather the fact that the man on the bench, Judge Wapner, was the veritable personification of a common-law judge. In the most fatherly and dignified manner, this Solomon of the small-claims court handed out justice and advice, making his audience believe, at least for as long as they were watching the show, that American ideals of equality and liberty for all are still alive and well. Wapner's decision-making was fast and authoritative. It combined a commonsensical assessment of what currently will or will not pass as acceptable behavior in American society with a belief in Higher Justice. What is hinted at in Wolfe and much debated in Turow here comes to full expression: the recognition that in the authoritative decision-making of a quasi-moral sort, so familiar to us from the Anglo-American common-law tradition, lies much of law's current appeal.

Having identified as a major reason for the popularity of these cultural products their preoccupation with law's meaning in contemporary America in general and the promise of unity and reconciliation inherent in the common law in particular, I shall then move on to discuss, in chapters five and six, the role that law has played and is still playing in the areas of race and gender. In *And We Are Not Saved* (1987) and *Faces at the Bottom of the Well* (1992), law professor Derrick Bell criticizes the belief among civil rights advocates that racism can be effectively fought with the enactment and subsequent enforcement of civil rights laws. Rather than keep searching for progress in American race relations via the courts, he claims, blacks and other minority groups would be much better off fighting their battle in the political arena. A former student of Bell's, Patricia Williams, disagrees with Bell and his critical legal views. What Bell and others forget when they wish to discard rights altogether, she maintains in *The Alchemy of Race and Rights* (1991), is that for blacks "rights" has always been an important symbol holding out a promise of empowerment. It is to this discussion among black scholars about the utility of a rights-based fight for racial equality that chapter five is dedicated.

Chapter six explores the issue of gender. Much like the battle for racial equality, the fight for equality between the sexes has been a legal one. The resulting focus on a morality of rights has been much debated by feminists, especially since Carol Gilligan began in the mid-eighties to talk about a female "different voice" and a female morality, not of rights, but of care and responsibility. Notwithstanding criticisms voiced against the law and legal reasoning for relying on and catering to male norms, however, most American feminists have never entirely abandoned the rhetoric of rights. What they have attempted, instead, is to find a workable synthesis or reconciliation of female and male values, connecting female interests in relationships to prior male frameworks emphasizing rights and differences between people. And in so doing, chapter six argues, they have relied on a common-law vocabulary which, in its combination of theory and practice, equity and equality, holds out a promise of incorporation and synthesis. One arena in which the tension between the promise of individual rights and a morality of care and a possible reconciliation of the two has been in focus over the past two decades is feminist detective fiction. Here I shall look at the novels of Sara Paretsky, in the development of whose protagonist from autonomous selfhood to a selfhood embedded within relationships we recognize the development advocated by many American feminists.

The topic under consideration in chapter seven is the abortion debate. The heated discussion concerning the right to choose versus the right to life is a prime example of an essentially moral and political, that is nonlegal, issue that invariably ends up being treated as if it were a legal issue. As in other contemporary American debates, the underlying assumption is that everything that is wrong can or must be made illegal. The key concern for everyone involved, I shall contend, is the question of control—who is or ought to be in control over that fateful decision whether or not to terminate a pregnancy: the individual woman or her medical doctor/family/community, the judicial or the legislative branch of the government, man or God? The pro-choice side rests its case on a right to privacy argument, that is, on a common-law argument. In this, one of the most important of contemporary debates, in other words, the common law sets the parameters for discussion, thereby showing its continued influence on American ways of thinking and arguing.

As in the preceding chapters, the theoretical and speculative parts will be followed by a "case study" of a cultural text. The text used in this chapter is Margaret Atwood's *The Handmaid's Tale* (1985). Projected into the near future, the Republic of Gilead described by Atwood in the novel is a curious mixture of a medieval-style theocracy and a futuristic dystopia in which individual initiative and autonomy have been severely limited. Decisions—essentially those concerning female reproduction—are made, not by the individuals involved, but by the leaders of Gilead. Atwood's message is that no matter how much we may dislike current tendencies to turn everything into a question of individual rights and may lament the destruction of communitarian impulses, the threat to modern democratic ways of thinking presented by such tendencies is only minor compared to that presented by the loss of autonomy as guaranteed by due process of law. Never one to miss an opportunity to criticize the United States and the influence on her native Canada of American popular culture, Atwood in this novel interestingly enough comes very close to vindicating American liberal notions of individuality and autonomy.

Chapter eight offers a discussion of William Gaddis's *A Frolic of His Own*. Gaddis is one of the most highly regarded, yet least read novelists in America. This may have to do with the fact that his novels are highly intellectual and therefore somewhat difficult to read. *A Frolic of His Own* from 1994 is much more accessible than his previous novels, however. It is also funnier and has earned for its author a much wider readership than its predecessors. With his fourth novel, Gaddis tapped into the popular fascination with law, which is everywhere in *A Frolic of His Own*. The main characters are all involved in one or more lawsuits, and they all seem convinced that the place to turn for answers, for definitions of right and wrong, is the country's justice system. Gaddis ridicules law-permeated America, and he suggests that whereas the legal system may once have been able to supply the kind of redemptive justice contemporary Americans are yearning for, it has become too wordy and bureaucratic to do so today. Yet his satirical attacks never obscure his affection for the law and for the people for whom it has developed into an ideology.

A Frolic of His Own is about old-fashioned themes such as divided selves, the originality of art, and the corruption of the ideal and the aspirational by the vulgar; in addition, the novel also deals with more contemporary themes such as the impact of multiculturalism on national and personal identity. Some of these themes have been dealt with before by Gaddis. What makes *A Frolic of His Own* significant within the context of this book, however, is the way in which Gaddis uses the law and the legal system as a point of departure for a discussion of the various cultural debates presently ravaging the United States.

Finally, in chapter nine the focus will be on the law and literature movement. An interdisciplinary invention which has emerged at American universities within the past twenty years and has become remarkably successful, this movement mirrors the general preoccupation with law and lawyers so evident in the texts explored in the preceding chapters. What we see here, it will be argued, is the academic equivalent of *The People's Court*. In a country as law-permeated as the United States, there is nothing puzzling about the fact that one of the most important current intellectual discourses involves the law.

The law and literature debate has evolved around the issue of interpretation. Beyond interpretation, I shall maintain, the real concern of the participants in the debate is whether the incorporation into the disciplines of law of postmodern critical literary theory and methods will endanger the modernist foundation for American self-identification, and whether law's promise of unity and integration, so central to modernist jurisprudence, will be removed by the condition of postmodernity. Faced with the threat to American unity and nationhood inherent in postmodern ways of thinking, most scholars recoil from embracing these ways of thinking in their entirety. What most of them end up doing is to perform a leap of legal faith—their awareness of and, especially in the case of scholars on the Left, their affinity with postmodern critical theories notwithstanding, they consciously choose to remain within a modernist frame of thinking. As in American culture at large, we see in the law and literature movement an effort to reaffirm the modernist legal foundation on which the American experiment rests. The language and way of arguing employed in the process have their origin in the common law.

Finally, a word about the attempt to bring together two fields of inquiry. Being interdisciplinary, as Stanley Fish once remarked, "is so very hard to do."[22] Addressing so broad a topic in so relatively few pages means that I will be painting with a broad brush. There will undoubtedly be texts or discussions from American cultural life that some readers will find missing. There will likewise no doubt be discussions in the coming chapters that to people with a legal background may seem somewhat superficial, but that people with an American studies background may learn something from—and vice versa. Let me say, therefore, with historian Jerold S. Auerbach, one of the first scholars within the humanities to show a serious interest in the law: "The examples in this book could easily be multiplied tenfold—without, however, decisively altering the conclusions. As I learned, fortunately before the book became my life's work, the patterns are more important than the particulars; it is the meaning, not the minutiae, that matters."[23]

22. Stanley Fish, *There's No Such Thing as Free Speech: And It's a Good Thing Too* (New York: Oxford University Press, 1994), 231.
23. Auerbach, *Justice without Law?*, 16.

"They Came to Lawyers, You Know, What Can You Do?"

American Exceptionalism and Judicial Activism

The concept of American exceptionalism—that is, the claim that America is not only different from other countries, but also unique in a fundamentally benevolent way[1]—has recently been the target of heavy criticism. Implicit in "exceptionalism," critics claim, is an attempt to characterize American society as a unified whole, and in a completely multicultural society any talk of a national character makes little sense. Historian Joyce Appleby is one critic who has taken issue with American exceptionalism. In her presidential address to the Organization of American Historians in the spring of 1992, she described it as a version, or rather perversion, of European Enlightenment ideas. The grand narrative of American exceptionalism, she argued, has been "America's peculiar form of Eurocentrism." It has ignored the "original and authentic diversity" in America's past, especially the colonial past, and has foreclosed "other ways of interpreting the meaning of the United States." It has cast into the shadows experiences of people whose errand has not been self-promotion and autonomy, and it has imbued

---

The title of this chapter is from Melissa Fay Greene, *Praying for Sheetrock* (New York: Fawcett Columbine, 1991), 175.

1. For an interesting reassessment of the debates concerning American exceptionalism in the light of the previous twenty years' scholarly inquiry, see Michael Kammen, "The Problem of American Exceptionalism: A Reconsideration," *American Quarterly* 45 (1993): 1–43.

with universality particular social traits—virtually all white and male. When looking at the American past and present through the lens of American exceptionalism, therefore, American historians and others have been blinded to the importance of the multicultural agenda, and the time has now come to move beyond exceptionalism "to recover the historic diversity of our past."[2]

For fashioning out of American exceptionalism an ideology that would unite all Americans, Appleby blames the country's lawyers. At the time of the Revolution, the few things that all Americans actually did have in common were British in origin and consequently had to be redefined. Among ordinary Americans, moreover, there existed no great wish to form "a more perfect union." What mattered to most people were local ties, local politics. When, therefore, nationalist leaders, most of whom were lawyers, took it upon themselves to turn American exceptionalism into a unifying ideology, they did not enjoy the support of the people:

> The case for a "more perfect union" was made in a lawyerly fashion by nationalist leaders, most of them lawyers. Outside of their circles, there were abroad in the land few common sentiments, fewer shared assumptions operating at the intimate level of human experience, and a paucity of national symbols recognizable from Georgia to Maine.[3]

Joyce Appleby is not the only critic to point to the role of law and lawyers in the creation of an exceptional United States. Nor is she alone in criticizing the general unwillingness to deal with America's multicultural histories. Unlike some of her colleagues, however, Appleby fails to point out that American common law and judicial activism are an important part of the legacy of America's colonial past.[4] The very multiculturalism that she celebrates in her presidential address has been fostered by activist lawyers and judges, most notably in the Civil Rights movement. Down through American history, the law and the courts, by providing social definitions for events and transactions, and by extending citizenship to previously "unwanted" groups of people, have con-

2. Joyce Appleby, "Recovering America's Historic Diversity: Beyond Exceptionalism," *Journal of American History* 79 (1992): 420, 431.

3. Ibid., 422.

4. See e.g., Gordon S. Wood, "The Origins of Judicial Review," *Suffolk University Law Review* 22 (1988): 1293–1307.

stituted one of the few fora or "things" all Americans have in common. "Can a multicultural nation of nearly a quarter of a billion people be a community?" asks Kenneth Karst in *Belonging to America*. His answer is a resounding yes; being an American essentially means adhering to the American civic culture and behaving according to that culture's norms. Karst's civic culture is made up of five elements: individualism, egalitarianism, democracy, nationalism, and tolerance of diversity, and what ties these elements together is an ideology, "a creed that is both manifested in our constitutional doctrine and shaped by it."[5] In Karst's version of American exceptionalism, that is, it is the law that translates ideology into behavior.

Lawrence M. Friedman has talked about an "American legal culture,"[6] Sanford Levinson about an American "faith community" centered around the Constitution,[7] and Mary Ann Glendon about American "rights talk" and "law-riddenness"[8]—others have referred to American legalism or legalization. Like Kenneth Karst, these commentators on American culture and society tend to see the law and its practitioners as protectors and translators into actual day-to-day behavior of American exceptionalism. This chapter will argue that any discussion about American exceptionalism will have to take into account the role of law and lawyers in American culture. Section one will focus, in a general and speculative way, on judicial activism. In a contemporary perspective, the term "judicial activism" is most often used about the period roughly from *Brown* v. *Board of Education of Topeka* in 1954 to *Roe* v. *Wade* in 1973—a period in which judges actively promoted social transformation to enforce new rights for African Americans and other minorities. In this rather specific sense, today's judges are not as activist as their predecessors thirty or forty years ago. But "judicial activism" has a deeper sense, too; it

5. Kenneth L. Karst, *Belonging to America: Equal Citizenship and the Constitution* (New Haven, Conn.: Yale University Press, 1989), 182, 31.

6. Lawrence M. Friedman, "American Legal Culture: The Last Twenty-Five Years," *St. Louis Law Journal* 35 (1991): 529. Reprinted in Stewart Macauley, Lawrence M. Friedman, and John Stookey, eds., *Law and Society: Readings on the Social Study of Law* (New York: Norton, 1995), 271–77. This legal culture is defined as "the attitudes and expectations of the public with regard to law."

7. Sanford Levinson, *Constitutional Faith* (Princeton, N.J.: Princeton University Press, 1988).

8. Mary Ann Glendon, *Rights Talk: The Impoverishment of Political Discourse* (New York: The Free Press, 1991).

refers to the idea of law responding to social need and social change and to a responsive judiciary committed to the protection of rights and the active inclusion of everyone, by law, in community life. In this deeper sense, the whole period after *Brown* may be seen as one period. In what follows, it is this deeper sense of judicial activism that is of interest.

As illustrations or case studies of how judicial activism works in practice, I shall then turn, in section two, to Melissa Fay Greene, *Praying for Sheetrock* (1991), and David L. Kirp, John P. Dwyer, and Larry A. Rosenthal, *Our Town: Race, Housing, and the Soul of Suburbia* (1995). The former is a study of how civil rights came to McIntosh County, Georgia, in the 1970s, and the latter tells the story of the creation of something like a right to fair housing in New Jersey over a period of two decades. In both books, judicial activism markets "a very new commodity: Law. For the poor"[9]—a commodity that seeks to desegregate, to include those who have hitherto not been seen as welcome additions to American society.

The assumption throughout will be that the arguments advanced by Kenneth Karst and other believers in American exceptionalism are ultimately more persuasive than are those of Joyce Appleby.

JUDICIAL ACTIVISM: THE THEORY

In an interesting article called "The 'Hegelian Secret': Civil Society and American Exceptionalism," Daniel Bell argues first of all that it does make sense to talk about American differentness, and second, that this differentness has to do with the United States' being a "complete *civil society,* perhaps the only one in political history." By "civil society" Bell means a society in which individual self-interest and a passion for liberty reign supreme. In such a society, no institutional structures—no state in a European sense—have been created "to shape and enforce a unitary will over and above particular interests." What has taken the place of a state in the United States, Bell argues, is a government or political marketplace, "an area in which interests contended (not always equally) and where deals could be made." The foundation for the American civil society has been inalienable, naturally endowed rights inhering in each individual rather than in a group or a community of people, and institutions have been created for the purpose of protecting these rights.

9. Greene, *Praying for Sheetrock,* 158.

Among such institutions, the Supreme Court has played a very special and very important role:

> Fortuitously, for it was not planned (nor were these powers specified in the Constitution), the Supreme Court became the final arbiter of disputes, and the mechanism for the adjustment of rules, which allowed the political marketplace to function, subject to the amendment of the Constitution itself—which then again was interpreted by the court. The Constitution and the court became the bedrock of civil society.

The Constitution, Bell suggests, has provided a social contract,

> a contract initially between the several states, yet transferred over time as a social contract between the government and the people. It may be the only successful social contract we know in political history, perhaps because the state was so weak and often non-existent.[10]

Americans have remained committed to constitutionalism and to the ideal of a responsive judiciary. From the Supreme Court down, courts have generally been perceived to have a special responsibility as arbiters, even legitimators, of change. The degree of authority that American judges exercise is unparalleled among modern Western nations. Americans tend to take this for granted, writes Gordon S. Wood,

> but any foreign observer is immediately overwhelmed by the extent to which the courts not only set aside laws passed by popularly elected legislatures but also interpret and construe the law in such a way as to make social policy. It is not simply the power of the Supreme Court, which tends to be the focus of our attention, but the power of all courts, both federal and state, to interpret the law in accordance with either written constitutions or fundamental principles of justice and reason that is impressive. Nowhere else in the modern world do judges wield as much power in shaping the contours of life as they do in the United States.[11]

10. Daniel Bell, "The 'Hegelian Secret': Civil Society and American Exceptionalism," in *Is America Different? A New Look at American Exceptionalism,* ed. Byron E. Shafer (New York: Oxford University Press, 1991), 60, 66, 62.

11. Wood, "Origins of Judicial Review," 1293.

Law professors and political experts engage in lengthy and complicated discussions from time to time as to the desirability for a modern democracy such as the American of having the courts resolve issues that are essentially political.[12] In other modern democracies issues concerning, for example, racial desegregation, abortion, or the relationship between religion and the government would be looked upon as political matters which ought to be determined by parliamentary legislation.[13]

When legal and political commentators criticize this exercise of judicial authority as unwarranted and issue warnings against judicial encroachment or usurpation, however, their criticism does not seem to meet with much approval from the general public. The staying power of the ideal of a responsive judiciary, as well as of the most important "tool" with which the Supreme Court pursues this ideal, judicial review, "is an undeniable historical fact," according to Kenneth Karst. He claims that we can talk about an American "natural-rights mentality"—a mentality that, "accompanied by a receptiveness to judicial review, has stayed rooted in the popular folklore for reasons only indirectly related to democracy, either economic or political."[14] As we shall see shortly, natural-rights doctrines such as substantive due process and its modern offshoots in the equal-protection field have their origins in the common law.

The Supreme Court first claimed the power of judicial review in *Marbury* v. *Madison* (1803). The practice of judicial review has been "so extraordinary, so pervasive, and so powerful," however, claims Gordon Wood, that we have to look beyond this particular decision to the history of American jurisprudence and American legal culture as a whole to discover its origins. In colonial America, old beliefs in law as something discovered, not made, lingered on long after such beliefs had

---

12. Cf. Geoffrey C. Hazard, who notes: "In case no one has noticed, it should be reported that these days some very intense debates are going on in political and legal philosophy. These debates concern what our society should be like and how decisions about it should be made, and particularly who should make those decisions. One of the primary issues of those debates is the legitimacy of what lawyers and judges do, particularly appellate judges and more particularly Supreme Court justices" ("Rising above Principle," *University of Pennsylvania Law Review* 135.1 [1986]: 153).

13. For an interesting recent attack on judicial activism see Susan V. Demers, "The Failures of Litigation as a Tool for the Development of Social Welfare Policy," *Fordham Urban Law Journal* 22.4 (1995): 1009–50.

14. Karst, *Belonging to America*, 222.

been effectively discredited in the mother country by positivist thinkers such as John Austin. The colonists "were much more conscious than their English cousins of the distinctiveness of the common law—as something set apart from statutory law and even from current English judicial decisions and precedents," and persisted in identifying the common law with "right reason or natural justice—with principles that existed apart from current English statutes and judicial decisions."[15]

The continued American preoccupation with the morality of law was a result of the ambiguities and complexities of colonial law. Judges had to take into consideration before handing down their decisions not only English legal sources (common-law reports, new judicial interpretations, and parliamentary statutes) but also local colonial statutes and judicial customs. Often, conditions would be so different in the New World that no suitable precedents could be found in English law, or local customs so undeveloped that judges had to take recourse to the immutable maxims of reason or justice. The extraordinary degree of judicial discretion that was needed under these circumstances paved the way for judicial review:

> Amidst the confusion and disorder of colonial law, lawyers and judges found that they had really no other basis except reason and equity for clarifying their law and for justifying their deviations from English practice. By resting their law on some principle beyond statutory will or the technicalities of the common law—on justice or common sense or utility—the colonists prepared the way for what we came to know as judicial review.[16]

With the exception of the infamous *Dred Scott* case in 1857, the Supreme Court made little use of its power to declare statutes unconstitutional until the late nineteenth and early twentieth centuries.[17] Prior to the Second World War, the Court reviewed mainly cases involving claims of economic right. It was only after the Second World War and in particular with *Brown* v. *Board of Education* that the Court started concentrating on the rights of the underprivileged.

15. Wood, "Origins of Judicial Review," 1296, 1299.

16. Ibid., 1302–3.

17. It should be noted, however, that the Court did strike down a number of *state* statutes before the Civil War.

The truth is, that where rights pertaining to fair criminal procedure, equal legal treatment, free expression, or privacy are concerned, the United States Supreme Court has only a slightly longer experience than a great number of other nations. For us, too the great expansion of personal liberties and civil rights began in the post–World War Two period.[18]

The *Brown* decision, says Kenneth Karst, is "our leading authoritative symbol for the principle that the Constitution forbids a system of caste." With the Warren Court's decision in favor of racial equality, the principle of equal citizenship was revived. That principle had become formal law when the Fourteenth Amendment was ratified in 1868. For almost a century, the Court had been reluctant to realize its potential, however, for fear of fundamentally changing the relation between the federal government and the states. When, after the Second World War, political leaders as well as the population at large showed a certain willingness to reconsider matters concerning race and equal citizenship, the Supreme Court responded. In the late 1940s and early 1950s, the Court handed down a number of decisions that had been unimaginable only a few years earlier.

The Justices who decided *Brown v. Board of Education* perceived the Fourteenth Amendment's guarantee of liberty and equality in the way every one of us perceives: through the filters created by the perceiver's acculturating experience. The Justices understood that the whole system of racial segregation was a betrayal of the central values of American civic culture. And political action, from the Niagara movement to the threatened march on Washington, had helped the Justices to understand.[19]

The revival of equal citizenship in *Brown* amounted to a formal redefinition of the national community. When Chief Justice Warren wrote the opinion for the Court in the *Brown* case, he recognized "the strong connection between the meaning of the Constitution and the national community of meaning that is the American civic culture." Of the five elements that make up Karst's civic culture, the most interesting—at least for the purposes of this chapter—is nationalism. The

18. Glendon, *Rights Talk*, 163.
19. Karst, *Belonging to America*, 74, 73. On the Court's reluctance to embrace the potential of the Fourteenth Amendment, see Karst, chap. 4.

civic culture defines the national community, Karst claims, and nobody has done more to uphold and protect that community than the country's judges. When committed to social change, these judges, and especially the justices on the Supreme Court, have been nation-builders—the prime example being *Brown,* which expanded the meaning and actual contents of belonging. "Validation of a claim of equal citizenship is not merely important to the individual claimant. It also forms part of the social cement that makes the nation possible." When legislatures have defaulted, courts and lawyers have reacted, thereby providing a "cultural glue," a frame that may hold all Americans together, however uneasily.[20]

Courts have been in a better position than have legislatures to defend the principle of equal citizenship. Not subject to majoritarian domination, courts have generally been insulated from partisan politics. Their point of departure being concrete cases, moreover, judges have acquired a way of thinking that emphasizes prudence or practical wisdom. The training in practical wisdom starts in the country's law schools, where students are exposed to the case method of instruction. What the case method essentially consists of, Anthony Kronman has argued, is forced role-playing. In reenacting concrete disputes by playing the roles of the original parties and their attorneys, students learn to be sympathetic to a whole range of different points of view. Ultimately, it is the role of the judge that is given priority. This has the effect, according to Kronman, of emphasizing the need to reach a "reasoned" and "publicly justifiable" conclusion to the problems at hand, thereby encouraging student interest in civic-mindedness.[21] In American civil society, or the political marketplace where individual interests contend, it has thus fallen to lawyers and judges to defend the public good. "If there are possibilities for some realization of the republican vision in today's polity, they appear to lie with the judiciary."[22]

The use of law as an instrument of "policy" and social engineering is a reconstruction of the common law.[23] Naturally preoccupied with the

---

20. Ibid., 18, 10, 29.

21. Anthony T. Kronman, *The Lost Lawyer: Failing Ideals of the Legal Profession* (Cambridge, Mass.: Harvard University Press, 1995), 117.

22. Karst, *Belonging to America,* 225.

23. See e.g., Harry H. Wellington, *Interpreting the Constitution* (New Haven, Conn.: Yale University Press, 1990), and Laurence H. Tribe and Michael C. Dorf, *On Reading the Constitution* (Cambridge, Mass.: Harvard University Press, 1991), for recent state-

most basic requirements of the law, the common law has provided from the very outset a useful vocabulary in which to talk about conceptions of individually centered justice. "As against the continental legal system with its powerful inquiring magistrates, Anglo-American legal procedure has been an adversarial one, with an emphasis on rights."[24] The common law and common-law judges have always been held in high esteem. Even though by far the majority of cases that reach the nation's courts are statute-law rather than common-law cases, American lawyers still tend to consider the common law the truest expression and repository of the most basic legal rights and principles. "Not even the most learned treatise can do justice to the fertility, variety, and ambiguity of the case law, its surprising ability to put out new shoots, or to turn an old theme to a fresh purpose. American judges at their best have been virtuosos of practical reason," as Glendon puts it.[25]

The common law dates back to the twelfth century and possibly beyond. Its boundaries have always been defined by prevailing community standards. What gave authority to the common law as a legal order entitled to the highest respect was the belief that it embodied centuries of human wisdom. Emphasizing continuity and peaceful incorporation of change rather than sudden and violent reform, and residing in the customs of the community rather than in the political system, the common law understood law as developing out of and along with the people. "Law by and large evolves; it changes in piecemeal fashion. Revolutions in essential structure are few and far between. That at least is the Anglo-American experience. Some of the old is preserved among the mass of the new."[26]

What all common lawyers share is "an emphasis on the ongoing cultivation of a concrete historical tradition."[27] This ongoing, dynamic, and incomplete tradition encompasses both theory and practice. The common law does not consist only of the legal doctrines derived from binding official legal sources such as statutes and precedents. Under the

---

ments to the effect that modern, activist judicial review is an inevitable (and by and large desirable) effect of the common-law method of adjudication.

24. Bell, " 'Hegelian Secret,' " 59.

25. Glendon, *Rights Talk*, 169.

26. Lawrence M. Friedman, *A History of American Law* (New York: Simon & Schuster, 1973), 14.

27. Bruce Ackerman, *We the People: Foundations* (Cambridge, Mass.: Harvard University Press, 1993), 24.

institutional principles that govern the common law, what Melvin Eisenberg calls "social propositions"—propositions of morality, policy, and experience—are relevant in all cases. One of the key questions in common-law reasoning concerns precisely the interaction of social and doctrinal propositions, and it is not difficult, Eisenberg claims, to see why such propositions must necessarily play an important part in common-law reasoning.

> The common law is heavily concerned with the intertwined concepts of injuries and rights, and moral norms largely shape our perception of what constitutes an injury and a right. Judicial consideration of policies furthers the courts' function of enriching the supply of legal rules: if the courts are to establish legal rules to govern future social conduct, it is desirable for them to consider whether those rules will conduce to a good or a bad state of affairs. Experiential considerations are necessary to mediate between policies and moral norms on the one hand and legal rules on the other.[28]

Not any and every social proposition is acceptable, however. Only "applicable social propositions" that it is "proper for a court to employ" will do.[29] And as we shall see in the following chapters, consensus as to what constitutes "proper" social, nonlegal propositions is no longer as stable as it used to be. For some, for example, the legal positivists, social propositions ought to be discarded altogether, whereas for others, such as the members of the Critical Legal Studies and Critical Race Theory movements, legal doctrines are hardly worth considering as entities in and of their own right but only make sense in connection with social propositions. More often than not, though, the question is one of degree rather than kind—what weight to give to each of the respective propositions. What concerns us here is the fact that the common law is, in its very nature, both material and ideological.

That the common law is not merely fact, but also inevitably has an intellectual and moral dimension, has to do with law being "custom transformed, and not merely the will or reason of the lawmaker. Law spreads upward from the bottom and not only downward from the

---

28. Melvin Aron Eisenberg, *The Nature of the Common Law* (Cambridge, Mass.: Harvard University Press, 1988), 1–2, 43.

29. Ibid., 43.

top."[30] What happens at the grass-roots level carries importance for decisions made at the top. Reflecting and defending on the one hand the interest of the ruling class, the law has provided protection against the misuse of power by that very class on the other.

> Law not only expresses and creates power but also serves to limit power. . . . Law expresses community norms and it applies them to particular situations by interpreting the norms in the light of community morality and other community understandings. The essence of a norm is that it constrains behavior, including the behavior of the powerful.[31]

It is in this doubly dualist nature of the common law, as it were—its being material but also ideological, and its spreading upward from the bottom and not merely downward from the top—that we may find the origins of judicial activism. In many ways, contemporary judges are merely doing what generations of common-law judges have done before them: adapting law to a changing society.

JUDICIAL ACTIVISM: THE PRACTICE

Praying for Sheetrock

Joyce Appleby would not find much support for her attack on American exceptionalism among the general public. As already mentioned, most Americans find in the very notion of American exceptionalism—and especially in its legal underpinnings—a viable path to effective inclusion in American society. This is reflected in the nation's cultural life. From the works of Scott Turow, John Grisham, and countless other writers of detective novels, through television series such as *The People's Court* and *L.A. Law,* to the works of "serious" writers such as William Gaddis and Margaret Atwood, the sacred principles of personal freedoms and rights as outlined in the Constitution are invariably invoked above or beyond the actual plots. A person's decency and human worth are tested against whether or not he or she still—deep down—believes in the American civic culture. If and when the average American stops believing in

---

30. Harold J. Berman, *Law and Revolution: The Formation of the Western Legal Tradition* (Cambridge, Mass.: Harvard University Press, 1983), 556.

31. Karst, *Belonging to America,* 194.

American exceptionalism and stops wanting to fight for it, these cultural works suggest, then things do not look good.

One revealing example is the story of a small southern community's awakening to civil rights in the 1970s, a story told in *Praying for Sheetrock* by Melissa Fay Greene. The development that takes place within just one generation is one from church to court. As the book unfolds, the devoutly Christian black community of McIntosh County, Georgia, who have been "blind and deaf to issues of civil equality, equal employment, and local corruption," discover that the law and its practitioners may actually be of more help to them in their fight for justice and equality than their church leaders.[32]

In the early 1970s, McIntosh County is a completely segregated community. Tom Poppell, the white sheriff, wields all power; he controls everyone and everything. He has been sheriff since 1948, when he inherited the office from his father, Sheriff Ad Poppell, and he rules McIntosh in much the same way that George Washington Plunkitt once ruled New York's Tammany Hall: by "honest graft." In return for votes, he protects and takes care of his constituents. He is famous all over the South, for example, for allowing the local population to loot the cargo spilled onto old U.S. Highway 17 through McIntosh County whenever trucks collide or suffer the mishaps of heavy interstate traffic. Oftentimes, such mishaps will be caused by Sheriff Poppell himself and his deputies, who will take possession of the scene and call in the locals once the truck driver has gone off in search of help. "Such redistribution of wealth," we are told, "invariably put the sheriff in an excellent mood" and earned him "ever-widening circles of supporters."[33]

Like most successful political bosses, Tom Poppell is a wealthy man. He has acquired his wealth in a number of illegal business transactions over the years. During his reign, McIntosh County has been converted into "a mini–Las Vegas, a mini–Atlantic City, a southern Hong Kong or Bangkok where white men came looking for, and found, women, gambling, liquor, drugs, guns, sanctuary from the law, and boats available for smuggling."[34] The locals do not condone Poppell's activities; indeed, most are sorry for the bad reputation these activities bring to McIntosh.

32. Greene, *Praying for Sheetrock*, 8.
33. Ibid., 3, 241.
34. Ibid., 14.

Yet, by playing Robin Hood from time to time and tossing the occasional bonus to law-abiding whites and blacks alike, Poppell has managed to stay in power, thereby continuing one of the longest-running sheriff's dynasties in the state's history.

Between the black and the white communities of McIntosh, there are "close and long-time connections . . . unlike anything in the North." Half of the population are white and for the most part they live in Darien, where they own all the major shops and businesses and occupy all the important offices. All the menial tasks are performed by blacks, the majority of whom still inhabit slave or sharecropper shacks to the north of Darien between the Atlantic shoreline and the pine woods. They live their lives much as they have since emancipation, trusting in the Lord to provide for their needs and relying on the sheriff to maintain the racial equilibrium.

> The historic black community of McIntosh lived in a sort of pale outside a century of American progress and success. They survived by raising vegetables and keeping chickens and pigs, by working menial jobs in Darien, and by fishing the network of tidewater rivers and blackwater swamps. They lived without plumbing, telephones, hot water, paved roads, electricity, gas heat, or air-conditioning into the 1970s.[35]

When finally the call for civil rights disrupts the silent understanding between blacks and whites in McIntosh, everybody—blacks and whites alike—has a hard time understanding how acquaintances, people they have known all their lives, now turn into adversaries. It all starts when Thurnell Alston, an uneducated and unemployed black man with a keen sense of justice, has finally had it. Years before he first hears about Martin Luther King Jr. and his fight for racial equality, Thurnell starts becoming conscious of the systematic attacks on his own dignity and that of his black brothers. In "a series of rude awakenings"—one of which consists of his overhearing Sheriff Poppell remarking how the "only way you can control the Negroes is to keep them hungry"—Thurnell undergoes a gradual but effective "education," "until the day he had heard and seen enough and could not, in good conscience, remain passive any longer."[36]

35. Ibid., 16–17, 20.
36. Ibid., 38.

What turns Thurnell's passive knowledge of racial discrimination into an active will to fight for change is the senseless shooting of a black man named Ed Finch by Darien's white chief of police, Guy Hutchinson. Annoyed at Finch, who is engaged in a loud and drunken quarrel with his girlfriend on the front porch of her house and refuses to be quiet when Chief Hutchinson tells him to, the chief simply sticks his revolver into Finch's mouth and fires. He then takes Finch, bleeding, to the jail, charges him with aggravated assault and drunk and disorderly conduct and leaves him without any medical attention. What chiefly upsets the black community is not so much the fact that a violent act is committed by a white person against a black neighbor—after all, the black community is used to far worse!—but rather the fact that all of this happens in broad daylight within a residential area.

> Clearly an attack such as Hutchinson's upon Finch was not allowed: the blacks were not, after all, to be slaughtered like hogs; the fiction was to be maintained of two separate societies living rather gingerly side-by-side, each with its own hub of social and business life. Such a vicious and unprovoked attack by the chief of police against a citizen was a violation of the unspoken social contract that allowed the whites and the outcast blacks to live in peace.[37]

The night Chief Hutchinson shoots Ed Finch, black McIntosh residents gather around Thurnell Alston, and from now on it is Thurnell to whom they turn for advice and leadership. Thurnell teams up with two old pals, Rev. Nathaniel Grovner and Sammie Pinkney. Together, these "Three Musketeers" set out to *do* something. For various reasons, all three of them have independent sources of income and thus need fear no economic reprisal from the sheriff and the rest of white McIntosh. They hold meetings around Thurnell's kitchen table, but also in church, where they try to raise the political consciousness of their devoutly Christian black brothers and sisters. At some point Sammie Pinkney, who as a former New York City policeman with experience of the American West and of Europe knows about the ways of the world, becomes impatient, however. Alston and Grovner's reiterating every evening in church "the same half-dozen painful facts," which are then swept away by the congregation "with another mighty hymn," does not

37. Ibid., 122.

get them anywhere.[38] Outside intervention is needed, Pinkney decides, so he contacts Georgia's controversial legal aid network, the Georgia Legal Services Program, and hires a lawyer.

Alston and Grovner are not immediately persuaded that the move from church to court is a wise one. Not long after their first appointment at the Brunswick Legal Services office, however, they find themselves commuting back and forth between McIntosh and Brunswick nearly every day. The meeting with the young legal aid lawyers, whom they initially view with much skepticism, turns out to be a revelation:

> The amazing thing, to Thurnell, was how quickly and easily the young white lawyers had named the ill health of the county; how they had listened as the three McIntosh men tumbled out their tales of poverty, underemployment, and a sense of being the untouchables in McIntosh's caste system. . . . It was as if he'd come to them delirious, a feverish child, and they had smoothed his hair, laid a cold cloth on his forehead, and explained to him that he had the mumps and this was the cherry syrup he must sip from a spoon to be all better.[39]

Time and again, Thurnell and his fellow Musketeers hear the white lawyers talk about and refer to one particular document: the American Constitution. This document, the lawyers promise, has something to say about every fight for equality—even when that fight occurs in such a faraway and seemingly insignificant place as McIntosh County, Georgia. The Constitution, the black men soon come to understand,

> was the white boys' Bible; and the lawyers quoted it often, chapter and verse, taking secular pleasure in its ornate language every bit as much as the rural people relished the antiquated resonance of biblical thou shalts and wherefores and cometh and goeths.[40]

For their part, the young white lawyers rejoice in the chance to leave their offices in Brunswick and do some active service in the black community. Fresh out of the nation's best law schools, these "young, upper-

38. Ibid., 151.
39. Ibid., 178–79.
40. Ibid., 180.

middle-class, mostly urban, mostly Yankee lawyers" have no idea what awaits them in the South. They are taken aback by the Third World conditions under which people, black and white, are still living and consider the challenges they meet in Georgia "akin to those of their friends who had joined the Peace Corps instead of VISTA and who now dwelled in Asian or African villages. The exoticism and foreignness of the surroundings were vivid, and they themselves were looked upon as bizarre implants." Their social commitment is genuine and deeply felt. They had gone to law school in the first place out of a desire to perform public service, and consider a legal career the best instrument for creating social change. Their will to live a judicially activist life is founded on an understanding of law as "self-evident truths about fundamental human rights," and when they set up shop in the small rural towns, they are "prepared to work heroic hours."[41]

The course upon which the lawyers decide to embark is to bring suit in federal court, contending that the electoral system for electing city and council officers presently in operation in the city of Darien and McIntosh County, respectively, dilutes the votes of black citizens. *The NAACP* v. *McIntosh County* is resolved with a consent order, which divides McIntosh into five voting precincts. As for the second voting rights suit, *The NAACP* v. *The City of Darien,* the Georgia Legal Services Program lawyers fail to convince Judge Alaimo of the Southern District that anything is wrong with the way the city of Darien runs its elections, and the judge dismisses the suit. The legal aid lawyers decide to try their luck a second time and appeal. This time they win; in October 1979 the U.S. Court of Appeals for the Fifth Circuit reverses, "and Darien, like McIntosh before it, was sliced into districts, including a majority-black district."[42]

The way is now paved for black citizens to run for both city and county office. The first to benefit from the court order that has created a majority-black district is Thurnell Alston. Running, at age forty-one, for county commissioner for the fourth time, he finally succeeds in placing himself squarely in the midst of McIntosh County politics. Politically, he is a success, forcing the white commissioners to dedicate the sparse budget to the most fundamental needs of the poor. What

41. Ibid., 161, 156.
42. Ibid., 219.

Thurnell has not anticipated, however, is that after his election, the black community, tired of fighting and wishing merely to go back to their lives, lose interest in him and his continued struggles with the white commissioners.

> In a strange collapse of vision, the election of Thurnell Alston to the County Commission now appeared to everyone to be the chief thing they had worked for, the ultimate victory. . . . He became, to the black people, simply the Commissioner; not the Barber, not the Undertaker, not the Preacher, but the Commissioner, as if the larger community had no more vested interest in his daily work than in anyone else's.[43]

Without the support of the close-knit black community, Thurnell is lost. None of what he has fought so hard for over the past years seems worth it. When furthermore he and his wife suffer the loss of a favorite son, Thurnell feels so alienated, so tired and depressed that he starts loafing and drifts in the direction of the criminal milieu in McIntosh. He is indicted on charges of accepting bribes and possessing and distributing drugs and eventually has to go to jail.

"What might have happened differently," muses one of the young white lawyers as the two voting rights suits are about to be filed, "if Sammie and Thurnell and Reverend Grovner . . . had contacted say, political organizers, the national NAACP or SNCC. There might have been a different approach to this stuff. But they came to lawyers, you know, what can you do?"[44] The question as to whether the course of events would have been a different one, had the Three Musketeers decided to fight in the political rather than the legal arena, is never addressed by Melissa Fay Greene. In fact, the author of *Praying for Sheetrock* does not even seem to find it a relevant question. The reader cannot help wondering if the backing of a political group or organization might not have prevented Thurnell's sad fall from grace. As far as Greene is concerned, however, the real heroes are the lawyers whose judicial activism makes it possible for Thurnell to embark on a political career in the first place. As the book closes, a black man has replaced Thurnell as county commissioner, a black woman is elected to the post

43. Ibid., 253.
44. Ibid., 175.

of superintendent of education, another black woman runs the tourism office, and yet a third black woman teller works in Darien's bank. Of course, says Greene, "it is not enough, but it is a beginning."[45]

Our Town: Race, Housing, and the Soul of Suburbia

Like *Praying for Sheetrock*, David L. Kirp, John P. Dwyer, and Larry A. Rosenthal's *Our Town: Race, Housing, and the Soul of Suburbia* is about the use of law to make America more inclusive. As the title implies, the issue discussed is zoning and its implications for the racial makeup of America's suburban landscape. We are in Mount Laurel, New Jersey—a state, we are told, that is the most suburbanized in the nation, and in which judicial activism is "the byword," New Jersey's Supreme Court justices having been "more openly political and politically strategic in their decrees than other states' judges."[46]

The story of Mount Laurel—the township and the landmark case—begins on a Sunday in 1970, when the congregation of the all-black African Methodist Episcopalian Church has invited the mayor of Mount Laurel to announce the town's response to a housing proposal that will open up suburban Mount Laurel to local, poor, and mostly black families. After praising the new prosperity that is fast changing small, rural Mount Laurel into a booming suburb, the mayor comes to the point: the township has no intention of ever approving the proposed housing project. Indeed, he goes on, " *'if you people'—you poor and black people, that is—'can't afford to live in our town, then you'll just have to leave.' "*[47] These words are like a slap in the face to the blacks present; the mayor as good as tells them that for them and their families, whose roots in Mount Laurel after all go back to before the American Revolution, there is no room. This leaves them no option but to move to the riot-torn slums of nearby Camden.

Appalled at Mount Laurel's rejection of the idea of housing for the poor, the minister of the African Methodist Episcopalian Church approaches Camden's radical Legal Services lawyers. Upon hearing about the mayor's message to the black population of Mount Laurel, the

45. Ibid., 175, 335.

46. David L. Kirp, John P. Dwyer, and Larry A. Rosenthal, *Our Town: Race, Housing, and the Soul of Suburbia* (New Brunswick, N.J.: Rutgers University Press, 1995), 65.

47. Ibid., 2.

Camden lawyers decide "to bring their equalitarian agenda to the suburbs." Like their colleagues in *Praying for Sheetrock,* these lawyers

> had gone to law school in the sixties, not with the intention of becoming
> partners in some stuffy Wall Street firm, but instead meaning to accom-
> plish a quiet social revolution in the nation's courtrooms. These children
> of the Warren Court era regarded the law almost as a secular religion, and
> they had faith in its power to undo injustice.[48]

With the involvement of the Camden Legal Services lawyers, the
housing controversy ceases to be a matter for the citizens of Mount
Laurel to settle among themselves. For the lawyers, affordable housing is
a matter of simple justice, and they see in the Mount Laurel controversy
a potential "frontal challenge to the ever widening divisions between
blacks and whites, as well as between the poor and everyone else."
Together with local community organizers they decide to take the controversy to the courts, contending that Mount Laurel's zoning ordinance
unconstitutionally excludes poor and minority citizens from affluent
neighborhoods. Among the local organizers, it is especially a black
woman by the name of Ethel Lawrence with whom the lawyers deliber-
ate as they pursue their legal course. Ethel Lawrence is the Thurnell
Alston of *Our Town.* The book is dedicated to her for, as the authors put
it, without her it "would have been simply an account of how policy gets
made, not a textured human drama as well." It is Ethel who first educates the authors on "the folk-ways and law-ways" of New Jersey, just as
it is her constant presence in court that serves to remind attorneys and
judges that real people, not just legal principles, are involved.[49]

When the lawyers file *Southern Burlington County NAACP et al.* v.
Township of Mount Laurel in May 1971, they have no idea that *Mount
Laurel,* as the zoning litigation comes to be collectively known, will
continue to be argued in court for a decade and a half, and will become
"the *Roe v. Wade* of fair housing, the *Brown v. Board of Education* of
exclusionary zoning." The first to hear the case is trial court judge
Edward Martino. Judge Martino is so overwhelmed by the stories told in
court by the township's poor of neglect and abuse on the part of Mount
Laurel's politicians that he pronounces Mount Laurel's zoning ordi-

48. Ibid., 3, 70.
49. Ibid., 70, ix.

nance unconstitutional on grounds of economic discrimination. Writing his opinion, Martino has to do some creative legal thinking as he has no New Jersey precedent to rely on. Instead, he "cobbled together an opinion that relied on dissents, decisions from other states, and law review commentary."[50]

Judge Martino's opinion, delivered in May 1972, is bold, though not as bold as the judgment delivered three years later by Justice Frederick Hall for a unanimous New Jersey Supreme Court. Upon the township's appeal of the trial court's ruling, the state Supreme Court decides to hear the case directly, skipping the intermediate appellate court. Picking up on Judge Martino's notion of economic discrimination, Justice Hall speaks of a moral obligation on the part of America's suburbs toward the poor and homeless and demands that "developing towns across the state rewrite their zoning laws so that private developers, taking advantage of federal subsidies and market forces, could build homes for a 'fair share' of the region's poor and moderate-income families."[51] As had been the case for Judge Martino before him, Justice Hall has no specific text other than the New Jersey Constitution's vaguely formulated concern for the general welfare to rely on in his call for constitutionally mandated municipal obligations.

The politicians are enraged at Justice Hall's demand for an ordinance providing "realistic opportunity" for affordable housing. They refuse to play this game of "judicial dictatorship" and submit a "farcical document, every bit as defiant of the judiciary as southern school districts' responses to desegregation in the 1950s and 1960s." To the lawyers' dismay, the trial court approves of the town's sham zoning changes, and they decide to mount a new Mount Laurel lawsuit. In *Mount Laurel II,* as the suit comes to be known, they are defeated at the trial court level, but vindicated by the New Jersey Supreme Court in 1983. The opinion delivered by Chief Justice Robert Wilentz himself gives "developers, lawyers, and poor families eager to prise open the suburbs expansive declarations of rights, detailed remedies to make those rights real, and even the apparatus of a new mini-administrative system to enforce them."[52]

The lawyers rejoice in Chief Justice Wilentz's public interest–oriented

50. Ibid., 3, 75.
51. Ibid., 77.
52. Ibid., 86–87, 93.

call for each town to take affirmative responsibility for its "fair share" of the state's poor. As it turns out, however, they rejoice too soon. Prodded into action by Wilentz's specific warning in *Mount Laurel II* that the Supreme Court will continue its judicial activism until the state legislature acts, members of the legislature start negotiating a compromise. After several failed attempts at reconciling liberal hopes of preserving in legislation the most central elements of *Mount Laurel II* with conservative plans of aborting the court's ruling, the legislature finally produces the 1985 Fair Housing Act. Along the way, Republican Governor Thomas Kean has done his best to transform "the fair-share problem *Mount Laurel II* had addressed into another kind of problem—runaway judges."[53]

The 1985 Fair Housing Act, it is generally understood, sends an unequivocal signal to the New Jersey Supreme Court that further judicial activism is neither needed nor wanted. It takes the high court barely six months to respond. In February 1986, in a case formally known as *Hills Development* v. *Bernards Township* but more commonly called *Mount Laurel III,* the Supreme Court unanimously upholds the new law. To some, this is a realistic, even pragmatically wise peace offering to the bench; to Ethel Lawrence and the Legal Services lawyers, who have made the cause of affordable housing central to their lives over the years, *Mount Laurel III* amounts to retreat, even capitulation, on the justices' part.

In the assessment of the authors of *Our Town,* neither response is entirely fair. The New Jersey Supreme Court must be commended first of all for forcing the legislature to recognize the state's responsibility to solve the housing needs of the poor, and second for knowing exactly how far to pursue a legally activist course without losing its autonomy and integrity. Unlike what has happened in other states where justices have been forced to resign for being too openly political, New Jersey's justices "have continued to be legal innovators, and appointments to the Supreme Court still stress professional competence, not partisan politics." On the other hand, *Mount Laurel III* raises questions about the high court's willingness and ability to keep a reform agenda going. Just as the court had demonstrated, in *Mount Laurel II,* a willingness to "craft broad remedies for systemic social problems and transcend the limitations of traditional litigation," it draws back and leaves the issue of

53. Ibid., 101, 123.

affordable housing in the hands of New Jersey's politicians, for whom the needs of the prosperous middle class have always been more important than those of the poor. The unfortunate result has been that Justice Hall's talk, in *Mount Laurel I*, of a moral obligation toward Mount Laurel's poor, essentially black population, has been conveniently forgotten, and that "there has been relatively little low- and moderate-income housing built in New Jersey since the Fair Housing Act was passed in 1985."[54]

For a brief moment, it looks as if a handful of judicially activist justices may succeed in forcing Middle America to commit itself to the principle of fair shares for the haves and the have-nots alike. But then the justices retreat from "that bold new conception of the commonweal," allowing Middle America to slip back into its old beliefs in the power of a free market economy to resolve America's problems. *Our Town* is very much about judicial activism—its potential for "defining and enforcing newly created social rights and obligations." Above and beyond the issue of whether affordable housing is a matter for the judiciary or for the legislature, however, it is the actual—and very real—needs of the poor, the human problem, that concerns the authors. At a time when "the very idea of our being a 'good society,' a city on a hill, commands little credence," and when "compassion, once a byword, has become a political liability," Kirp, Dwyer, and Rosenthal ask, to whom are the poor going to look for support? Until Middle America finally wakes up and recognizes that help is needed, "it is vital that the idealists keep talking the talk."[55] And for the time being there seem to be more idealists among America's judges than among its politicians.

CONCLUDING REMARKS

Down through American history, the common law has served as a basis for social and political inclusion. As some critics see it, the inclusiveness enabled by the common law has had the unfortunate effect of undermining multicultural identity. According to historian Joyce Appleby, for example, it is the very inclusiveness of the common law, and not merely its use as a tool of WASP exclusivity, that has threatened multiculturalism. To such attacks on legal universalism, other critics have responded

54. Ibid., 147, 113, 159.
55. Ibid., 173, 79, 174.

that legal universalism has in fact enabled the nation's subcultures to seek and obtain integration. Kenneth Karst is one such critic who has attempted in his writing to demonstrate that

> not every form of "legal universalism" threatens to undermine the na-
> tion's subcultures. To one who self-identifies within a culture or a social
> group partly or wholly defined by race or sexual orientation, equal cit-
> izenship implies that she can belong to America and at the same time
> keep that particularized orientation if she wants it. An increasing recog-
> nition of the mythical qualities of racial or sexual orientation identity
> should make no difference at all to the antidiscrimination component of
> the guarantee of equal citizenship. Nor should the recognition of race as a
> myth be taken to undermine the constitutional or statutory foundation
> for race-conscious group remedies that are appropriate for group-based
> harms. In the end, both the antidiscrimination principle and race-
> conscious remedies should be seen as the instruments of integration. Not
> "assimilation" in the sense of identity lost, but integration in the sense of
> a reality renamed, an identity renewed, a myth retold.[56]

Karst's attempt to combine legal universalism with the search for particularized identification, in which so many of America's diverse cultures have been engaged over the past many years, is an important and interesting one, as I have argued in this chapter. It is an effort, moreover, that is reflected in a variety of American cultural works. Two recent examples are Melissa Fay Greene's *Praying for Sheetrock* and David L. Kirp et al.'s *Our Town*. For Thurnell Alston and Ethel Law-rence, the black protagonists of *Praying for Sheetrock* and *Our Town* respectively, the fight to be included into American society is a long and arduous one. Not knowing at first where to turn for support and under-standing, they approach the Legal Services programs of their respective states. The idealism and willingness to fight for a better and more just society that characterize the young white lawyers who staff these pro-grams impress the two protagonists. As they befriend these lawyers, they cannot help but be swept along by the lawyers' belief in the law's ability to do good. The law of the land, they come to believe, is there for them too.

56. Kenneth L. Karst, "Myth of Identity: Individual and Group Portraits of Race and Sexual Orientation," *UCLA Law Review* 43.2 (1995): 369.

Central to the authors of *Praying for Sheetrock* and *Our Town* is the belief in a responsive judiciary—the belief that in a civil society such as America, the courts will have to step in to protect the rights of the underprivileged. Both books illustrate how intimately the idea of American exceptionalism is related to the role of law and lawyers in American society. It is especially since World War II that Americans have come to associate judicial responsiveness with an expansion of constitutional rights for America's needy. Earlier, the country's judges were not always instrumental in extending the rights of citizenship to previously unwanted groups of people. After *Brown,* however, the ideal of a compassionate judiciary has served to remind the nation that what makes America exceptional are not only certain constitutional rights and liberties, but also the very idea that such rights are for everybody—high and low, white and nonwhite, man and woman. When therefore critics such as Joyce Appleby attack the notion of American exceptionalism for *ex*cluding down through American history all that is nonwhite and nonmale, they miss the point.

II

Of Human Vanity, Multiculturalism, and American Legalization

Tom Wolfe's *The Bonfire of the Vanities*

When, on his way back to Manhattan from Kennedy Airport where he has picked up his girlfriend Maria, Sherman McCoy, the protagonist of Tom Wolfe's *The Bonfire of the Vanities,* takes a wrong exit, he gets lost and ends up in the Bronx. This is Sherman's first meeting with the Bronx, and it turns out to be nothing less than a catastrophe. A wealthy Wall Street stockbroker with a very WASP background, Sherman McCoy has lived his life under conditions as remotely different from those of any child growing up in the Bronx as can possibly be. The distance between McCoy's Manhattan—that of his business address, Wall Street, as well as his private one, Fifth Avenue— and the Bronx may not be great in geographical terms; in economic and psychological terms, however, it is enormous. In the Bronx, McCoy encounters "the other" America, the poor, nonwhite, and violent America from which his sheltered background has successfully shielded him until now, when he is well into his thirties. He, or rather his girlfriend Maria, runs down and mortally wounds a young black man—an accident for which Sherman later gets all the blame and is put on trial. Puzzled and frightened, Sherman does not quite know how to relate to the Bronx and to the accident, and it is Maria who finally has to enlighten and explain to him what it is all about:

Sherman, let me tell you something. There's two kinds a jungles. Wall Street is a jungle. You've heard that, haven't you? You know how to handle yourself in that jungle. . . . And then there's the other jungle. That's the one we got lost in the other night, in the Bronx. . . . You don't live in that jungle, Sherman, and you never have. You know what's in that jungle? People who are all the time crossing back and forth, back and forth, from this side of the law to the other side. You don't know what that's like. You had a *good* upbringing. Laws weren't any kind of a threat to you. They were *your laws,* Sherman, people like you and your family's. . . . And let me tell you something else. Right there on the line everybody's an animal—the police, the judges, the criminals, everybody.[1]

It is "right there on the line" where "everybody's an animal" that the action of *The Bonfire of the Vanities* takes place. Centered on the investigation leading up to Sherman's trial, the trial itself, and the motives, norms, and values of the people involved in it, the novel traces the effects on everyday life and the relationships between people of a society in which justice and the law are "a game. If [you] won, terrific. If [you] lost . . . well, on to the next war."[2] In modern America, Tom Wolfe implies, where pluralism reigns supreme and where one can no longer talk about culture or the law in the singular, there is a war going on—a war between the various (sub)cultures in which human dignity and basic fairness and justice get lost. Interested only in furthering its own particular needs and ends, each group scrupulously, and with no thought for people outside the group, uses, or rather misuses, the law and the legal system. Whoever succeeds in getting the law *and* the press—when the mass media enter the scene, things get totally out of hand—on his or her side wins the game.

It is apt that Tom Wolfe in his panorama of contemporary New York makes use of the law and the legal system as the arena in which the battle between the various cultures is fought out. By using the legal system as a microcosm of all of American society, he underscores and intensifies his criticism of that society. When the law and the legal system—those ultimate bastions of liberal democracy—have become tainted and corrupt, something very serious indeed is the matter with American culture and society.

1. Tom Wolfe, *The Bonfire of the Vanities* (New York: Bantam, 1987), 275.
2. Ibid., 552.

In what follows, *The Bonfire of the Vanities* will be used both as a point of departure and as a sort of checklist to illustrate how far things have gone, so to speak. It will be argued that by making the one exception to the pitiful collection of corrupt New Yorkers with whom we are presented in the novel, Judge Kovitsky, a member of the legal profession, Wolfe points beyond the law and the legal system itself toward the present mistreatment of that system by its servants as the root of the problems he describes. The general principles of fairness and decency for which Kovitsky is willing at great personal risk to stand up are the same principles for which, as we shall see in the following chapters, Scott Turow's Sandy Stern and Martin Gold, Judge Wapner of *The People's Court,* and Sara Paretsky's V. I. Warshawski spend their professional lives fighting. As they were originally conceived, there is nothing wrong with the promise and ideal of law, these writers suggest.

THE COMMON LAW:
HISTORICALLY AND AS PORTRAYED BY TOM WOLFE

In *The Law of the Land,* Charles Rembar outlines how

> Three features mark the Anglo-American legal system as different from all others. One is the extent to which *our law is formed in litigation.* Cases in court do more than what would seem their normal function, which is to settle specific controversies by applying rules of law. They also in large measure generate the rules. Our law comes not just from Parliament or Congress speaking broadcast to the public politic; it comes also from judges speaking to the litigants before them (though everyone had better listen). Another peculiar feature is the way we conduct these cases: *we pit antagonists against each other,* to cast up from their struggle the material of decision. A third—and largest in the public consciousness—is *the trial by jury.*[3] (italics mine)

In the following, I will concentrate on these three features. As the first of these, judge-made or common law, is crucial to an understanding of the other two, it will receive more careful attention. Thus, section one will deal with the common-law aspect of the Anglo-American tradition—historically and in general, first, and then as reflected in *The Bonfire of*

3. Charles Rembar, *The Law of the Land: The Evolution of Our Legal System* (New York: Harper & Row, 1989), 116.

the Vanities. Section two will be about the adversary system and section three about the trial by jury.

What distinguishes the Anglo-American legal system from other systems is the tradition of common law. At first, in the twelfth century or earlier, an expression of usage, custom, and precedents slowly and continuously evolving, as we saw in chapter one, the common law in later centuries came to be seen not only as part of history, but also as part of Nature, or Divinity. Whether validated by custom, Nature, or God, the common law resided outside of court; the judge's duty was to discover and declare it, not to assume that he could design or make it.

The equation of common law with a fixed, customary standard resulting in a strict conception of precedent remained largely unchallenged until the late eighteenth century. Beginning sometime in the 1780s, however, American jurists began to question the original natural-law foundation of common-law rules and instead to call for codified rules. The result was, as Morton J. Horwitz puts it, that the common law was "dethroned"[4] from the position it had occupied in the jurisprudence of preceding generations, including the revolutionary generation. In the latter, several common-law lawyers were among the heroes—John Adams and Thomas Jefferson, just to mention two of the more prominent ones. Indeed, it was lawyers who mostly drafted the state and federal constitutions, and whether in town, city, state, or national government, it was lawyers who occupied the majority of the seats. "Unlike some later revolutions, and some earlier colonial Utopias, the new republic did not try to do business without lawyers."[5]

As the belief in the law as an eternal set of principles expressed in custom and derived from natural law began to be eroded in the late eighteenth century, so did the faith in the impartiality of the judges. What underlay the demands for codification was the growing suspicion that much of first the English and then the American common law was a mere product of the whim of judges. Impartiality and objectivity could only be reached through a codification of all laws—a codification, moreover, whose legitimate foundation would no longer be the inherent rightness or justice of the law, but rather the consensual will of the

---

4. Morton J. Horwitz, *The Transformation of American Law, 1780–1860* (Cambridge, Mass.: Harvard University Press, 1977), 11.

5. Lawrence M. Friedman, *A History of American Law* (New York: Simon & Schuster, 1973), 94.

people. Attempting as far as possible to fit the common law into an emerging system of popular sovereignty, "judges came to think of the common law as equally responsible with legislation for governing society and promoting socially desirable conduct. The emphasis on law as an instrument of policy encouraged innovation and allowed judges to formulate legal doctrine with the self-conscious goal of bringing about social change."[6] Ironically enough, the attempts made in the nineteenth century by means of statutory, codified laws to curb the power of individual judges to "make" the law according to their moods and whims only led to a deeper penetration into society of the official legal system, and thereby to the politicization of the courts and the entire judicial branch of the government that has played such an important role in bringing about the law-permeated society as we know it today.

What more than anything else made the courts, and especially the Supreme Court, a force to be reckoned with was the explosion of judicial review in the nineteenth century. Judicial review was first asserted in the 1803 landmark decision *Marbury* v. *Madison,* where Chief Justice John Marshall and his colleagues declared an act of Congress unconstitutional. The degree of power exercised by the courts and especially the Supreme Court is unique in judicial history; no other country has given its courts such extraordinary power. It is also somewhat puzzling. The president is elected; so are Congress, state legislators, and governors. Only Supreme Court justices and other federal judges are not elected, but appointed for life. Yet these unelected justices and judges are given the power, through judicial review, to nullify some acts of an elected president and the elected representatives of the people assembled in Congress or the legislatures of the states—"the feature of American law that remains most difficult and most important to explain is why a country committed to democratic political and social principles continues to repose important law-making functions in the judicial branch of the government."[7] How the courts achieved such power, and whether it is proper that they exercise it, are questions that have been much debated by lawyers and legal historians over the past two hundred years.

That the "legalization" of American society has many drawbacks, most critics seem to agree. First and foremost, the range of controversies

6. Horwitz, *Transformation of American Law,* 30.

7. Geoffrey C. Hazard Jr. and Michele Taruffo, *American Civil Procedure* (New Haven: Yale University Press, 1993), 3.

brought to court is truly astounding. By 1980, lawsuits were being filed in the fifty state court systems at the rate of five million a year. A fair number of these suits were—and still are—both flippant and absurd, like the case of a high school girl suing her gym teacher after breaking a finger in a softball game, or a twenty-four-year-old man suing his parents for "malpractice of parenting."[8] "Sue Thy Neighbor" may indeed, as Jerold S. Auerbach claims, be "the appropriate modern American inversion of the Biblical admonition."[9] Second, American society is witnessing a real mania for lawmaking, an inflation of laws. Ralf Dahrendorf, as we saw, has called this inflation of laws and the accompanying growth of norms, sanctions, and institutions "hypernomia," a phenomenon he describes in this way: "Our law books . . . are cluttered with texts which confuse rather than clarify, spread uncertainty rather than certainty, and weaken confidence in the institutions of law by not being applied. . . . The plethora of sometimes incompatible rules and often unenforceable sanctions makes immobility likely even without any special effort to comply with the letter of the law."[10] The word "certainty," or perhaps rather "uncertainty," is important here. A fundamental requisite of law, certainty is jeopardized by the mass production of laws. If people cannot be certain not only that the laws will be precisely worded, but also that they will be lasting—that what is valid today will also be valid tomorrow—then how can they go about the everyday business of their lives? "A legal order is such precisely because it allows the addressees of its norms to plan their course of life, to be forewarned as to where the red and green lights are placed," as Giovanni Sartori puts it.[11]

The negative effects of legalization are thus considerable. The complaints that most writers on the topic voice notwithstanding, however, everybody seems to acknowledge that law and order of some sort are the key to ensuring that the fundamental democratic rights of every citizen are preserved in a modern, pluralistic society. To most Americans, in fact, legalization signals that American democracy is alive and well.

8. I have taken this figure and these examples from Jethro K. Lieberman, *The Litigious Society* (New York: Basic Books, 1981), 4–5.

9. Jerold S. Auerbach, *Justice without Law? Resolving Disputes without Lawyers* (New York: Oxford University Press, 1983), 12.

10. Ralf Dahrendorf, *Law and Order,* The Hamlyn Lectures (London: Stevens and Sons, 1985), 146.

11. Giovanni Sartori, *The Theory of Democracy Revisited,* vol. II (Chatham, N.J.: Chatham House, 1987), 325–26.

Jethro K. Lieberman, for example, has called the American obsession with law a "clarion of social health" and has dedicated *The Litigious Society* to tracing "this democratization of our legal system," permitting, at least in theory, everyone to sue for anything, thus making the law "the common possession of the whole citizenry."[12] Lieberman agrees with the critics of legalization that the judicial branch of the government has become increasingly politicized, but rather than viewing this with alarm, he is pleased at the courts' growing (political) influence. For if it had not been for the courts, he claims, there would have been no progress in such areas as civil rights, abortion, and environmental policy.[13] In an age that concerns itself with welfare and "fiduciary duties,"[14] and in which the law "has evolved from a negative or prohibitory institution ('Thou shalt not . . .') to one that declares positive and affirmative duties ('Thou shalt . . .')," the courts have been charged with a great governmental burden. Legal standards, rather than definite and precise rules, have increasingly become the norm, and the resulting imprecision gives rise to litigation. What tends to be happening in practice is that the courts are in fact doing the job that Congress ought to be doing, that of concretely defining what the legal standards mean. This serves Congress well, Lieberman further claims, as it leaves all the politically controversial decisions to the courts:

> Especially in the era of single-issue politics, with conflicting demands crushing legislators, the safest course is to avoid writing laws altogether or to enact legislation that is murky, ambiguous, and that holds out hope that the protagonists may yet win in court—as, of course, someone eventually will, to the anguish of the loser and the accompaniment of their

12. Lieberman, *Litigious Society*, 7, 18, 24.

13. Cf. Marc Galanter, who reminds us that "The effects of litigation include an admixture of benefits as well as costs—as do the alternative ways of handling such troubles; the net effects of each type cannot be ascertained by deduction or supposition" ("The Day after the Litigation Explosion," *Maryland Law Review* 46.3 [1986]: 38).

14. Lieberman explains the term in this way: "This term is used loosely. In a strict sense, a fiduciary is one who stands in a special relationship to another, as a trustee of an estate stands toward the estate's beneficiary. . . . It is possible to interpret much of the changing face of the law as an attempt to charge a variety of relationships with a fiduciary character: the trend toward a standard of strict liability from one of negligence in manufacturers' liability to purchasers and users, the increasingly broad sweep given by the courts to the ancient term *fraud*, industrial liability to the public for the effects of pollution, and so on" (Lieberman, *Litigious Society*, 20–21 n.).

cries that the courts have continued to tread where they are incompetent or unwanted.[15]

The solution to the problems of litigation is therefore not to make the courts apolitical, but to make Congress more responsible to the needs of the people.

With *The Bonfire of the Vanities,* Tom Wolfe has enlisted in the ranks of critical commentators on American law-permeation. He has furthermore enlisted in the ranks of scared whites who, feeling they are losing their white supremacy and that something has to be done about it, tend toward bigotry and racism, and this seriously mars his otherwise very interesting account of life in contemporary New York. In the Wolfean universe, litigation and the legal system are a far cry from Lieberman's "hallmark of a free and just society." The words "just" and "justice" hardly exist for the people involved in the Sherman McCoy case except to further private goals and ambitions. Nobody is interested in the facts of the case—what actually happened to whom and why—and it would not have developed into such a politically hot and explosive issue in the first place had it not been for District Attorney Abe Weiss, who is up for reelection and needs to show "the laboratory of human relations," as he calls the Bronx and its inhabitants, that he is aware of and wants to do something about racial problems. Likewise, to Peter Fallow, the journalist who gets things started by his insinuating articles in the gossipy *The City Light,* the McCoy case arrives on the scene at exactly the right time and enables him to escape a rather miserable existence and make it to fame and fortune. If there is a winner in the novel, it is Fallow; when the book closes, he has won the Pulitzer Prize for his coverage of the McCoy case and has just married the daughter of his boss, the wealthy Sir Gerald Steiner. Assistant District Attorney Larry Kramer, who is put on the case, sees it as his opportunity to "do something . . . to break out of here . . . to rise up from this muck"; Tom Killian, Sherman's lawyer, earns a lot of money and prestige from the case; and the black community, under the leadership of the charismatic Reverend Bacon, sees the case as their opportunity to get back at white injustice and make a political statement. The list could easily be extended; in short, everybody concerned is grateful—for personal reasons and/or to further a

15. Ibid., 122, 190.

particular political principle—to get a shot at "that much-prized, ever-elusive, and, in the Bronx, very nearly mythical creature, the Great White Defendant." As the mayor's right hand, Sheldon, sums it up toward the end of the novel:

> The McCoy case has become one of those touchstone issues in the black community. It's like divestiture and South Africa. There *are* no two sides to the question. You suggest there might be two sides, and you're not even-handed, you're biased. Same thing here. The only question is, is a black life worth as much as a white life? And the only answer is, white guys like this McCoy, from Wall Street, driving their Mercedes-Benzes, can't go around running over black honor students and taking off because it's inconvenient to stop.[16]

What Tom Wolfe presents us with is thus a "jungle" in which there is no difference between law and politics, in which law *is* politics. Right and wrong, good and evil are determined, not according to abstract, general rules of fairness and justice, but according to what the law allows or can be interpreted to allow one to get away with. What does or does not look good in the press or in court—that is what counts. One way or another, everybody is participating in a contest, a game for power, and whether one's game is the press, the law, investment, or men,[17] the underlying principle is "the Favor Bank." Sherman's lawyer, Tom Killian, describes it in this way: "Everything in the criminal justice system in New York . . . operates on favors. Everybody does favors for somebody else. Every chance they get, they make deposits in the Favor Bank. . . . A deposit in the Favor Bank is not *quid pro quo*. It's saving up for a rainy day."[18]

As the McCoy hit-and-run case takes on more and more of a political complexion, the facts as well as the person, Sherman McCoy, are forgotten, even ignored. The treatment McCoy gets when he is finally put on trial is out of proportion to his offense; it is clear that he is made an example of, "the white defendant in the Bronx getting the same treatment as everybody else." Only, he is treated *worse* than a nonwhite

16. Wolfe, *The Bonfire of the Vanities*, 391, 48, 396, 586.

17. Cf. Sherman's description of Maria: "She's a gambler. She's not the type to play it safe. She likes to mix it up, and her game is—well, it's *men*. Your game is law, mine is investment, hers is men" (617–18).

18. Ibid., 400–401.

person in the same position. But then again, as Sheldon explains to the mayor when he thinks that they are being "kind of rough on this guy, McCoy," what can Sherman expect, having "hit the wrong kind of kid in the wrong part of town driving the wrong brand of car with the wrong woman, not his wife, in the bucket seat next to him. He doesn't come away looking so wonderful." We may like or dislike Sherman—and it is very hard *not* to dislike this arrogant, selfish, and self-righteous "Master of the Universe"—and we may think that the treatment he receives serves him right. But that is not the point; the point is that the color of Sherman's skin ought to be immaterial, and that justice demands he be given the same treatment as anybody else. For, as Judge Kovitsky reminds Assistant District Attorney Larry Kramer during the trial, "what makes you think you can come before the bench waving the banner of community pressure? The law is not a creature of the few or of the many. The court is not swayed by your threats."[19]

If there is any human dignity and decency left in the "jungle" of *The Bonfire of the Vanities,* it is to be found in one of the minor characters, the aforementioned Judge Kovitsky. We first meet Myron Kovitsky, who is "about sixty, short, thin, bald, wiry, with a sharp nose, hollow eyes, and a grim set to his mouth," when he and Larry Kramer are yelled at and ridiculed because of their Jewish background by a group of prisoners in a van outside the Bronx County Building. Whereas Kramer, who is more offended at being called "bald-headed" than at being called "Hymie," chooses passively to wait until things have calmed down, Kovitsky heads straight for the van. When he stares at the window trying to make out his enemy and then *spits,* it stuns and ultimately silences the chorus in the van. Impressed at the fury and the courage of the little judge and depressed at his own passivity, Kramer then and there makes up his mind "to seize the Life for himself." That this Life turns out to be having an affair with a juror on one of his cases, "the girl with the brown lipstick," only serves to underline the difference in personality between the petty and selfish Kramer and the more broad-minded Kovitsky.[20]

In the climactic last scene of the novel, where a huge crowd has gathered on the grand staircase and the sidewalk of the Bronx County Building to show their displeasure at Kovitsky's having dismissed the in-

19. Ibid., 587, 676.
20. Ibid., 42, 44, 48.

dictment of Sherman McCoy, we again see the brave little judge in action. Mumbling to himself, "They don't know how bad this is . . . I'm their only friend, their only friend," he is once again ready, at great personal risk, to confront the crowd and give them his version of justice and fairness. This time, nothing comes of it, however; realizing that the crowd is too big, Kovitsky wisely, if dismayed, turns back. Without the support of the public, even the best and most fair of judges cannot prevail. This is indeed bad, Wolfe implies; just as it is bad when amid the ensuing storm of protest in the black community, District Attorney Abe Weiss brings the charge of reckless endangerment against McCoy before a second grand jury and obtains a new indictment, whereupon the Bronx Democratic organization refuses to renominate Judge Kovitsky.

It is interesting that Tom Wolfe, in his indictment of the legalization of American society, should have the one halfway-decent character belong to—of all professions—the legal one. Whether or not this reflects the enormous veneration in the Anglo-American tradition for the courts and their judges, built up over centuries of common law practice, is hard to say. The fact remains, however, that with his fine human qualities, Kovitsky does suggest the existence, even in these legalistic times, of just and capable practitioners of the legal profession.[21]

THE ADVERSARIAL FRAMEWORK OF THE COMMON LAW

In addition to the common-law tradition, Charles Rembar lists as a feature peculiar to the Anglo-American legal system "the way we conduct these cases: we pit antagonists against each other, to cast up from their struggle the material of decision." Historically, the adversary system has developed out of the wish to learn the truth about a case by leaving it to the litigants to provide the court with facts. As evidence and argument took over the role formerly played by lance and shield in the trial of combat, rules and standards were needed. These rules had to be clear and understandable to everybody involved, during the trial itself as well as before and after, so that the litigants could prepare themselves and be assured of the fairness of the procedures. In this match of liti-

21. It is interesting that in the film version of *The Bonfire of the Vanities,* Judge Kovitsky—here curiously enough transformed from a Jew to an African American—plays a much more prominent role than in the novel. The potential for fairness and human decency merely hinted at in the novel is underscored in the film, notably when Kovitsky delivers his "go-home-and-be-decent" sermon at the very end.

gants, we have what Rembar calls an "umpire-judge," as opposed to the "magistrate-inquisitor" of Continental law. Whereas the latter can do as he pleases and ask whatever questions he deems necessary, the former is restricted by the rules of the game; not every question may be asked, not every document taken into consideration. Which of the two systems is more just is, of course, debatable. One may argue on the one hand that a trained magistrate may have a better chance through his inquiries at getting to the bottom of things than do untrained jurors, who act as an audience to the performance of lawyers and their witnesses. And one may argue on the other that, by leaving everything to the skill of counsel in producing facts and presenting the law, the adversary system stands a better chance of generating fair results. Whichever argument one prefers, however, the fact remains that the adversary system is deeply embedded in the history of Anglo-American law and therefore hard to change.[22]

As already touched upon, the adversarial framework of litigation not only raises the question of fairness in connection with legal procedure; it also raises questions of a more general kind concerning the human values and conduct encouraged in the process. Does the definition of a disputant as an adversary foster hostility and competitive aggression rather than helpfulness and trust, and does the struggle until there is a clear winner and loser destroy rather than preserve the relationship between individuals or groups of people? These are questions brought up by critics of the law-permeated society. In a pluralistic society, where conflicts easily arise over differences in interests and outlooks on life, and where litigation increasingly becomes "the all-purpose remedy that American society provides to its aggrieved members," these questions are accentuated. For, as Auerbach puts it:

> Pluralistic societies, which value flexibility and change, can easily accept conflict as healthy. Its open expression is assessed as a measure of vigor, not an index of maladjustment. Basic assumptions are seldom threatened by disagreements where pluralism is the basic assumption (unless, of course, pluralism itself is challenged). It may even be difficult to distinguish tolerance from indifference; all points of view are possible because none really matters.[23]

22. See Rembar, *Law of the Land,* 321, 405.
23. Auerbach, *Justice without Law?,* 10, 34.

What critics of the adversary system should not forget when they point to the way in which the system nurtures rabid partisanship, however, defenders of the system argue, is that it seems, by and large, to be the least harmful and most legitimate means in this democratic and pluralistic day and age of seeking and winning one's just deserts. Besides, given the values and norms of American culture, an adversary system is unavoidable.

> There is no question that the adversary system invites and requires partisanship. Indeed, that is the system's very design. Yet it is difficult to believe that litigants would behave otherwise in the individualistic and competitive American culture, with its moralistic sentiments and its legalistic politics. . . . Party partisanship in litigation is of a piece with the peculiar American attribute that combines aversion to constituted authority with deep commitment to the ideal of law.[24]

If Jerold S. Auerbach and other critics diagnose the malady of modern America as legalization and the adversary system run wild, Tom Wolfe gives us a living illustration of that malady in *The Bonfire of the Vanities*. The concrete symptoms are a ruthless fight for power and fear. In fact, one might argue, *The Bonfire of the Vanities* is Fear writ large. In the Prologue, we are given a glimpse of diverse and heterogeneous New York:

> Come down from your swell co-ops, you general partners and merger lawyers! It's the Third World down there! Puerto Ricans, West Indians, Haitians, Dominicans, Cubans, Colombians, Hondurans, Koreans, Chinese, Thais, Vietnamese, Ecuadorians, Panamanians, Filipinos, Albanians, Senegalese, and Afro-Americans!

The underlying question here as throughout the novel is addressed to the Sherman McCoys of this world: "Do you really think that this is *your* city any longer? Open your eyes! The greatest city of the twentieth century! Do you think *money* will keep it yours?" In an almost apocalyptic manner, the mayor of New York (who is, of course, up for reelection) predicts that "Harlem rises up . . . All of black New York rises up!" And then, he warns, "you'll get to know them all right! They'll come see you!" More than anything else this is white fear—Tom Wolfe's fear?—of losing

24. Hazard and Taruffo, *American Civil Procedure*, 101–2.

power to nonwhites. At the beginning—that is, before the accident—
Sherman McCoy thinks he has found the way to cope in New York. In
contrast to his father, who would always take the subway to work, Sherman takes a taxi for, as he puts it, "*Insulation!* That was the ticket . . . If
you want to live in New York . . . you've got to insulate . . . meaning
insulate yourself from those people." After the accident, of course,
things change. Sherman is hurled into the "wasteland," "the darkness,"
and "the jungle" of the Bronx and black New York.[25]

The racial threat and the accompanying fear are both physical and
mental. It is physical when Larry Kramer and his colleagues at the Bronx
County Building have to order sandwiches, because "they were terrified
to go out into the heart of the Bronx at high noon and have lunch in a
restaurant!" And it is physical when the British journalist Peter Fallow
does not like to take the subway home because he fears "the squalor."
Most of all, however, the fear is physical for Sherman and Maria in the
climactic scene leading up to their accident:

> Two young men—black—on the ramp, coming up behind him . . . *Boston
> Celtics!* . . . The one nearest him had on a silvery basketball warm-up
> jacket with CELTICS written across the chest . . . He was no more than
> four or five steps away . . . powerfully built . . . His jacket was open . . . a
> white T-shirt . . . tremendous chest muscles . . . a square face . . . wide
> jaws . . . a wide mouth . . . What was that look? Hunter! Predator! . . . The
> youth stared Sherman right in the eye . . . walking slowly.

Real though this fear is, the mental or psychological fear on the part of
the white man of losing out in the power game between the races is even
stronger. Thus, Larry Kramer, when wondering about his career pros-
pects, cannot help musing, "What did they have to look forward to? . . .
Sooner or later the Puerto Ricans and the blacks would pull themselves
together politically, and they would seize even Gibraltar and everything
in it. And meanwhile, what would he be doing?"[26]

If whites are afraid of blacks, blacks know exactly how to use this fear
to their advantage. Rather than investing in welfare programs or another
day-care center for the children of Harlem, whites are, in fact, as Reverend Bacon puts it, investing in the "souls" of the black people, attempt-

25. Wolfe, *The Bonfire of the Vanities*, 7, 56, 86.
26. Ibid., 135, 186, 89, 136.

ing to "control the steam," the "*righteous* steam building up in their souls, ready to blow." This white wish to make up for past sins and to stave off as long as possible "that wild and hungry steam" produces money, a lot of money which can then be invested by Reverend Bacon and his people—in, among others, the investment banking house of Pierce & Pierce, Sherman McCoy's former place of employment. And just as Bacon knows how to turn the McCoy case into a political statement for black power, so he is adept at getting the most out of white fears.[27]

Between the fear of the whites and the (mis)use of this fear by the blacks, there is not much to choose. The former will eventually lose the power game, Tom Wolfe implies, but will that change anything for the better? As long as the engine driving each person or group is selfishness, greed, and fear, everybody will have conflicting interests and will see his or her fellow man/woman as a potential enemy. From being originally a democratic and fair way to ensure that all the facts are brought out in a trial, the adversary system has, *The Bonfire of the Vanities* tells us, developed into a general outlook on life that will destroy us all if we do not take care.

THE TRIAL BY JURY

As the third and last feature that marks the Anglo-American legal system as different from all others, Charles Rembar mentions "the trial by jury." The question of its origin is confused, but historians tend to agree that one accused of a crime has had the right to jury trial since the early thirteenth century. Accusation by grand jury—the interposition of grand jury action between suspicion and trial—seems to be even older, dating back to the Assize of Clarendon, 1166. Back then, of course, it was not the jury as we know it today. It was a group of neighbors directed by the king who, rather than sit and listen to the evidence given by others, were supposed to act on their own knowledge of the facts. The king or his people would ask the jurors for information about local conditions, and the jurors would then render judgment based on local sentiment and understanding. The idea of proving a case in court came later, as did the idea that in order for the trial to be fair and just, the jurors ought to have no prior knowledge of the facts and preconceptions of the verdict they

27. Ibid., 158.

would eventually render. This means that precisely the things that today would disable a person from serving as a juror were then incorporated into the process. The ultimate function of the jury is the same, namely determination of the facts, "but the present method is antipodal to what it was when the jury system started."[28]

To the men behind the American Revolution, the right to trial by jury was of prime importance. It was mentioned specifically in the documents that preceded the Constitution—the resolutions adopted in 1766 by the Stamp Act Congress, in 1774 by the First Continental Congress, and in the Declaration of Independence itself. In the Constitution, it appears twice; first in the main body of the document, Article III, Section 2: "The trial of all crimes, except in cases of impeachment shall be by jury"; and then in the Sixth Amendment, which lists jury trial first among the rights of a defendant: "In all criminal prosecutions, the accused shall enjoy the right to a speedy and public trial, by an impartial jury of the State and district wherein the crime shall have been committed." As for what is probably the oldest and most fundamental right of the accused, the right not to be put to trial for a crime unless accusation is made by a duly assembled grand jury, we find it stated in the Fifth Amendment: "No person shall be held to answer for a capital, or otherwise infamous crime, unless on a presentment or indictment of a Grand Jury." It is no wonder, therefore, that the trial by jury looms large and has come to be associated with basic democratic rights in the public consciousness.

The present use of the jury is much debated, however. Those who defend it refer to its democratic aspects (its being the vox populi), and to the fact that it has helped shape the character of the law. Those who oppose it, on the other hand, say that it is slow and inefficient in that it takes up much more time than would a trial before a judge alone. Furthermore, jurors may, because of their inexperience, be biased and unable to see through lawyers' tricks and rhetoric. Of these more negative aspects of the jury, Tom Wolfe reminds us. In *The Bonfire of the Vanities,* we meet both types of jury, the petty or trial jury and the grand jury, and in his descriptions of both, Wolfe deals the concept of the jury as a protection of the citizenry against unscrupulous members of the legal profession a heavy blow. What has happened over the years, Wolfe

28. Rembar, *Law of the Land,* 129. In this as well as the following two paragraphs, I am relying on Rembar, chs. 5, 13, and 14.

claims, is that this concept has "become a joke." In fact, a grand jury hearing is nothing but "a show run by the prosecutor." Thus, with rare exceptions:

> A grand jury did whatever a prosecutor indicated he wanted them to do. Ninety-nine percent of the time he wanted them to indict the defendant, and they obliged without a blink. They were generally law-and-order folk anyway. They were chosen from long-time residents of the community. . . . Mainly you used the grand jury to indict people, and in the famous phrase of Sol Wachtler, chief judge of the State Court of Appeals, a grand jury would "indict a ham sandwich," if that's what you wanted.

Both the director and the star of this "show," the prosecutor has the stage all to himself. And for somebody like Assistant District Attorney Larry Kramer, this is a choice role. Having rehearsed his actors well, he succeeds in sinking Sherman McCoy "like a stone," whereupon he leaves the grand-jury room "in the state of bliss known chiefly to athletes who have just won a great victory."[29]

If the grand-jury hearing is an ego-boosting contest for Larry Kramer—a contest in which justice and the actual facts of the McCoy case are secondary—the jury trial of the "Herbert 92X case" to which we are witnesses earlier in the novel is no less so. The typical Bronx jury, we hear, is

> Puerto Rican and black, with a sprinkling of Jews and Italians . . . Bronx juries were difficult enough for a prosecutor as it was. They were drawn from the ranks of those who know that in fact the police are capable of lying. Bronx juries entertained a lot of doubts, both reasonable and unreasonable, and black and Puerto Rican defendants who were stone guilty, guilty as sin, did walk out of the fortress free as birds.

In addition to the regular black and Puerto Rican contingent, however, this particular jury also includes Miss Shelly Thomas. Even before we are told her real name, Miss Thomas is referred to by Larry Kramer as "the girl with the brown lipstick," a "rare flower" about whom he daydreams. Getting a date with her is the prize he hopes to win, and when he performs in court, he performs for her with this aim in mind. The

---

29. Wolfe, *The Bonfire of the Vanities*, 628–29, 636.

link here as elsewhere in the novel between sex and power is very strong—for the male contestants of the game of law or investment, the reward is sex. The zeal and aggressiveness of Assistant District Attorney Kramer in "this nickel-and-dime Bronx manslaughter case" amazes the regulars. They do not realize that this is not just any case for Kramer; there is a prize to be won, and he wins it. What happens to Herbert 92X and to his colleagues in the courtroom, he could not care less.[30]

Kramer not only uses the law to gain access to Shelly Thomas. Once he has obtained his first date with her, he also plays upon certain privileged information about the developing McCoy case to woo and impress her. The role he hypocritically acts is that of the politically and morally conscious servant of justice who wants to get to the bottom of this case:

> You know what this case is? It's a signal, a very important signal to the people of this city who think they are not part of the social contract. You know? It's about a man who thinks that his exalted station in life relieves him of the obligation to treat the life of someone at the bottom of the scale the way he would treat somebody like himself. . . . This case is *so* important, on every conceivable level, not just in terms of my career. It's just a . . . I don't know how to say it . . . A whole new chapter. I want to *make a difference,* Shelly.

What really concerns him as he is thus performing for Shelly is the thought that "Imagine! Him! The budding star of the McCoy case—and no place—no place at all! in the very Babylon of the twentieth century!—to take a lovely willing girl with brown lipstick"![31]

Not much is left of the old common-law ideal of the jury as a safeguard for the accused by the time Tom Wolfe is done with it. A far cry from the pillar of democracy, the fundamental right of the accused mentioned not just once or twice, but three times in the Constitution, the jury trial—petty as well as grand—has by now degenerated into just another arena for the power games of selfish and self-righteous lawyers. A former symbol of all that is best in the American tradition, this proud legal institution has shrunk to a scary—but perhaps fitting—emblem of modern, law-permeated American society.

30. Ibid., 132–33.
31. Ibid., 534–35.

CONCLUDING REMARKS

The picture that Tom Wolfe paints of modern America is not a pretty one. *The Bonfire of the Vanities* tells us that we live in a world devoid of human dignity and decency—a world where selfishness and vanity reign supreme. There is a war going on between the various ethnic groups for power and social recognition, the results of which are fear and aggression. This war is not only fought out in the streets; it is also fought out in the courts and the legal system. For, as Ralf Dahrendorf puts it, "whereas the class struggle of the past century was primarily about economics, the struggle for the social contract is about law."[32] As this struggle continues, the attitudes of individuals and groups toward one another as well as toward more general political, social, and moral issues are increasingly shaped by the legal vernacular. Encouraged by the adversarial framework of litigation, people see their fellow men and women as potential adversaries, even enemies—focusing on differences rather than similarities, competitiveness rather than mutual helpfulness.

Wolfe's treatment of the war between the ethnic groups is, however, somewhat problematic. His and his white main characters' fear of losing power to the nonwhite population of New York not only has certain embarrassing racist undertones; it also tends to obscure the *real* issue, that of assuring justice to *every* citizen, regardless of gender, race, and class. As Wolfe describes it, the criminal justice system in New York seems to be working according to what one might call law by race. Together with the "Favor Bank" system of "I'll-scratch-your-back-if-you'll-scratch-mine," the constant emphasis on race and on fear of losing authority successfully effaces whatever abstract principles of justice and fairness once existed in the American republic. Rather than calling for justice for everyone, Wolfe tends to call for (a return to) white justice only, thereby becoming a proponent of a kind of inverted law by race. In this respect, *The Bonfire of the Vanities* is itself a symptom and not a cure of the malady it describes.

By pointing to the deterioration of such key institutions of the Anglo-American legal tradition as the adversary system and the trial by jury, and to the accompanying loss of justice and fairness so fundamental to the common law, Tom Wolfe voices the key concerns of the critics of the legalization of the American society. Even if we are wary of the effects

---

32. Dahrendorf, *Law and Order*, 150.

of legalization and would prefer to reorient our society toward more community-based values—toward "justice without law" and "law without lawyers"[33]—we ought to keep in mind, however, that this presupposes a homogeneity and a willingness to subsume individual needs under those of the community at large, which hardly exist in contemporary American society.

In the midst of all the corruption and moral decay in contemporary New York, there is one character—albeit a minor one—who seems to have preserved at least some measure of decency and honesty: Judge Kovitsky. It is but a faint shimmer of hope with which Wolfe leaves us, a vague hint that in the judge's courageous behavior and willingness to stand up and fight for general principles of fairness and impartiality lie the possibility of reconciling differences and reaching agreement in multicultural America. In making Kovitsky a member of the legal profession, Wolfe indicates that the problems described in *The Bonfire of the Vanities* do not originate with the legal system per se, but rather with its corrupt practitioners, for whom personal gain counts more than justice and fairness.

33. I am referring to Auerbach's *Justice without Law* and Victor H. Li's *Law without Lawyers: A Comparative View of Law in China and the U.S.* (Stanford, Calif.: The Portable Stanford, 1977). Both writers are of the opinion that "law begins where community ends" (Auerbach, 5).

III

The Education of Scott Turow

An Analysis of *One L, Presumed Innocent, The Burden of Proof,* and *Pleading Guilty*

L ooking back, toward the very end of *One L,* at his first year at
Harvard Law School, Scott Turow states how "it was an experience of great extremes. What was bad was awful. But what was
good often approached the ideal." All in all, therefore, "it was the best
year in the education of this person." When he had first arrived in
Boston a year earlier and had met his peers in what would be the
Harvard Law School class of 1978, he had been aware that the next three
years would be demanding ones. Especially the first year, he had heard
from others, would be a "time of trial and initiation," a period in which
the newcomers not only would face an immensely difficult and seemingly endless workload but would also "typically feel a stunning array of
changes taking place within themselves." What he had not been quite
prepared for, though, was the extent to which that first year would bring
out and force him to confront some of the more negative sides of his
personality. Of his wish in the end to gain the competitive advantage
over his peers, his anything but innocent striving to achieve, and his
jealousy at the success of even his closest friends, he would have preferred to remain ignorant. But then, as he dryly remarks, "I suppose that
is part of the education too."[1]

In addition to meeting his own personal enemy during his education

1. Scott Turow, *One L* (New York: Warner Books, 1977), 269, 3, 275.

at Harvard Law School (HLS), Turow also meets what one might call his professional enemy: the method and philosophy of the school of legal positivism as personified by one of his professors, Rudolph Perini. From initially admiring Perini's teaching skills, knowledge, and wit, Turow comes, as the year wears on, to question and eventually deeply resent the Socratic method to which Perini stolidly adheres and the message about the law as a wholly analytical and rational science that informs his teaching. Conversely, his initial frustration with another professor, William Zechman, is transformed into admiration as it dawns on him that the unwillingness on Zechman's part to provide any clear-cut answers to legal problems is due, not to an ineptitude as a teacher and scholar, but to the realization that there are no answers, but only legal rules that are the product of human interpretation and thinking about political and moral principles. The concept of law presented by Zechman and later also by another of Turow's favorites among his teachers, Professor Nicki Morris, and set up by Turow as an alternative to Perini's teaching of law as an analytical science, is that of the common law—law continuously in touch with, not downgrading or sidestepping as irrelevant to the uniqueness of legal thought, what is going on in society at large.

The education of Scott Turow, it will be argued in this chapter, is an education in or about the common law. At Harvard, as at most other law schools, the first year offers very little choice. The curriculum is composed of six required courses—Torts, Contracts, Property, Civil Procedure, Criminal Law, and Legal Methods or Argument—and one elective course. Most of the laws of tort, contract, and property derive from decisions made by the courts. In addition, many of the underlying principles of the criminal law and civil procedure remain embedded in the case law, even though nearly all of it is now in statutory form. Furthermore, even where the foundation for the law is to be found in acts of Congress, the interpretation of such legislation is a matter for the courts. No wonder, therefore, that "cases and opinions form the very center of a law student's world." Indeed, the Harvard Law School prepares lawyers, as it says on the first page of the HLS catalog, "to practice 'wherever the common law prevails'."[2] Both as a body of propositions concerning particular areas of law and in a wider sense as a method or

2. Ibid., 16, 24.

conception of law worked out in these particular areas, but now suffusing everything in American law, the common law is the heart of first-year legal education.

Based as it is on a journal Turow kept throughout his first year at HLS and written immediately upon the conclusion of that year, *One L* necessarily gives to the personal part of Turow's education a high priority. Yet, in interweaving a description of his encounter with his personal enemy with a discussion about Perini versus Zechman, positivist versus common-law jurisprudence, he expands a personal statement into a more general statement concerning law and American society. His technique is not unlike the one used a hundred years before by Henry Adams. In his Preface to *The Education of Henry Adams,* Adams tells us that he has used his own personal history as "a tailor's manikin," that his life's experiences are merely the garment meant to show "young men, in universities or elsewhere," to whom he believes that the record of his experiences may be instructive, "the faults of the patchwork filled on their fathers."[3] For Turow, as for Adams before him, the personal history becomes an emblem of the national history.

What Turow learns during his first year as a law student is not merely to master the basic skills of the legal profession. He learns to look at the world and the problems facing us all in a certain "lawyerly" way. "The law. The law. I've probably not been as thoroughly taken by something since I hit puberty," as he reflects after having survived the first demanding semester.[4] To the intensity with which he has come during that first crucial year to live with or in the law, the publication of first *Presumed Innocent* (1987) and then *The Burden of Proof* (1990) and *Pleading Guilty* (1993) bears testimony. In all three novels, the discussion about Perini's legal positivism and Zechman's more common-law-oriented way of thinking resurfaces. Much as in Tom Wolfe's *The Bonfire of the Vanities,* the legal world and its practitioners are used by Turow as a lens through which society at large is scrutinized. The focus is on a kind of spiritual crisis affecting the legal profession. Technical competence—and greed— have taken the place of a set of values prizing good judgment and a public-spirited devotion to the law. At fault, Turow suggests, is the

3. Henry Adams, *The Education of Henry Adams* (Boston: Houghton Mifflin, 1918, rpt. 1973), xxx.

4. Turow, *One L,* 169.

Perini school of legal positivism, with its aloof disinterestedness in issues of morality and politics. Having practiced law for a while, he has become even more convinced than he was as a law student that the Zechman-Morris view of law as custom transformed is the only morally defensible one.

What makes Turow's novels different from and perhaps somewhat more substantial than the average detective novel is their author's general interest in the law as a discipline and the role it plays in modern American society. When the protagonist of *Presumed Innocent* rhetorically asks, "If we cannot find the truth, what is our hope of justice?"[5] he voices the central concern of the novel and its author. In addition to providing his audience with a look behind the scenes, as it were, a look into that world of the law which exerts such a powerful attraction on the layman, Turow touches upon one of the most sensitive and essential of all issues: the issue of truth and justice. And it is this combination of suspense, information about the law, and moral concern with law and justice which, one may speculate, has endeared Scott Turow to the American public.

Whether or not Scott Turow is in fact "the bard of the litigious age" that *Time* made him out to be in 1990,[6] he has in his novels succeeded in calling attention to that area of tension where law, politics, and morality meet and at times overlap. Beyond and above the actual plots of *Presumed Innocent, The Burden of Proof,* and *Pleading Guilty* there is a discussion going on—a discussion about what will happen to "our only universally recognized system of telling wrong from right" if it loses its universality and degenerates into a political power game for ambitious attorneys. For better or for worse, Turow seems to say, our present legal system, this "bureaucrat of good and evil," is all we have;[7] it's the best we can do in these diverse and pluralistic times where every person and group is fighting for his or its own rights. If we give up every pretension of searching for a truth and justice applicable to and recognized by all, we will have no forum left where we can communicate and solve our problems.

5. Turow, *Presumed Innocent* (New York: Warner Books, 1987), 3.

6. Paul Gray, "Burden of Success: As a High-powered Lawyer and Novelist, Scott Turow Has Become the Bard of the Litigious Age," *Time,* June 11, 1990. Today, Turow would probably have to share that status with John Grisham.

7. Turow, *Presumed Innocent,* 2.

LEARNING TO LOVE THE LAW: *ONE L*

Uncertain at the opening of *One L* as to whether the decision he has finally made to leave behind his teaching position at Stanford in order to pursue a career in the law is the correct one, Scott Turow seeks out friends and acquaintances who he knows have themselves thought of going to law school, and with whom he therefore feels he can share his thoughts and feelings. One such friend tells him that "if I was going to law school, I would be going because I wanted to meet my enemy. I think that's a good thing to do. And if I wanted to meet my enemy, I would go to Harvard, because I'd be surest of meeting him there." Though Turow does not immediately understand what his friend intends the phrase "meeting my enemy" to convey, the phrase keeps coming back to him until he realizes that "somehow it summed up the feelings I had about law school: the fear, the uncertainties, the hope of challenge, triumph, discovery."[8] This realization helps him, makes him more sure that his decision to go to Harvard is the right one for him to make at this point in his life. Yet it is only when he has almost survived his first turbulent year that the true significance of the phrase hits home. Meeting—and successfully confronting—his enemy, he finally understands, is what a good deal of his education at Harvard, his learning to think like a lawyer, is all about. In what follows, I will take a look first at the personal and then at the professional enemy with which Turow has to contend as a One L.

Turow's first reaction to Harvard is a mixture of pride and insecurity. He is proud to have been accepted into the Law School, to be among the inheritors of its "tradition of excellence," but he is not sure that he is quite up to that tradition. As he meets his new classmates, he is amazed at their intellectual backgrounds, the range of their achievements and their "personal force." There are moments during those initial days, as he sums it up, "when, awed by the geniality and talents of my classmates, I felt proud, and sometimes startled, that I had been included at all." His classmates being as brilliant and as used to succeeding as they are, it does not surprise him that the atmosphere, in as well as outside the classroom, is loaded with an intense demand for achievement. There is something about the Harvard Law School, as one of his tutors suggests, "which inspired people to use their capacities fully, to do things in

8. Turow, *One L*, 12.

a way that would make them proud of what they'd done and of themselves." At this early point, Turow finds such orientation toward success
or excellence positive, even admirable, and has every intention of taking
HLS and its "standard of achievement" quite seriously. It is only later,
after he has witnessed in himself and others some of the more negative
effects of this standard, that he becomes suspicious of the pretense of the
"Harvard-love at HLS."[9]

It all begins with Contracts, Professor Perini, and the Socratic
method. The Socratic method allows a professor to call on a student
without warning and question him or her in front of the entire section
of one hundred and forty people. To most students, it is a harrowing
experience to be thus selected out of the blue for intense questioning.
Despite student discomfort and protest, many law professors still defend
the Socratic method, arguing that it makes students familiar with the
specialized kind of behavior in which they will one day have to engage as
attorneys. For Scott Turow, the overwhelming feeling at the beginning is
"one of incredible exposure . . . In using the Socratic method, professors
are informing students that what would normally be a safe personal
space is likely at any moment to be invaded."[10] As it turns out, some
professors practice the method more religiously than others. Professors
Mann and Morris, for example, often lecture or wait for volunteers to
answer their questions. Not so Rudolph Perini, who seems determined
from day one to live up to his reputation as the toughest professor on
campus.

Perini does not waste his time. Upon entering the classroom on the
first day of classes, he barely offers a few introductory remarks before he
produces a pencil, points it at the seating chart and sharply orders a poor
student called Karlin to state the facts of the case of *Hurley* v. *Edding-
field*. Karlin is battered with questions, and when he does not get an
answer quite right, he is harassed and ridiculed. To Turow's amazement
and increasing alarm, the rest of the class plays a willing audience to
Perini's horrendous treatment of their classmate, laughing and cheering
as Perini makes one joke after another at his expense.

> I was bothered by the mood which had taken hold of the room. The
> exorbitance of Perini's manner had seemed to release a sort of twisted

9. Ibid., 19, 22, 71, 237.
10. Ibid., 31.

energy. Why had people laughed like that? I wondered. It wasn't all good-natured. It wasn't really laughter *with* Karlin. I had felt it too, a sort of giddiness, when Perini made his mocking inquiries . . . What the hell went on here? I was thoroughly confused, the more so because despite my reservations the truth was that I had been gripped, even thrilled, by the class. Perini, for all the melodrama and intimidation, had been magnificent, electric, in full possession of himself and the students . . . He was, as claimed, an exceptional teacher.[11]

Turow's enthusiasm for Perini and his teaching does not last long. After having been exposed to his openly inconsiderate behavior toward his students for a while, Turow begins to resent him. And as toward the end of the second semester, in what Turow sees as a misappropriation of his teacher's power, Perini uses the classroom to select and interrogate candidates for three summer research assistantships, his resentment grows into outright hatred. "I hated him now, and I thought less of HLS because he was here." Beyond the mere rudeness and inhumanity at the heart of the Socratic method employed by Perini, it is the cultivation of rational, analytically argued opinions, the substitution of dry reasoning for emotion, that bothers Turow. What they are learning as One Ls, in Perini's class in particular and to a lesser extent in their other classes, he and his classmates feel, is "a grimly literal, linear, step-by-step process of thought," a way of thinking foreign to them all and somehow changing them into something they do not want to be.[12]

One of the earliest signs that a change for the worse is taking place comes during interview season, when Turow and his classmates get their first glimpse of what the future might hold in store for them. Having been politically involved in both the civil rights and the antiwar movements of the 1960s and early 1970s, Turow views corporate practice as embracing "a regime of power to which I'd long objected." As he sees older students walking around campus wearing suits and ties, heading for interviews with representatives of some of the biggest and wealthiest law firms in the country, however, he feels vaguely tempted and wonders whether he will be able, when it gets to be his turn to be interviewed, to

11. Ibid., 43.

12. Ibid., 236, 81. Cf. also Turow's reflections upon meeting Perini for lunch: "He remained much the man behind the lectern—probably the most practiced human being I've ever met, the person who most desires to have his world in perfect order" (118).

turn down all the advantages that working for a big law firm entails. "That I was already feeling that kind of temptation," he tells us, "irked and pained and surprised me."[13]

Somehow, as Turow soon realizes, things just seem to push that way. Though hardly ever directly voiced, there is a tacit assumption at HLS that for the best and brightest graduates, the money, prestige, and power offered by the big firms make corporate law practice the obvious career choice. What is likewise taken for granted is that everyone will want "to make the Review." Becoming a member of the *Harvard Law Review,* One Ls are given to understand, is the height of achievement and excellence at HLS. In the beginning, the whole fuss about the Law Review makes no sense to Turow. The rewards of Review membership— faculty contacts and judicial clerkships—do not sound worth it, he thinks, compared to the obligations and the long hours of work a student will have to put in.

As the year wears on, however, avoiding the race for the Law Review becomes more and more difficult. Whenever that HLS standard of achievement is referred to either by a member of the faculty or by one of the students, mention of the *Harvard Law Review* inevitably seems to follow. Conjectures as to who will make it are constantly made. When finally the names and grades of those who actually have made the Law Review leak out, Turow cannot help but feel "cheated." Though his grades are good, they do not make him one of the top five or six people in his section to be elected to join the Review. Knowing that he should feel lucky at being among the best 25 percent, he is still "nagged by a desire for more," his "sense of jealousy and denial [leaving him] dizzy for a day."[14] When it comes to making Law Review, no less than when it comes to securing for himself one of those prestigious and lucrative jobs in a big law firm, Turow is forced to acknowledge at the end of the year that he has fallen prey to the HLS striving for excellence.

> What had been suppressed all year was in the open now. All along there had been a tension between looking out for ourselves and helping each other; in the end, I did not expect anybody—not myself, either—to renounce a wish to prosper, to succeed. But I could not believe how

13. Ibid., 91, 92.
14. Ibid., 275, 274, 275.

extreme I had let things become, the kind of grasping creature I had been reduced to—I had finally met my enemy, I figured, face to face.[15]

Even as Turow is thus meeting his personal enemy, he never for a moment wishes himself back at Stanford. "Harried, fearful, weary," as his learning to love the law leaves him, he nonetheless "never resisted that sensation of being taken, overwhelmed." The expectation that had brought him to HLS in the first place, "that a knowledge of the law would somehow amplify my understanding of the routines of daily life," is instantly fulfilled and remains fulfilled throughout. At the end of the year, as much as at the beginning, he has "the perpetual and elated sense that I was moving toward the solution of riddles which had tempted me for years." Not all his classes address the kinds of questions he finds relevant, however. As his hostility toward Professor Perini increases, he loses interest in Contracts, putting off as far as possible the work for the course. Instead, he focuses his interest and energy on first Torts and Professor Zechman and, in the second semester, on Civil Procedure and Professor Nicki Morris.[16]

Toward the end of the first semester, as he is beginning to feel a growing resistance to HLS, and his fellow students and professors are becoming "known quantities," there is only one class that he is thoroughly pleased with: Torts. After having felt unable to cope, like his classmates, with Zechman's constant bombardment with questions and crazy hypotheticals and refusal to give any clear answers, Turow is hit one day with the realization that "there were no answers. That was the point, the one Zechman—and some of the other professors, less tirelessly—had been trying to make for weeks. Rules are declared. But the theoretical dispute is never settled." Reassured that he no longer has to look for and be frustrated at missing clear-cut and well-defined answers to the legal problems he encounters, Turow becomes so excited in Zechman's class that he "literally cannot sit still."[17]

After Christmas, Nicki Morris carries on where Zechman left off. Unlike Torts, Civil Procedure is taught over two semesters. As the second term begins Morris embarks on a "kind of wide-ranging philo-

15. Ibid., 260, 262.
16. Ibid., 48, 49.
17. Ibid., 99, 98–99.

sophical tour" which, rather than underscore the uniqueness of legal thought, sees law's search as profound and wide-ranging. Here, as in Zechman's class, Turow feels the gap between legal ideas and those he has encountered in other fields of study close down. Things make sense in Morris's class to an extent that they never do in Perini's. To Morris, moreover, more than to any other professor at HLS, the students' well-being matters. He willingly shares his time with them and tries as best he can to lessen their anxiety about grades. Every time Turow comes to Morris's class, therefore, "all that rapturous discovery of the first six weeks returned." In the end, it is also Morris who puts into words Turow's feelings and thoughts about the law:

> "The law," Nicki said at one point in the second term, "is a humanistic discipline. It is so broad a reflection of the society, the culture, that it is ripe for the questions posed by any field of inquiry: linguistics, philosophy, history, literary studies, sociology, economics, mathematics."[18]

It is the willingness on both Zechman's and Morris's part to acknowledge and base their teaching on the uncertainties and contradictions inherent in the law that makes them Turow's favorites. Unlike Perini, these two professors show no desire to bring under control, or rationalize, that which is random or arbitrary. They do not teach that "there is always a reason, always a rationale, always an argument," but rather that human choice is arbitrary, and that the interpretation of the law, based as it is on such choice, is subjective. Precisely because both see the law as "a reflection of the society, the culture," they never expect the law to successfully resolve the fundamentally chaotic nature of human feelings and behavior. Toward the end, reflecting back on the professional education he has received, Turow sees the pursuit of definition and sureness, associated in his mind with Perini's view of law as a science, as "another of those forces which could make me less a person than I'd like to be, that foe I'd come here to meet."[19]

The difference between Perini's approach to the law and that of Zechman and Morris is not immediately apparent to Turow. The way in which Zechman transforms a case into a hypothetical may differ some-

18. Ibid., 198, 200.
19. Ibid., 272–73.

what from Perini's "kind of step-by-step analysis," he reflects during his first weeks as a law student, but the pattern of each class is by and large the same—"in each course, that process of comparing and distinguishing in order to flesh out the law is usually somehow repeated." This experience on Turow's part of an underlying similarity between his classes is due to the fact that in all these classes, including the ones like Civil Procedure and Criminal Law, the subject matter of which is now mostly in statutory form, the professors rely on the case-study method. For nearly a century now, American law schools have adhered to this method, which insists upon the reading and discussing in class of actual cases as the best way to learn the law. The tenacity with which law schools nationwide have held on to this common-law method of teaching even as more and more areas of the law are becoming codified is remarkable. Turow's awe at being a part of this "grand tradition" notwithstanding, he initially experiences the teaching of the common law as one big "jigsaw puzzling," a process far easier

> to describe than it is to practice. The common law is crazy and cases go off in all directions. You can never quite jimmy all of them into place—up and down, back and forth. Hopping from minutiae to the big picture. That process is now fully in gear which is supposed to teach us to think like lawyers.[20]

By the middle of October, however, Turow is beginning to "see patterns in what I'm learning, rather than just a series of abstruse doctrines." No longer frantically grabbing at anything that can make the law more manageable, he is able at this point to enjoy the turn most classes are taking for the more speculative, even philosophical. Zechman, and later Morris, in particular, now tells his students not to bother too much with all the dry details but instead to focus on "those philosophical, political, economic, and other pragmatic concerns which justify the rules and usually pass under the name of 'policy'." With the exception of Perini's class, little of what goes on in classes centers around the memorization of rules. Learning a law course, Turow has come to see, somewhat resembles the methodical job of designing and then building a house nail by nail:

20. Ibid., 77, 16, 77–78.

Putting up the struts, the walls, the roof; rule/policy/theory; trying to remember exactly how each of the layers joins and fits . . . And when you get to the roof raising, when the course has really begun to fall together, with the term-long mysteries dissolving and the basic patterns becoming clearer and clearer, the study can seem as gratifying as it was boring in the rule-storing phase.[21]

There is only one problem with the "policy" orientation of Zechman's and Morris's classes: it will be of only limited use to the students at exam time. For decades, exams at HLS have consisted mainly of so-called issue-spotters which demand of the students a detailed mastery of the predominant common-law rules. Though many professors agree with the students that some sort of discuss-the-case essay would more adequately reflect what has actually been going on in the classroom during the semester, issue-spotters are not easy to get rid of. As exam time nears in January, there is therefore no way around it—rules have to be memorized. This is dull work and not nearly as rewarding as figuring out the policy rationales behind the rules. As it turns out, even Zechman's Torts exam contains an issue-spotter. This leaves Turow feeling "bitter and cheated." What has been tested, he feels, is not the depth of the students' mastery of the law. "Intellectual quick-draw contests," all the exams, Torts included, have been "frantic exercises that seemed to place no premium on the sustained insight and imagination which I most admired in others, and when they occurred, felt proudest of in myself."[22]

After the final exams at the end of the second semester, Turow does not experience the same kind of frustration. Having had to work less hard in the second than in the first semester, and having had to struggle less with comprehending the material, he does not feel the "victim of my own excesses" this time. Also, and perhaps just as important, he does not feel the same lack of correlation between what is tested and what he has spent all those hours studying for in relation to one of the most important tests, Perini's. Contracts is the last exam; indeed, as Turow dryly remarks, "it is only fitting that [Perini] provided our travail at the end." The way in which Perini has taught Contracts throughout the year, as "one rule followed by a million exceptions," leaves no guesswork as to what is needed for his exam: a tedious and prolonged effort at memori-

21. Ibid., 92–93, 171, 172–73.
22. Ibid., 171, 179, 180.

zation.[23] This, then, is perhaps the only positive thing that may be said about Perini—his teaching of the law as a science matches his final test. In the end, however, this does not, cannot make up for the rigidity of his teaching. Having focused on the uniqueness of legal thought—on that which sets the law apart from rather than that which makes it a part of the rest of society—and having avoided the kind of rule/policy/theory reasoning so typical of Zechman and Morris, Perini has made of a common-law course an exercise in positivist jurisprudence. What he has left out, we are given to understand, is the soul of the common law.[24]

PRESUMED INNOCENT, THE BURDEN OF PROOF, PLEADING GUILTY, AND THE LOSS OF PROFESSIONAL RESPONSIBILITY AND INTEGRITY

Presumed Innocent

In *The Lost Lawyer: Failing Ideals of the Legal Profession,* dean of Yale Law School Anthony T. Kronman describes a spiritual crisis affecting the American legal profession. He attributes this crisis to the collapse of what he calls "the lawyer-statesman." This ideal has lost much of its appeal over the past twenty-five years, and *The Lost Lawyer* constitutes an attempt on Kronman's part to revive it. A devoted citizen who "cares about the public good and is prepared to sacrifice his own well-being for it," Kronman's outstanding lawyer or lawyer-statesman "excels at the art of deliberation as others excel at writing, singing, or chess. The lawyer-statesman is a paragon of judgment, and others look to him for leadership on account of his extraordinary deliberative power." The excep-

23. Ibid., 179, 267.

24. An interesting comparison may be made between Turow's *One L* and Chris Goodrich's and Richard D. Kahlenberg's more recent accounts, in *Anarchy and Elegance: Confessions of a Journalist at Yale Law School* (Boston: Little, Brown, 1991), and *Broken Contract: A Memoir of Harvard Law School* (New York: Hill and Wang, 1992), respectively, of their experiences with legal education. Much like Turow's, Goodrich's and Kahlenberg's books are personal stories about the loss of a moral vision of learning or service. There are twenty-five years between Turow's and Goodrich's and Kahlenberg's stories. Yet, the initial amazement followed by resentment at discovering that learning to think like a lawyer means losing one's soul described by Goodrich and Kahlenberg is very similar to that recalled in *One L*. The high expectations Goodrich and Kahlenberg had—even in the early 1990s—upon entering law school are remarkable and tell us something about the persistence in the general population of a legal "mystique."

tional persuasive powers that distinguish the lawyer-statesman from the average lawyer may not be accounted for in terms of professional excellence and accomplishment only. Most fundamentally, Kronman argues, what makes of an ordinary lawyer a statesman are certain temperamental qualities or traits of character, the most important of which is the trait of prudence or practical wisdom. The ideal of the lawyer-statesman, that is, is "an ideal of character," a virtue. The professional standing of the lawyer-statesman "is as much to be explained by who he is as what he knows."[25]

To a certain extent, the lawyer-statesman ideal is a child of the Enlightenment. Its most important roots are to be found in a very different intellectual tradition, though, namely that of the common law:

> The lawyer-statesman ideal was partly shaped by an Enlightenment enthusiasm for system and order. But it was also deeply rooted in the common-law tradition that historically had taken a more skeptical view of systematic law reform and stressed the wisdom of proceeding on a case-by-case basis instead. . . . For all its Enlightenment rationalism, the lawyer-statesman ideal viewed the work of lawyers through the prism of the common law. It conceived their primary task to be the argument and adjudication of concrete disputes, and it placed a high value on the character-virtue of practical wisdom that task requires.[26]

It is during that first year of law school when students are exposed for the first time to the case method of instruction that they receive their most basic training in prudence or practical wisdom. Students may well react to the case method the way Scott Turow did, with bafflement and frustration, but most of them will eventually come to appreciate "the way in which it functions as an instrument for the development of moral imagination." The justifications normally given for the continued reliance on this common-law method of instruction even as more and more areas of the law have become codified—that the case method offers the most economical way of giving students a feel for controversies involving boundary problems that cannot be decided by already well-defined principles, that it teaches students to apply the law to concrete, real-life dilemmas, or that it promotes rhetorical skills of fundamental

---

25. Anthony T. Kronman, *The Lost Lawyer: Failing Ideals of the Legal Profession* (Cambridge, Mass.: Harvard University Press, 1993).

26. Ibid., 20–21.

importance to a practicing lawyer—are all correct, but they do not go to the heart of the matter. What the case method essentially consists of, says Kronman, is forced role-playing. In reenacting concrete disputes by playing the roles of the original parties and their attorneys, students learn to be sympathetic to a whole range of different points of view. At the same time, however, since the role that they most often are asked to play is that of the judge, the case method compels them to stand back, as it were, from whatever feelings of sympathy and understanding they may have just entertained and instead assume a disinterested judicial point of view. In this way, the case method "works simultaneously to strengthen both the student's powers of sympathetic understanding and his ability to suppress all sympathies in favor of a judge's scrupulous neutrality."[27]

The process is a complex one. Ultimately, it is the role of the judge that is given priority over the other roles the students are invited to play. This has the effect, according to Kronman, of emphasizing the need to reach a "reasoned" and "publicly justifiable" conclusion to the problems at hand, thereby providing "its own counterweight to the student's growing acceptance of complexity and pluralism in the realm of values, and block[ing] the slide to what might otherwise become the cynical celebration of arbitrariness." The judge's interest ideally being broader than that of the parties involved, the case method, in emphasizing the judicial point of view, encourages student interest in civic-mindedness as well as in the soundness of the legal order. When it works as it is supposed to, therefore, the case method

> sets students on a middle course, strengthening their moral imagination and encouraging them to take a more cosmopolitan view of the diversity of human goods, while also reinforcing, through its insistence on the priority of the judicial point of view, the habit of civic-mindedness that is the only reliable antidote to the cynicism into which all cosmopolitanism threatens to decline.[28]

In recent years, that is, since the late 1960s, the virtue of practical wisdom—the central virtue of the lawyer-statesman—has increasingly come to be viewed as "an embarrassed virtue."[29] Young lawyers merely

27. Ibid., 113.
28. Ibid., 117, 160–61.
29. Kronman calls his first chapter "An Embarrassed Virtue."

laugh or shake their heads at the talk of a possible connection between the virtue of statesmanship and the everyday circumstances of law practice. This has already had and will continue to have disastrous consequences, Kronman warns, for the American legal profession, but also for the American nation. Since about two-thirds of America's political leaders have traditionally been trained as lawyers, the loss of the belief in prudence or practical wisdom as the central virtue of a lawyer will mean that the political leaders of the future will be less qualified to lead than were their predecessors. "Like ripples on a pond, the crisis of values that has overtaken the legal profession in the last twenty-five years must thus in time spread through the whole of our political life with destructive implications for lawyers and non-lawyers alike."[30] What is at stake for Kronman, that is, is nothing less than the well-being of American democracy itself.[31]

Considering the central role that judges play in the legal profession as a whole and the way in which students learn, as a result of the case method, to adopt as their own the perspective of the judge, one of the most disturbing consequences of the collapse of the ideal of the lawyer-statesman, as Kronman sees it, is the weakening of "the sense of personal responsibility that has always been considered an essential condition of judicial integrity in the Anglo-American system of law."[32]

As a former prosecutor in "Operation Greylord," a federal investigation into corruption in the Illinois courts, Scott Turow has had firsthand experience of the demise of the character-virtue of personal responsibility and public-spiritedness that the ideal of the lawyer-statesman stresses. The story of corruption and deceit that unfolds around Judge Larren Lyttle in *Presumed Innocent* may very well be based on the investigation into the finances of a circuit court judge, who was subsequently sentenced to eighteen years in prison for soliciting more than $200,000

30. Kronman, *Lost Lawyer,* 4.

31. Compare Christopher A. Darden's reflections about the O. J. Simpson trial in *In Contempt.* Bitter at the way in which a murder trial turned into a forum for discussing racial prejudice, Darden notes how "sometimes when I am teaching law courses now, I'll look up at my students and wonder what we are teaching them. Am I instilling the respect and responsibility they should have for the law? Because it should be the most important thing for them about being a lawyer—more important than trial technique or billable hours." Christopher A. Darden with Jess Walter, *In Contempt* (New York: Regan Books, 1996), 223.

32. Kronman, *Lost Lawyer,* 325.

in corrupt payments, among other crimes, which Turow led near the end of his tenure in the United States Attorney's office.[33] In the trial of Rozat "Rusty" Sabich, as in any other trial, we are told in *Presumed Innocent*, there are many issues where "a judge is within legal boundaries no matter what he does. The authorities support a ruling for either side."[34] The trustworthiness and moral integrity of a Larren Lyttle is therefore critical.

When Rusty Sabich is told that His Honor, Larren Lyttle, has been selected as the trial judge for his lawsuit, he is delighted. As former chief deputy district attorney, Rusty has often encountered Lyttle in court and knows that he is "the defense lawyer's dream":

> The habits of twenty years as a defense lawyer, in which he regularly manhandled and belittled prosecutors and police, have never left him on the bench. And beyond that, he has the black man's authentic education in the countless ways that prosecutorial discretion can be used to arrogantly excuse unreasoning caprice. The random and complete injustices which he witnessed on the streets have become a kind of emotional encyclopedia for him, informing each decision that is made almost reflexively against the state.

Having this "handsome, mercurial, extraordinarily prepossessing" judge preside over his case is a good omen, Rusty feels—perhaps the only one in the hopeless situation in which he finds himself, being charged with the murder of his colleague and former mistress, Carolyn Polhemus. Having the tables turned on him, so to speak, being all of a sudden that defendant about whom, as a prosecutor, he has often been "preoccupied, imagining how it would feel to sit there, held at the focus of scrutiny," scares him and makes him think of Kafka. At odds with his wife, who feels he has betrayed her and their little son by having an affair with Carolyn, and unable to communicate with his former colleagues and friends during his trial, Rusty is not too sure whom he can confide in and receive support from. Who, in this world of lawyers—"among the sophisticates and hacks, the collection lawyers in their rayon suits, the bankruptcy moguls, the divorce-court screamers, the gold-chained dope lawyers or the smooth likes of Sandy Stern, the big-firm 'litigators' who

33. See Jeff Shear, "A Lawyer Courts Best-Sellerdom," *New York Times*, June 7, 1987.
34. Turow, *Presumed Innocent*, 307.

perform even routine courtroom tasks in pairs"—can he trust, who believes in his innocence?[35]

As it turns out, Judge Lyttle is indeed true to his reputation. On various occasions he rules for the defense, thus indirectly helping Rusty and his lawyer, Alejandro "Sandy" Stern—"one of this town's finest defense lawyers"—proceed with Rusty's case. Most important, he ends Rusty's ordeal after no more than a week's trial by setting him free due to lack of evidence on the prosecution's part. In addressing the jury, Lyttle states his reasons thus:

> No man ought to be brought to trial without sufficient evidence that some fair people might conclude beyond a reasonable doubt that he is guilty. I think justice requires that. And I think that in this case justice has not been done. . . . No person should be held on trial on evidence such as this. I have no doubt that your verdict would be a ringing not guilty. But Mr. Sabich should not have to live with this specter a moment longer.[36]

Noble as this piece of rhetoric may sound, there is a somewhat hollow ring to it when it is taken into consideration that Judge Lyttle stands to gain almost as much as Rusty does from an early dismissal of the case. If the truth about the missing B-file (B for "bribery of law enforcement officials") mysteriously hovering over the entire trial had come out—that it was Larren Lyttle himself, in collaboration with Carolyn Polhemus, who took money from people in exchange for "making cases go away," as the police officer Lipranzer puts it—then he might as well have forgotten all about his dreams of a future on the federal bench. Even though Sandy Stern, who Rusty thinks has carefully orchestrated Lyttle's move for dismissal by constantly bringing up and wanting to go into the B-file, assures Rusty that Judge Lyttle entered a proper decision and that Rusty would have been acquitted anyway, he cannot help feeling somewhat let down. There has, in his opinion, been a sad absence of legal and moral standards, and he does not approve of Stern's subtle ways of creating pressure on Lyttle. About the outcome of the trial, Rusty says to Stern, "I'll always wonder."[37]

It is not only that Judge Lyttle misuses his professional authority to

35. Ibid., 180, 195, 196, 2, 148, 195.
36. Ibid., 170, 366.
37. Ibid., 49, 355, 381.

dismiss Rusty's case early for fear of having his doubtful acts of the past laid bare that bothers Rusty. It is also the fact that "Larren was taking," that "the judge was doing it too" which he deeply resents, just as it had "pissed off the coppers back then." Described by a former colleague as "a non-political guy. A professional prosecutor. Stable. Mature. Somebody everyone can depend on," and considering himself "a person of values," Rusty is disgusted by the selfish motives that can often be discerned behind his colleagues' acts:

> God, I think politics is dirty. And the police department is dirtier. The Medici did not live in a world fuller of intrigue. Every secret alliance in the community comes to bear there. To the alderman and your bookie and your girlfriend . . . Every one of them needs a break. And you give it. In a big-city police department, at least in Kindle County, there is no such thing as playing by the book.[38]

Whether one is a policeman, a coroner, or a district attorney, one's best bet seems to be playing for one's own team. "Justice in the Middle West" does not seem to be faring too well with law enforcement officials such as county prosecutor Raymond Horgan, who is up for reelection and can think of nothing else; his brash opponent, Nico Della Guardia ("a smart-ass ethnic kid," in Rusty's opinion); and Rusty's successor, Tommy Molto, "the kind of prosecutor that the D.A.'s office too often breeds: a lawyer who can no longer make out the boundaries between persuasion and deception, who regards the trial of a lawsuit as a series of gimmicks and tricks." To all these lawyers—Judge Lyttle included—the law is a strictly technical tool to be handled and controlled at will.[39]

His own professional integrity and disillusionment with the way of his colleagues notwithstanding, Rusty Sabich is himself morally culpable, hurting his wife when he becomes obsessed by his mistress. As he realizes, part of the blame for the murder of Carolyn, committed by his wife, Barbara, in an attempt to save their marriage, falls on him. When Sandy Stern advises him not to judge others too harshly and to remember that "not all human misbehavior is the result of gross defects of character. Circumstances matter, too. Temptation," he has the case of Judge Lyttle in mind. He might just as well have been talking about

38. Ibid., 357, 15, 33, 94–95.
39. Ibid., 173, 317.

Rusty, however. When it comes to the personal sphere, it seems, Rusty's moral principles crumble somewhat. Keeping in mind his rejoinder to Stern's talk about mitigating circumstances, that "tolerance doesn't require an absence of standards," the reader cannot help wondering, for example, how, as a trained prosecuting attorney, he can justify keeping the truth about the real murderer to himself and even contemplate living on with this murderer as if nothing had happened.[40]

The obsession Rusty had felt with Carolyn was, we are told, raging mad and utterly devastating:

> I was shattered. Riven. Decimated. Torn to bits. Every moment was turmoil. What I'd struck upon was old and dark and deep . . . I was like a blind ghost groping about a castle and moaning for love . . . I wanted in a way I could not recall—and the desire was insistent, obsessive, and, because of that, somewhat debased.

This is the language of melodrama. Carolyn is described as the whore, the conniving temptress who leads men to sin—"she was a cunt," says one of the policemen. "You know . . . out for herself. She was sleepin her way to the top, right from the git-go. Anybody coulda seen that."[41] No move—sexual or political—was too low for her to make to get her way. Like the other men she had had affairs with—Raymond Horgan and Larren Lyttle, just to mention two—Rusty was nothing more to her than a means to political power. Yet, Rusty stubbornly keeps maintaining throughout that there was more to his fascination for her than the purely sexual—and morally "debased"—aspect. It was partly, he claims, her pain that attracted him to her. Whether we believe Rusty or not, the impression we are left with of Carolyn is one of a totally unscrupulous person—a person who, because of being fatally attractive to men and using this power to her advantage, is seen by her (male) author as being one step further removed from the path of common moral decency than her male colleagues. On the list of morally reprehensible lawyers in *Presumed Innocent,* Carolyn takes the lead.

In the lawyerly world of Scott Turow's first novel, nobody seems to be entirely "above temptation." Politically manipulative and constantly forgetting their moral responsibility as "functionar(ies) of our only uni-

40. Ibid., 374, 380.
41. Ibid., 114.

versally recognized system of telling wrong from right," the lawyers we encounter seem to have forgotten that there is such a thing as truth and justice, and that it is their job to look for it. Apart from Rusty Sabich, who, as we have seen, has at least some measure of professional decency and honesty left, the only possible exception to the sorry lot of corrupt lawyers in the novel is Sandy Stern. This may be the reason why Scott Turow decided to make him the protagonist of his second novel.

The Burden of Proof

Unlike most of the other lawyers in Scott Turow's novels, Sandy Stern, counselor for the defense in *Presumed Innocent* and protagonist of *The Burden of Proof,* believes that there is a connection between law and morality and that as a lawyer he has a moral responsibility to care for those who are in trouble. Throughout his successful career, Stern has for the most part "allowed himself the luxury of a clear conscience." As a young lawyer he did at times have to do things for money—things that today he no longer cares to recall. "But one of the clearest grains in his character as a lawyer was the desire to let his clients know that he did not wade in the same polluted waters they did." By steering clear of the various pitfalls confronting a lawyer eager to prove himself, and by avoiding becoming the "winking collaborator" of any of his clients, Stern has earned for himself a reputation as an honest, fair, and accessible lawyer—somebody who cares about justice and about giving a fair treatment to all his clients, rich or poor.[42] In his professional life, therefore, the keywords have been uprightness, honesty, and moral integrity.

The professional ideal to which Stern aspires is not unlike that of Anthony Kronman's lawyer-statesman. Moreover, for Stern, as for Kronman, the idea of law is intimately tied up with the idea of America. Stern had come to the United States from Argentina when he was thirteen years old, and

> He was one of those immigrants who still became weak with sentiment— and gratitude—on the Fourth of July. What an idea this country was! The flourishing of the liberal democracies, with their ideal of equality, remained in his eyes, along with advances in medical care and the invention of movable type, humankind's grandest achievement of the millen-

42. Turow, *The Burden of Proof* (New York: Farrar, Straus, Giroux, 1990), 52, 198.

. nium. His life in the law—at the criminal bar, in particular—was somehow bound up with those beliefs.[43]

With "its substance, its venerated traditions, and its relentless con-
templation of social relations," the law seems to Sandy "capable of
providing one set of proposed answers" to the problems of modern
society. Being a defense lawyer, helping out people who for one reason
or another are in trouble, is a calling to him. When he receives a tempting offer of becoming federal prosecutor, he carefully deliberates but
eventually declines. He "could not. No. Could not," for:

> No person Argentine by birth, a Jew alive to hear of the Holocaust could
> march in the jackboots of authority without intense self-doubt; better to
> keep his voice among the voices, to speak out daily for these frail liber-
> ties, so misunderstood, whose existence, far more than any prosecution
> marked us all as decent, civilized, as human. He could not abandon the
> credo of a lifetime now.[44]

"To be an *American*"—that was what Stern wanted more than anything else when he first came to the United States as a young immigrant.
Many years later, when we meet him in first *Presumed Innocent* and then
The Burden of Proof, he has by and large achieved this goal. Apart from a
slight accent, not much is left from his earliest years in Argentina. The
means he chose to become an American was the law, and once he has
made it as a lawyer, he "adore[s] the practice of law," which enables him
to defend those "frail" American liberties. He may wonder from time to
time about his "mad devotion to people who balked at paying fees, who
scorned him the moment a case was lost," but never for a moment does
he doubt that he may do something valuable for his fellowman as a
defense lawyer.

> Some spoke of the nobility of the law. Stern did not believe in that. Too
> much of the grubby bone shop, the odor of the abattoir, emanated from
> every courtroom he had entered. It was often a nasty business. But the
> law, at least, sought to govern misfortune, the slights and injuries of our
> social existence that were otherwise wholly random. The law's object was

43. Ibid., 371.
44. Ibid., 252, 131–32.

to let the seas engulf only those who had been selected for drowning on an orderly basis. In human affairs, reason would never fully triumph; but there was no better cause to champion.[45]

When it comes to the personal sphere of Stern's life, however, things are more complicated. If he has made it as a lawyer, he has failed utterly as a husband and father. Having "lived decades never wholly knowing what was occurring behind Clara's composed and gracious facade," Stern is taken completely by surprise by the suicide of his wife. For years, Clara had had "spells" or "moods," but they were always allowed to pass. He had prided himself on his "discretion," but now he cannot help blaming himself for failing "to notice in the bed beside him a woman who in every figurative sense was screaming in pain." As he attempts to unravel the painful mystery of Clara's death, he is forced to confront all that he truly does not or has not wanted to know about his marriage, family, and career. He realizes, for example, that without Clara's mediating influence, he does not know how to communicate with his children. And when he finds out that it was his brother-in-law Dixon with whom Clara had an affair many years ago which resulted in her contracting herpes, the sad truth is finally brought home to him that "this drama, all of the play, had transpired entirely out of his presence. He roamed offstage in Kansas City. In the arms of his own jealous mistress. Absorbed in the role he liked best, he had managed to miss the signal events of his lifetime." This estrangement from his wife and his children is the price he has had to pay for a flourishing career as a lawyer.[46]

Ironically enough, the lesson Stern learns from his wife's suicide and all the events that follow is not unlike the one he himself taught Rusty Sabich in *Presumed Innocent*, that it is human to err but not impossible to make up for the mistakes one has made. It is not, the narrator of the novel tells us, that human beings are willfully evil; it is just that, "by whatever name—self-interest, impulse, anger, lust, or greed—we are inclined that way." Our tragedy is to know that we will never change, but we do have a duty all the same to try as far as possible to overcome our weaknesses. At this, we may occasionally succeed—especially if we are given a second chance.

45. Ibid., 8, 426, 202.
46. Ibid., 384, 412, 384.

"Do you believe," [Helen] asked, "that we are doomed to repeat the same mistakes all our lives?" "There is that tendency," [Stern] said. But, of course, if he believed that the soul would forever be a slave to its private fetishes, why had he come to the U.S.? Why did he cry out for justice for those who were the most often unredeemable? What, indeed, had he spent these months trying to transcend? "But I also believe in second chances."[47]

Stern is given a second chance in more than one way. The isolated man who used to look at the world from afar and who would draw a certain comfort from stillness has disappeared by the end of the novel. Thrown together with and forced to relate to friends and family members in a more direct way as a result of his wife's death, Stern ends up taking a much more active part in the lives of the people around him.

Pleading Guilty

Like Sandy Stern, the first-person narrator and protagonist of Scott Turow's third novel, McCormack "Mack" Malloy, is offered a second chance. But unlike Sandy Stern, Mack Malloy decides against accepting this chance. *Pleading Guilty* tells the story of Mack's personal and professional downfall. Mack is an "ex-drunk former copper" turned corporate lawyer who works for one of Kindle County's top law firms. He was once a fairly successful litigator, but over the past few years his career has been going downhill. When the novel opens, he is mostly "doing odds and ends for (the) other partners . . . trying cases they are too busy for."[48] When Bert Kamin, one of Mack's partners, disappears along with $5.6 million from a fund established to settle a massive air-disaster class action, Mack is assigned the sensitive task of finding Bert and the money.

Much is at stake, for the law firm as well as for Mack himself. The $5.6 million fund was set up by the firm's most important client, Trans-National Airlines (TNA), which for some time has shown dissatisfaction with the work done by the firm's lawyers and has hinted that it plans to change law firms. Evidence of embezzlement might give TNA the best possible excuse for seeking legal expertise elsewhere and leave the firm without its most significant source of income. And should Mack fail to locate Bert and the money, his own well-paying job will be in

47. Ibid., 511, 514.
48. Ibid., 51.

serious danger. The situation is critical, and Mack has no choice but to "take on Mission Impossible and buy myself a job."[49]

At this point in his life, Mack is, as he himself admits,

> a troubled individual . . . kind of a wreck from all directions—overweight even by the standards of big men who seem to get some latitude, gimpy on rainy days because I ruined my knee while I was a copper . . . My skin, from two decades of drinking hard, has got that reddened look. . . . Worse is what goes on inside. I have a sad heart, stomped on, fevered and corrupted, and a brain that boils at night in a ferment of awful dreams.

In the middle of a midlife crisis as he is approaching fifty, Mack is full of bitterness that nothing turned out the way it was supposed to. His wife has left him for her lesbian lover, their only son is a monster with whom he has no relations to speak of, and neither the career as a famous artist nor that of a star litigator of which he used to dream when he was younger has materialized. Apart from his missing partner, Bert, who "is sort of like the way people figure me, smart but basic," and his other partner and subsequent lover, Emilia Bruccia or Brushy, he does not really get along with anybody. He spends most of his time feeling sorry for himself, refusing to get involved with anything or anybody. Watching others go about their jobs with genuine interest and concern makes him feel "a spy, a clandestine agent from somewhere else" who takes "no part in the joy that everybody here seemed to feel in belonging." Why is it, he wistfully asks himself, that "they cared and I didn't?"[50]

It is especially the commitment of his two partners, Brushy and Martin Gold, to their jobs, the firm, and the law in general that stirs in Mack feelings of envy and regret at his own withdrawn existence. Brushy and Martin are alike in many ways; both highly intelligent and loyal, they can be ruthless if they have to. They are "lawyer[s] every waking hour. . . . Something in the law is always at hand and on [their] mind[s]." For Brushy, the law, "all this right and wrong . . . is nifty," and Mack cannot help feeling somewhat jealous of the fact that it is the law—and not Mack himself—that is the real love of her life. As for Martin, "the man I love," he is

---

49. Turow, *Pleading Guilty* (London: Viking, 1993), 36.
50. Ibid., 16, 19, 26, 109.

one of those men who abound in the legal profession whose brains seem to make them a quarter larger than life. His mind is always zipping along at the speed of an electron. You sit down with him and feel surrounded on all sides.[51]

Accompanying Martin's impressive intelligence, Mack tells us, is a remarkable grasp of human nature. Engaging in a conversation with Martin is like entering a contest that you know you cannot win. Martin obviously enjoys the sense of superiority and power that this gives him.[52] But that does not alter the fact that he is "your veritable Person of Values, a lawyer who does not see the law as just business or sport." Martin sits on a number of do-good committees and takes active part in local politics. This enables him to attract a lot of clients, but

> it's not just the sense of being important by attachment that excites him. It's also what his clients want to know: right or wrong, allowable or no. He's the navigator, the person with the compass, the man who tells the high and mighty, if not about morals, then at least about principles and rules.[53]

It is precisely this belief on Martin's part that he is involved in activities that are fundamentally sound and good to which Mack is drawn. Compared to his own shallow existence, Martin's life looks utterly fulfilling, glamorous, and worthwhile. As Mack describes Martin, we are reminded, once again, of Kronman's ideal of the lawyer-statesman. Realizing that the reader may find his glowing account of Martin somewhat exaggerated, Mack gets embarrassed and feels the need to explain "how it is."

> It's easy to be a poet sitting behind the gates of a university or a monk in a monastery and feel there is a life of the spirit to which you are dedicated. But come into the teeming city, with so many souls screaming, I want, I need, where most social planning amounts to figuring out how to keep them all at bay—come and try to imagine the ways that vast unruly

51. Ibid., 57, 173, 63.
52. Ibid., 63. "Martin would not be mistaken for Mother Teresa. Like anybody else who has whizzed along the fast track in the practice of law, he can cut your heart out if need be."
53. Ibid., 171, 171–72.

community can be kept in touch with the deeper aspirations of human-kind for the overall improvement of the species, the good of the many and the rights of the few. That I always figured was the task of the law, and it makes high-energy physics look like a game show.[54]

When, toward the end of his investigations into the disappearance of Bert Kamin and the $5.6 million, all the evidence seems to point toward Martin as the one who has been masterminding the whole thing, Mack is crushed. He confronts his former hero with his suspicion that Martin has cut an ugly deal with TNA to improve the firm's relations with its biggest client. Martin does indeed plead guilty—not to cutting the deal, however, but to trying to preserve the firm. As it turns out, Martin has done nothing wrong; on the contrary, he has acted like a true lawyer-statesman. It is consequently now Mack who has to plead guilty: "I'd misjudged Martin and his complexities. You wouldn't call his conduct saintly, but he'd done better than I thought—and, God knows, a hell of a lot better than me."[55]

When Mack realizes that he has been wrong about Martin, it is too late, however. Having located the money, he has already transferred it to his own account. Bitterly disappointed at Martin's conduct and com-mitted to his "own kind of rough justice," Mack had been acting with the "fixed intention to smite Martin and the whole smarmy scheme." He had contacted the one person he knew could be counted on to act on his information about Martin: Carl Pagnucci. A member of the Man-agement Oversight Committee, Carl had intimate knowledge of the firm's problems with TNA and "had already been making contingency plans" in case TNA decided to move on to a different law firm. When Mack had proposed that Carl approach the chief executive of TNA and tell him the truth about Martin, he had known that Carl would see this as a wonderful opportunity to "salute the flag and steal the client." By making it look as if he were acting, on behalf of the firm, out of a moral obligation toward their client, he would make sure that his candor would be remembered by TNA in the future. "Moving on, he would take some of TNA's work with him, even as [the firm] sank."[56]

What Mack had been banking on was Carl's utter selfishness, his will

54. Ibid., 172.
55. Ibid., 356.
56. Ibid., 333, 334, 333.

to save himself at all costs. On wife number four and driving one modified Formula One car after another, Carl loves life in the fast lane. Every soul for itself, Mack tells us,

> is Carl's creed. He worships at the altar of the free market. The same way Freud thought everything was sex, Pagnucci believes all social interaction, no matter how complex, can be adjusted by finding a way to put a price on it. Urban housing. Education. We need competition and profit motive to make it all work.[57]

Carl, we are quickly given to understand, is not Mack's favorite among his partners. Carl is the kind of lawyer you can cut a deal with, the kind of lawyer who sees the law as just business or power. Yet it is Carl whom Mack turns out to resemble the most. His commitment to "rough justice" does not last long. Attempting to give him that second chance in which Stern believed, both Martin and Brushy try to tell Mack that there is still time, but he absolutely refuses to give the money back. As we leave him, he is heading off to Pico Luan, promising to be drunk for the rest of his life. In the end, he is so "tired of being myself—of fucking things up the way I do" that he cannot help thinking "how great it would be to start new. A really clean slate. It's the only thing left that excites me."[58]

Like *Presumed Innocent* and *The Burden of Proof, Pleading Guilty* is about human aspirations and human fallibility. The ideal of Anthony Kronman's lawyer-statesman, we recall, has everything to do with human character. For Scott Turow, too, a lawyer's professional standing "is as much to be explained by who he is as what he knows." And the way in which the personalities of his characters are shown to us is by means of their views on and relation to the law and matters of a legal nature. The law is the pillar on which Scott Turow's morality plays rest.

CONCLUDING REMARKS

In his provocative and interesting contribution to the debate about professional responsibility, *The Lost Lawyer,* Anthony T. Kronman attempts to revive the common-law ideal of the lawyer—whether judge, attorney, or scholar—as practitioner of prudence or practical wisdom.

57. Ibid., 176.
58. Ibid., 318, 199.

Fearing that this is a somewhat futile attempt, he merely hopes, as he puts it in his Introduction, to help individuals "find a way to honor this ideal in their own careers . . . by searching out the cracks and crevices in which a person devoted to the ideal of the lawyer-statesman may still make a living in the law." On such individual lawyers, "the continued existence of the lawyer-statesman ideal—even marginally, interstitially, contrapuntally—depends."[59]

Kronman may well be too bleak in his assessment of the current situation. Judging from the popularity of Scott Turow's novels, the television show *The People's Court* and other courtroom shows, the recent surge of feminist detective fiction, and other contemporary cultural "events"—some of which will be discussed in the following chapters—the soul of the common law is alive and well, if not among all American lawyers, then very much in the popular consciousness. To Scott Turow, as to Kronman, there is every reason to warn against the dangers of an antiprudentialist or positivist takeover of American legal education. Most of the lawyers we meet in his novels are the product of the ideal of scientific law reform or the positivist approach to law as exemplified in *One L* by Professor Perini. For these lawyers there is no such thing as an internal morality of law, no specific moral purpose for which our legal system exists. They may occasionally use such terms as justice, responsibility, rights and duties, law and order, but they use them with the knowledge that they cannot be more than provisional, something to be created and re-created continuously to meet the needs of professional practice. Yet, the very fact that Turow manages to fix on something noble, to endow at least a couple of these characters with selfless and dignified motives—the cynical power and other games they are playing with each other notwithstanding—suggests the survival even into this legal positivist day and age of an older belief in professional integrity.

Professors William Zechman and Nicki Morris in *One L*, Deputy District Attorney Rusty Sabich in *Presumed Innocent*, perhaps in particular the protagonist of *The Burden of Proof*, Sandy Stern, and Martin Gold in *Pleading Guilty*, are the exceptions that prove the rule, so to speak, in the positivized lawyerly world that Turow creates for his readers. For Stern as well as for Gold, the American way is intimately tied up with the idea of law—nowhere are the rights and freedoms of the individual better and more properly seen to than in the letter of the law.

59. Kronman, *Lost Lawyer*, 7.

Caring not only for the formal requirements of valid law, but also for its moral content, Stern and Gold embody and keep alive the spirit of the common law—a spirit, admonishes Turow, that all American lawyers would do well not to forget.

Though more powerful than Tom Wolfe's, Turow's commitment to the promise and ideal of law must struggle for expression. Interestingly enough, for example, none of the more promising or hopeful characters in his three novels are judges. With *The Laws of Our Fathers* from 1996, however, this has changed.[60] Here, for the first time, Turow "allows" the central figure in his novel to be a judge. We have met Her Honor, Judge Sonia Klonsky before. In *The Burden of Proof*, she plays a brief but important part as a young assistant district attorney with whom Sandy Stern almost falls in love. Like Larren Lyttle, who is exposed as a morally corrupt judge in *Presumed Innocent*, Judge Klonsky, in *The Laws of Our Fathers*, presides over an aborted murder trial that does not reveal the truth about the murder in question, but unlike Lyttle she struggles hard to maintain her integrity. Turow's series consequently now ends with a figure not so far removed from one of the most unabashedly affirmative legal figures in American culture, Judge Joseph Wapner of *The People's Court.*

60. Turow, *The Laws of Our Fathers* (New York: Warner Books, 1996).

IV

Law as Soap Opera and Game Show
The Case of *The People's Court*

I n his introduction to *The Tolerant Society*, Lee C. Bollinger expresses dissatisfaction with current explanations and theories of the modern concept of freedom of speech. What most explanations and theories regarding the importance to modern American society of this concept fail to understand, he claims, is that "while the interpretive authority over the free speech principle has become part of the legal realm, the free speech idea nonetheless remains one of our foremost *cultural* symbols. It is suffused with symbolic significance."[1] The idea of free speech has, in fact, become an integral part of the American character and mentality, and it is important to realize that this broader social symbolism interacts in numerous ways with the strictly legal process of interpreting and applying the principle.

It is to an analysis of the reciprocal relationship between the legal analysis and the cultural symbolism of freedom of speech that *The Tolerant Society* is dedicated. The conclusion that Bollinger reaches is that freedom of speech is a highly complex enterprise which has acquired in modern American society a more involved function than the "classical" one of preventing the state and federal governments from interfering in the democratic process, or protecting the right and access to free speech for minorities against tyrannical majorities. Since the

1. Lee C. Bollinger, *The Tolerant Society* (New York: Oxford University Press, 1986), 7.

beginning of this century, free speech has developed into a forum for defining certain fundamental intellectual values and certain preferred behavioral patterns in modern, pluralistic America. The idea of free speech addresses broad, general questions, that is, speaks to the intellectual, moral, and political makeup and character of American society.

> Besides their concrete and particular consequences, which sometimes, to be sure, are considerable, free speech cases also constitute fundamentally symbolic social activity. They are like theater, especially classical Greek drama, in which extreme behavior takes place that is socially defined through the context of the litigation stage. Sometimes the value of a given case is to be found more in its dramatic potential than in its particular factual importance. This perspective helps to account for a highly interesting feature of First Amendment jurisprudence: it includes an extraordinary number of disputes that, looked at in isolation, seem nothing short of trivial and socially inconsequential.[2]

Bollinger's point that the idea of free speech is one of the foremost "cultural symbols" of modern America is well taken and important. The question is, in fact, whether it may not be expanded to apply beyond the idea of free speech to the role of the law, lawyers, and the legal system as a whole. In a thoroughly law-permeated society such as America, it is the law in *all* its manifestations and not only the concept of freedom of speech that has become a "cultural symbol." Bollinger's argument may therefore be taken one step further, as it were. If the idea of free speech addresses broader questions of general importance in modern American society, it is but a symptom—albeit a very important one—of an even wider phenomenon: the peculiar and powerful fascination that the law, lawyers, and the legal system in general hold for the average American. "The law," says Kenneth Karst in *Law's Promise, Law's Expression,* "says something important about the meanings of America. The point of law is the state's official stamp of approval. . . . Law is seen as an official statement of the meanings of behavior, an authoritative pronouncement of public values. . . ."[3]

One of the longest running and most popular syndicated series on American television ever, broadcast daily and seen by more than twenty

2. Ibid., 169–70.

3. Kenneth L. Karst, *Law's Promise, Law's Expression: Visions of Power in the Politics of Race, Gender, and Religion* (New Haven: Yale University Press, 1993), 19, 18, 50.

million Americans, was *The People's Court*. The participants in this show, which premiered in the 1981–82 season and ran through the 1992–93 season, were "real" people who had chosen to have their cases heard not by a "real" court, but by Judge Joseph A. Wapner on *The People's Court*. This mixture of fact and fiction (as a retired judge, Wapner was as "real" as the rest of the participants on the show) became so popular that Judge Wapner reached the status of a folk hero. Some commentators, speaking only half in jest, suggested him for appointment to the Supreme Court. In the film *Rain Man*, one of his ardent fans, Dustin Hoffman, portrayed the autistic Raymond as a Wapner fan ("Oh, oh. Time for Judge Wapner"), and in June 1989 a *Washington Post* survey announced that many more Americans, by a margin of 54 percent to 9 percent, knew Wapner's name than that of William H. Rehnquist, the Chief Justice of the Supreme Court.[4]

The People's Court dealt primarily with the most mundane aspects of daily life: sick pets, improperly cleaned laundry, overcharging repairmen, and the like. Its phenomenal following and acclaim may therefore not be accounted for in terms of its spectacular quality; rather, it seems to be precisely the everyday nature of the litigants and their grievances that made it so popular. This chapter will discuss *The People's Court*, its interest in law in action and in controversies resolved before our very eyes without a script. The main argument is that the popularity of this "authentic television innovation"[5] was due not only to its aura of realism and genuine human conduct, but also to its "timing": its being exactly the right kind of show in a day and age that is thoroughly law-permeated and obsessed with personal rights and rights of redress. *The People's Court* may not have had much in common with classical Greek drama, but it displayed precisely the kind of theater discussed by Bollinger in connection with free-speech cases, "in which extreme behavior takes place that is socially defined through the context of the litigation stage" and which "includes an extraordinary number of disputes that, looked at in isolation, seem nothing short of trivial and socially inconsequential."[6] The subtext of *The People's Court* was a highly interesting discussion about the role of the legal system, moral values, and preferred behavior in modern, pluralistic, and law-permeated America.

4. This information is from *Current Biography Yearbook,* 1989, 606–9.
5. Alan Dershowitz, "The Verdict," *American Film,* Dec. 1987, 15–18.
6. Bollinger, *The Tolerant Society,* 169–70.

AMERICAN TELEVISION AND COURTROOM SHOWS

Up through the 1980s and 1990s, daytime television has displayed an increasingly crowded courtroom calendar. Amid game shows and soap operas, several syndicated shows have offered entertainment in the form of real or simulated law cases. It began in 1981 with the debut of *The People's Court*, whose innovative concept was to show actual small-claims cases being argued on camera. Originally conceived by Stu Billett and John Masterson in the mid- to late-1970s, about the time the California Judicial Council authorized the presence of television cameras in the courts, the show became an immediate hit. Before it went on the air, however, the concept of *The People's Court* had been turned down by several networks including NBC. Keeping up faith in this "combination of soap opera and game show," Billett and Ralph Edwards, who had by now teamed up with Billett, finally succeeded in persuading ABC that the show "was perfect for access fringe time, a transition from soap operas to the reality of the news."[7]

The immediate and continuing success of *The People's Court* indicated an abiding audience interest in courtroom shows. In 1984, this success was accordingly followed up by a revival of a series from the 1950s and '60s, *Divorce Court*. Two years later, two additional TV-tribunals were convened, *Superior Court* and *The Judge*. In addition, there have been periodic specials like "You, the Jury," with viewers watching a staged trial and using their telephones to vote on the verdict, and prime-time programs like *L.A. Law*, which in two years went on to become one of the highest-rated shows on American television, and *Night Court*. One of the latest inventions is *Judge Judy*, a half-hour show taped in Hollywood which premiered in September 1996. Before going to Hollywood, Judge Judith B. Sheindlin spent almost thirty-five years in New York City's family courts as a prosecuting lawyer and then as a judge dealing with child abuse, juvenile crime, and foster care.

For those who wanted still more, Courtroom Television Network started broadcasting court proceedings live in 1991. By then, most states had passed laws that allowed television cameras into courtrooms, and it was not difficult for Steve Brill, the founder of Court Television, to find backing for "the idea that the new network would be a cross between

---

7. Stu Billett, quoted in Curt Schleier, " 'People's Court' Endured Long Trial before Verdict," *Advertising Age,* Jan. 10, 1985.

C-Span and soap opera." The purpose of the new channel, Brill claims, "is to show the workings of the third branch of the government [and] make what lawyers do understandable to the public." Cases are chosen not for sensationalism but because they concern an important legal principle or controversy. Together with his three coanchors, who are all law school graduates, Fred Graham, former legal correspondent for CBS News and recruited by Brill to anchor and help promote the new network, provides constant explanations of legal procedures and jargons. In addition, various outspoken courtroom celebrities discuss prosecution and defense strategies. Interestingly enough, considering that for hours on end the television screen may show little more than a lawyer's back, this new cable offering has had high daytime ratings ever since it made its debut. But then again, as Brill puts it, "the legal system is the way we fight our battles in this society."[8]

As previously mentioned, *The People's Court* was seen by twenty million viewers nationwide each day and was consistently among the top-ten syndicated programs.[9] Other courtroom shows have not enjoyed this kind of popularity, even though they too have had high ratings. Two cases were presented per episode, both drawn from small-claims courts in the Los Angeles area. In each case, the parties would be given a chance to present their side of the matter at hand, whereupon Judge Wapner would briefly withdraw to his chambers before giving his ruling. In one half-hour show, that is, commercials and stations breaks left Judge Wapner approximately twenty minutes in which to administer justice. Wapner's decision was final, since the litigants on the show agreed to waive their right to proceed in a real courtroom. Stu Billett, who produced the show, had a staff looking through small-claims court records for likely cases. If a case appeared interesting, both parties were contacted and interviewed "to make sure they can articulate their case and that they care about it."[10] About fifty interviews were conducted every week for twenty-five cases. Unlike real courts, *The People's Court* paid all monetary awards.[11] If the plaintiff won, the producers paid the judg-

8. Steve Brill, quoted in Marlys Harris, "Making Crime Pay," *People*, Apr. 20, 1992, 96.
9. Lisa Belkin, "Realism of the Courtroom Captivates TV-Audiences," *New York Times*, July 22, 1987.
10. Stu Billett, quoted in Schleier, " 'People's Court.' "
11. The limit in a small-claims case was $2,000.

ment and $50 to the defendant. If the defendant won, both litigants split the $500 fund set aside for each case by the producers. In either case, no one lost except in principle.[12]

In addition to Judge Wapner, each episode of *The People's Court* featured Rusty Burrell, the armed, uniformed bailiff of the show who was entrusted with administering the oath, and the "reporter," Doug Llewelyn. Burrell used to serve as bailiff in the Los Angeles County Sheriff's Department, which made his presence on the show as "authentic" as Wapner's. Llewelyn was the show's only professional actor. A former Washington, D.C., news anchorman, he did the introductions, occasionally polled the studio audience for its reaction, and conducted brief interviews with the litigants after their trial. Llewelyn was also the one who ended each episode of *The People's Court* with a standard warning to the viewers: "Remember, if you're involved in a dispute with another party and you can't work it out, don't take the law into your own hands. You take them to *The People's Court!*" Just as it did for Wapner himself, the show's overwhelming success made celebrities of Burrell and Llewelyn. When it came to Wapner's charismatic personality and cult hero status, however, Burrell and Llewelyn never measured up. There was only one superstar on *The People's Court*!

Why is it, then, that so many people were so interested in watching two persons argue in front of a third? What made a show that dealt primarily with the most mundane aspects of daily life so enormously popular? It had a popularity, moreover, that extended beyond the average viewer to practitioners of the legal profession itself. Rumor has it, for instance, that former Supreme Court justice Thurgood Marshall had a habit of withdrawing to his chambers to watch *The People's Court,* just as Harvard Law School professor Alan Dershowitz, "along with some other law professors I know who shall remain nameless," tried to catch as many episodes of the show as he could. The show's phenomenal following and acclaim was "well-deserved," says Dershowitz.

> *People's Court* is a truly great show—an authentic television innovation. There are no actors, no phony tears. The disputes are believable. The disputants are actual. The passions are genuine. And the reality shows through. Judge Wapner is an arbitrator in robes who dispenses rough

---

12. See Susan Barron, "Lights! Camera! Justice!" *The Washingtonian,* July 1989, 115.

justice, cuts through the verbiage, splits the difference, and detects bull-shit with a seemingly unerring ear. Unlike too many "real" judges, Wapner has no agenda other than to do justice among the litigants who have elected to appear before him. And justice he does, in a manner calculated to instill confidence in winners and losers alike. If only real courts were as fair.[13]

The realistic quality and mundaneness upon which Dershowitz bases his verdict in favor of *The People's Court* is the quality most often referred to by fans of the show. Somehow, it seems, there is something reassuringly familiar about the very banality of the human condition played out before us. The problems that people on *The People's Court* had are everyday problems—problems that every one of us may very well already have had or may someday get. As Dershowitz also mentions, much credit was due to Judge Wapner himself. To many viewers, the man on the bench was the main attraction. Handing down binding decisions with the benign authority of a man who had heard it all during his twenty years on California municipal and superior courts, Wapner exuded competence and confidence. When faced with a legal dilemma, Wapner loyalists would much rather turn to this Solomon of small-claims than to, say, Chief Justice Rehnquist.

Wapner himself did not seem to mind that he developed into a kind of father figure. As he repeatedly stated, he perceived his primary function to be educational. "The show educates people in basic law. It shows that in cases where the claim is monetarily small, they have a place to go. And it teaches people how to present a case."[14] That other judges often told him how small-claims litigants came to their courtrooms better prepared for having watched his show made him satisfied that he was fulfilling a need. More than having brought a whole new forum, small-claims courts, and thereby the possibility of vindicating even the seemingly most insignificant of wrongs, to the country's attention, however, Wapner prided himself on enhancing the public's perception of the judiciary. "There may well have been judges who know better about the relationship of law and economics or other new studies in law," he tells us in *A View from the Bench*. "But I was a judge whom people could trust

13. Dershowitz, "The Verdict," 15.
14. Joseph A. Wapner, quoted in *Current Biography Yearbook,* 1989, 609.

to see problems to their heart and offer a fair resolution. That was the reputation I cherished."[15]

It is clear from his "recollection of a life in the law," as he called *A View from the Bench,* that the law was not just the law to Joseph A. Wapner. Whenever the law forgets about human compassion and plain common sense, it becomes heartless. That is when the judge has to step in and correct the balance, making sure that he puts his own eyes and ears and good sense into the case before him. "Look for the truth of a case with your own eyes," Wapner admonishes. "The law is not supposed to be run like a machine, with inanimate facts being put in one end and an inanimate verdict coming out the other end. The law has a person there to enforce it and render judgments. Let that *person* have something to say." Even with a good judge, though, who can bring equity to the law, going through a trial may not always be the best, fastest, and most efficient way of dispensing justice. It is, of course, essential to have a legal system with adequate safeguards of constitutional rights, but much too often a trial will consume vast amounts of money, time, and human energy without leading to a fair solution of the problem at hand. Wapner therefore declares himself an eager advocate of settlements. "A settlement is almost always preferable to a trial and that is the most basic of legal truths."[16] Whether on the bench rendering judgments or off the bench negotiating his way to a settlement, therefore, the judge is the all-important person. This is how it was in the old common-law system, and this is how it was in the (TV) world of Joseph A. Wapner. No wonder he came across as the competent jurist and benign father figure!

In addition to the realism and mundaneness of *The People's Court* and the role played by Judge Wapner, commentators list as a third reason for the appeal of the show a certain voyeuristic impulse in most people: the enjoyment of seeing other people's problems and of comparing one's own with other people's lives. Finally, viewers may have thought that they were getting free legal advice simply by turning on their TV set. Encountering on an episode of *The People's Court* a problem that looked similar to one of their own may have persuaded viewers that they did indeed have a case. And if those viewers decided to take their cases to court, they would know how best to present them. All in all, judges and lawyers claim, the program increased public awareness of court pro-

15. Wapner, *A View from the Bench* (New York: Penguin Books, 1987), 163.
16. Ibid., 26–27, 162.

cedures and the law and inspired small-claims litigants to come to court better prepared, thereby affecting the standard of acceptable courtroom behavior.[17] "People see that there is a forum for settling grievances besides using a two-by-four," as Sol Wachtler, former chief judge of the State Court of Appeals in New York, puts it. "People see a court in action, administering justice fairly, albeit in a commercial context. It acts as a primer."[18]

Changes have unmistakably come about in the past fifteen years as a result of *The People's Court.* Not everyone agrees that these changes are for the better, though. It may well be that the program has helped increase public awareness of the law, critics concede, but what has also increased is the caseload of once-obscure small-claims courts. And in contemporary law-permeated America, court dockets do not exactly need to be more clogged than they already are. Furthermore, the quality of the cases taken to the country's small-claims courts after the debut of *The People's Court* has suffered, these critics say. "Lawsuits over the thickness of a slice of pizza, for heaven's sake"—how much more frivolous can it get?[19] Then there is the example set by the procedure of the show as well as by Judge Wapner himself. "To the extent that people don't realize that they must pay if they lose or that they presume the award will be executed immediately if they win, the show is giving litigants a misimpression of life in small-claims courts."[20] Judge Wapner's knowledge of the law is judged insufficient by certain critics, just as his demeanor on the bench is looked upon as too showmanlike and sarcastic. According to such critics, in short, Wapner and *The People's Court* cast a shadow over the real courts. To such accusations Wapner would commonsensically and good-naturedly answer that "if the good in something outweighs the negative, then it's a plus. If we demystify the small-claims court process, then it's all to the good."[21] And to the twenty million fans of *The People's Court,* "the good" does indeed by far seem to have outweighed "the negative"!

17. See Lisa Belkin, "Realism of the Courtroom."

18. Quoted in ibid.

19. Judge Mikva, U.S. Court of Appeals for the District of Columbia, quoted in Margot Slade, " 'The People's Court': The Case for and against It," *New York Times* (The Law), May 5, 1989.

20. Tom Lawrence, presiding justice of the peace in Harris County, Texas, quoted in ibid.

21. Quoted in ibid.

Judge Wapner no longer rides the television circuit. Interestingly enough, however, *The People's Court* has returned to television in a new version with former New York City mayor Ed Koch presiding over the court. Produced by Ralph Edwards and Stu Billett, the same team that was responsible for the original series, the updated *People's Court* originates from New York. The new version, which premiered in September 1996, is longer (one hour) than the old one, but the format remains the same. Two or three cases are heard per episode. The series draws on ordinary people who have filed grievances with small-claims court in and around New York City, but who have opted to have their cases heard and mediated by Koch, whose decision is final and binding. An integral part of the show's updated format is its interactivity. During the show, co–executive producer and on-air legal anchor Harvey Levine engages in discussions with viewers who feel strongly about a case or a legal issue. Also, *The People's Court* has its own website that allows participants to preview the next day's trial and vote in favor of either the plaintiff or the defendant.

The decision to resurrect *The People's Court* is an obvious attempt on the part of its producers to cash in on the phenomenal success enjoyed by the original show. But for anyone to try to follow in Judge Wapner's footsteps is a serious challenge. Whether or not Ed Koch is up to it, it is still too early to say.

READING POPULAR CULTURE

> Films, like all cultural-intellectual creations, participate in their society's public conversation . . . To understand and evaluate any cultural comment one has to listen as closely as one can to what is said and to understand as far as possible how that reverberates within the general cultural conversation in which it occurs.[22]

As David Grimsted reminds us, the reading of popular culture requires looking as closely at the text as the reading of any other kind of culture does. Rather than uncritically taking over the sharply drawn dichotomies—high and low, elite and mass—of what he calls "the classical debate," or the definition of all mass culture as an illustration of the

---

22. David Grimsted, "The Purple Rose of Popular Culture Theory: An Exploration of Intellectual Kitsch," *American Quarterly* 43.4 (Dec. 1991), 543.

dominant, self-evident ideology of capitalism and/or patriarchy of "postclassical theories," the critic must respect the complex nature of cultural consumption. Excluding wide areas of culture from serious consideration simply because they are popular, commercial, mass-marketed, and easily understandable merely serves to assert "the superior discrimination of the critics, most of whom despise or despair over mass culture's emptiness and baleful influence from political perspectives ranging from Mandarin to fundamentalist, from proto-fascist to Marxist to democratic." Only by leaving behind elitist/intellectual snobbery and preconceived notions of quality, only by meeting the popular text with an open mind may we "*learn* in a way almost never encouraged in the classic debate: to see better, to make some unexpected connections, to have to reshape a bit of one's history, memory, and judgment. . . ."[23]

One possible place to start is with the question of what a particular artifact—say *The People's Court*—means to the several million people who used to watch it. This is one of the most difficult and elusive, but also one of the most important questions in the ongoing debate about popular culture. The methodological problems are considerable. How does one go about determining the ways in which popular culture interacts with the lives of ordinary people who enjoy and consume it, are drugged or stimulated by it? How can one gain understanding of the emotional and intellectual richness that popular culture may have and may encourage? As we have seen, it is not hard to learn what Alan Dershowitz and his fellow lawyers and critics think about *The People's Court*. But when it comes to the average viewer who is not asked to write an essay in *American Film* about his or her reaction to the show, things become more difficult. One critic who has attempted to look more closely at audience discourse is Janice Radway. In the following, I will take my lead from Radway's reading of the romance and Grimsted's reading of *The Purple Rose of Cairo*. Unlike Radway, I do not have any empirical data to work from, but will approach the question of what *The People's Court* meant to its audience and to American culture from a theoretical angle.

A "combination of soap opera and game show," one of the creators and producers of *The People's Court,* Stu Billett, once called the show. "You're sucked in right away. You want to know who's telling the truth.

---

23. Ibid., 557, 560.

And you start judging their demeanor from the time they walk in."[24] To Alan Dershowitz, as we heard, the show was "an authentic television innovation." Both correctly perceived, that is, that *The People's Court* did not fit into any already existing category of media event, but was an assemblage of bits and pieces of other forms into a new structure. Though bordering on the soap-operatic in its emphasis on everyday, often domestic, concerns and its somewhat didactic nature, the program was the very opposite of a soap opera in its resolution of problems and movement toward closure. According to Robert C. Allen, soaps not only "lack any semblance of dramatic unity, but their lack of ultimate closure renders them narratively anomalous."[25] As we shall see, it is precisely Judge Wapner's ability to simplify and solve problems that his viewers appreciated the most.

Another important piece of the bricolage that became *The People's Court* was the element of realism so highly valued by most fans of the show. The actual disputants and cases notwithstanding, that realism was somewhat "embellished," as we saw, when it came to the payment of all monetary awards and the quick and efficient settlement of grievances. In real life, things do not always work this smoothly. The show's aura of realism was furthermore tempered, I would argue, by an element of something that for want of a better word I will call "melodrama." As Christopher Prendergast once told us, " 'melodrama' and 'realism' occupy a common space" in that melodrama, on stage as in fiction, answers primarily to the need to escape from the strains and stresses of our everyday existence. "The dream offered by melodrama is thus neither prophetic nor analytic; it is reassuring and predictable, enacting a fantasy of wish-fulfillment within a plane that is an idealized version of the real world." Central to the idealization offered by melodrama is "a set of simple, unambiguous moral presuppositions" that spring from and speak to our longing for an ordered moral universe. Melodrama works in simple ways toward the triumphal assertion of the rule of moral law: the happy ending guaranteeing the victory of good over evil.

> The dominant function of melodrama appears, therefore, to be that of making available an uncomplicated moral reading of the universe, and of

---

24. Stu Billett, quoted in Schleier, " 'People's Court.' "

25. Robert C. Allen, *Speaking of Soap Operas* (Chapel Hill: University of North Carolina Press, 1985), 14.

locating the subject in a secure world of moral representations, free from doubt, uncertainty, ambiguity.[26]

At the same time as melodrama is moving toward the articulation of a stable and reassuring universe, however, the real moving force of the form is the villain. Much as people long for order and stability, historians of stage melodrama have observed, they seem to be attracted to danger and violence. In most of us, it would appear, there is a clash between what Prendergast calls "the fantasy of mastery" and "the fantasy of destruction," between fear and revulsion at that which is morally wrong and secret enjoyment of it. This tension can only be repressed but never resolved within the melodramatic mode itself, as the mode is firmly committed to the ultimate victory of the good. "In respect of its involvement with evil, melodrama is founded upon a dialectic of gratification and repression: it partially gratifies an impulse to destruction, but at the same time, through its insistence on triumphant virtue, represses any acknowledgment of that gratification."[27] Smoldering discontent and urges toward disorder notwithstanding, the melodramatic mode is predominantly conservative, pacifying.

Now, it would be overstating the case to assert that *The People's Court* was melodrama incarnate. The small claims argued over were hardly of a nature to merit heroic fighting—often, it was even hard to establish which party was right and which wrong. Nor did most litigants seem to be made of the stuff for such heroic fighting. If we do not find "hyperbole," "ensuring that each side of the moral polarity is represented in an extreme, intensely magnified form," we do, however, find at least a touch of the second elementary rhetorical figure of melodrama mentioned by Prendergast, "antithesis." Again, the very nature of the small-claims discussions may perhaps not be said to serve "to organize the universe in terms of the preconceived polarities of good and evil,"[28] but antithesis and theatricality or drama were certainly built into the adversarial framework of the court proceedings. Things could get quite rough on *The People's Court;* it was not unusual for Judge Wapner to have to call two litigants to order. For even though some of the cases on the show may have looked petty to outsiders—"lawsuits over the thickness

26. Christopher Prendergast, *Balzac: Fiction and Melodrama* (London: Edward Arnold, 1978), 184, 7, 8.

27. Ibid., 11.

28. Ibid., 8, 7.

of a slice of pizza, for heaven's sake"[29]—we should not forget that they were very real and very important to the parties involved at that moment. Indeed, it was this adversarial quality of the show which more than anything else made it look like a kind of game show—"you're sucked in right away. You want to know who's telling the truth," as Stu Billett said.[30]

Most of all, however, it was the role played by Judge Wapner that lent to *The People's Court* its aura of melodrama. On the show, the resolution of problems was not left to the person with the problem, who might, after all, make a mistake. It was put in the capable hands of the omnipotent judge whose decision was final. "There's a finite end to the story. Most of us would love to have that in our lives."[31] The ultimate function of this Solomonic father figure was to provide gratification by putting a lid on any urge toward discontent and disorder, thereby ensuring that order was (re)established. Joseph A. Wapner personified, I would argue, "the fantasy of mastery," making what Prendergast terms "the dream of the paternal discourse" come true. Chief interpreter of the law and hence master of intelligibility within the universe of *The People's Court,* Wapner was "the figure who transacts nothing less than 'reality' itself" to the viewer.[32] That "reality," or rather version of reality, was readily graspable, because it was made to look simple and unequivocal. Within the integrated unit of the show, the essential principles of the social contract itself were maintained. When pronouncing a judgment, Wapner often embarked on moralizing, even sermonizing soliloquies on justice, human relationships, friendships, and loyalties. To a late-twentieth-

29. See note 19.

30. Billett, quoted in Schleier, " 'People's Court.' "

31. Peter Locke, cofounder of Atlantic/Kuschner Locke Inc., producers of *Divorce Court.* Quoted in Belkin, "Realism of the Courtroom."

32. Prendergast, *Balzac,* 181. Cf. also Duncan Kennedy, who in his introduction to *A Critique of Adjudication (fin de siècle)* (Cambridge, Mass.: Harvard University Press, 1997) writes about the importance of the figure of the Judge in American culture—a figure who carries "multiple resonating meanings and associations, under- and overtones of mystic power." Some of the Judge's mythic role models, he continues, are "God, the good Father of a large family, the King, and Solomon. His (or her) more mundane comrades are the clergyperson, the police officer, the doctor, the therapist, and even the airline pilot. Describing the Judge in gender-neutral language distorts the figure, because he is one of the multiple archetypes of virtuous male power, defined by semiotic contrast with the Mother, the Sybil, the Nurse, the Virgin Sacrifice, and other images of female virtue and power" (3).

century pluralistic and litigious American audience, such soliloquies were reassuring and encouraging. It made the struggle of everyday life easier to be told that there is nothing fundamentally wrong with the otherwise much-criticized American nation, its legal system, and its people. "The glory of America is that we are a nation governed by laws and not by the whims and caprices of men and women. But the glory of American law is that it has room in it for the best qualities of men and women"[33]—thus speaks a true descendant of the old proud and venerable common-law tradition.

What the average viewer got from watching *The People's Court*, I would suggest, is not unlike what Janice Radway's romance readers get from reading romances and Cecilia gets from watching *The Purple Rose of Cairo:* affirmation that love, respect, and fair treatment are the proper human values, "forgetfulness combined with hope that the boring, messy, and scary can be formed toward the soothingly meaningful, affirming both new possibilities and old values." Wapner may have been fatherly, and he may at times have bullied the litigants, but he very rarely did so without showing respect for the dignity of the common man or woman. By expressing over and over again his touching belief in truth and justice and in the workings of that major bastion of American democracy, the legal system, he "asserts what democracy needs to believe: the life humans choose can involve the beautiful, decent, and worthwhile."[34]

In *Reading the Romance,* Radway poses the question of "whether the romance should be considered fundamentally conservative on the one hand or incipiently oppositional on the other." When viewed by the readers themselves, the act of romance reading can be conceived as combative and compensatory. By reading a book they spend time on themselves rather than attending to the needs of their family. Their own pleasure comes first, and their "romance reading addresses needs created in them but not met by patriarchal institutions and engendering practices."[35] At the same time, however, romance reading may well be a vicarious activity, serving to disarm the need for real and dramatic change by successfully meeting it in the realm of fiction.

33. Wapner, *A View from the Bench,* 3.
34. Grimsted, "Purple Rose," 565, 567.
35. Janice Radway, *Reading the Romance* (Chapel Hill & London: University of North Carolina Press, 1984), 209, 211.

This question of contestative versus conservative may also be raised in connection with *The People's Court*. Judge Wapner's pride in educating his audience about the ways of the law, and his colleagues' affirmation that the people who come before them in the country's various small-claims courts seem to be the better prepared for having watched the show, indicate that the program did indeed plant certain seeds of rebellion and willingness to act. As Wapner was thus instilling faith in his audience that it was within their reach to seek redress for even the smallest of wrongs inflicted upon them, however, he was simultaneously maintaining a distinctly paternal and pacifying presence in the court. The message he delivered was the seemingly ambivalent one of "by all means take your problems to court; but once here you will bow to my authority as a representative of the law." In this way, the potentially liberating quality of the show was tempered by an emphasis on the authority of the existing system. While claiming to "demystify" the legal system, Wapner was in fact preserving the ideological and political status quo.

And that, as I have previously suggested, was precisely what the viewers of *The People's Court* liked about it. Unlike most of Janice Radway's romance readers, the fans of *The People's Court wanted* to see that the system works, *wanted* to be told that the old American dream of a legal system accessible to all is still true. To the viewers of the show as indeed to the American public at large, it was and still is obvious that they are surrounded by intense social problems, not the least serious of which spring from a struggle on the part of various ethnic and minority groups for power and social recognition. This struggle is not only fought out in the streets; it is also fought out in the courts and the legal system. As this fight continues, the results of which are all too often fear and aggression, the attitudes of individuals and groups toward one another as well as toward more general political, social, and moral issues are increasingly shaped by the legal vernacular. In modern, pluralistic America, whether the issue at stake is civil or human rights, abortion, AIDS, or the environment, the place to seek vindication is the courts, more than it is the political system. To believe in the legal system is therefore to believe that a solution to the most important problems of the day may be found.

As a forum to fight out major societal battles, a "meeting-place" for the various groups of the American society, the courts may or may not work in a satisfactory way, but they are *there*. In the area of small claims, of everyday grievances, *The People's Court* functioned as one such meeting-place, bringing people together so that they could state their problems. Within the four walls of this curious mixture of fact and fiction, for about half an hour every day, decisions were made and justice seen to in an efficient, straightforward, and unproblematic way, just as moral directions were given as to the proper way to behave and the proper values to hold in today's America. How reassuring amid the seething tensions and social problems of contemporary America, to which the viewers of the show would have to return after that half-hour was up!

CONCLUDING REMARKS

> Small claims is a procedure designed to permit ordinary citizens to bring claims for money with minimum legal formality. . . . The ideal sought in small claims procedure is simplicity and efficiency without legal technicality. The complaint can be written in hand and need be only an informal narrative of the dispute. . . . Trial is held by a judge without a jury and is conducted by informal conversation, the judge seeking to mediate as well as to adjudicate.[36]

The producers of *The People's Court* could not have found a better person to preside over their show than Joseph A. Wapner. A silver-haired retired judge whose twenty-year career on the bench began in the Los Angeles Municipal Court, Wapner was the embodiment of "simplicity and efficiency without legal technicality." "*Eminence grise*," "Solomonic father-figure," and "pillar of stability" are some of the expressions used about him by his fans. Millions of viewers tuned in daily to *The People's Court*, and the show's success has made Wapner's name a household word to most Americans. What his fans appreciated about him was his ability first of all to take seriously even the most unremittingly mundane legal claims and to treat with respect the people who advanced these claims, and second his ability to render his judgment in an authoritative, though straightforward, way. Wapner obviously believed in what he was doing; his viewers sensed his determination to preserve the reputation of the legal calling and his honest wish "to mediate as well as to adjudicate."

36. Geoffrey C. Hazard Jr. and Michele Taruffo, *American Civil Procedure* (New Haven, Conn.: Yale University Press, 1993), 167.

In the aspects of Wapner's demeanor, professional as well as personal, to which his fans refer in order to explain why he became one of the most enduringly popular father figures on American television, it is not hard to recognize the traits that used to be attributed to the common-law judge. Advocates of *The People's Court* often mention the realistic quality of the show—its featuring real people arguing real cases—as the main reason for its popularity. Appealing as the stark realism of the show may have been, however, it has been argued in this chapter that its main attraction is to be found in Wapner's willingness and ability, in the best common-law manner, to provide resolutions to seemingly insoluble problems.

In his long tenure on *The People's Court,* Wapner became for the American public a unique icon of legality. He stood for the idea that the law will hear everyone, that everyone can turn to law, though the matter at hand may seem small. He embodied what people long for in their judges: the alert protection of rights, in case after case, or, to put it in a different way, judicial activism in the deeper sense of actively including everyone, by law, into community life, as described in chapter one. Like Tom Wolfe's portrayal of Judge Kovitsky and Scott Turow's depiction of Sandy Stern, Judge Wapner and his popularity testify to the deep commitment of the American people to the ideal of law, the faith that litigation will remedy injustices. When at his best, Wapner inspired in his viewers a belief in impartial justice and fairness—a fairness which invariably took as its point of departure the concrete, real experiences of the men and women appearing before him. And in thus preaching—and practicing—a symbiosis of theory and practice, he followed in the footsteps of generations of common lawyers before him.

V

Race and Law

Promising Alchemical Reaction or Dangerous Trap?

Toward the end of *Tracks,* Louise Erdrich has one of her two
narrators and main characters, old Nanapush, stand for tribal
chairman. The year is 1924. Having in his own lifetime seen
"more change than in a hundred upon a hundred [years] before,"
Nanapush has realized that the only way to prevent any further decima-
tion by disease and demoralization by drink among his tribesmen, the
Chippewas of North Dakota, any further selling off of their forest re-
serves for a quick profit, is to learn to "write letters" and send them off to
their proper destination. For, "once the bureaucrats sink their barbed
pens into the lives of Indians, the paper starts flying, a blizzard of legal
forms, a waste of ink by the gallon, a correspondence to which there is
no end or reason." By 1924, the Chippewas have become "a tribe of file
cabinets and triplicates, a tribe of single-space documents, directives,
policy," and only by becoming a "bureaucrat myself," Nanapush tells us,
may he learn how to "wade through the letters, the reports" by means of
which the white authorities exert their power over the Indians.[1]

Nanapush's turning bureaucrat is but the last of a number of manifestations throughout *Tracks* of his ability to survive. While Pauline, the
other narrator of the novel, who provides a starkly different version
of events, breaks down under the accumulated horrors following the

---

1. Louise Erdrich, *Tracks* (London: Pan Books Ltd., 1989), 2, 225.

white man's conquest of the plains and the peoples on them, Nanapush adapts. Without ever forgetting "the passing of times you will never know,"[2] and without losing his sense of humor and compassion, he simply avails himself of and puts to good use the white man's most powerful instrument of authority, the legal document.

Nanapush and his tribe's sense that survival in the white man's world entails an understanding of the law and the legal system is an experience shared by most Indian tribes in the late nineteenth and early twentieth centuries. As the frontier kept moving westward in the nineteenth century and more and more settlers became interested in acquiring land for farming on the Great Plains, the government sought to regulate relations with the Indians in a number of treaties. Though honored mostly in the breach, these treaties served an important function:

> [T]he nation's avowed recognition of Indian rights distinguished it in principle from previous settlers of the New World and other lands whose prevailing method of expansion consisted of the wholesale slaughter of aboriginal peoples . . .
>
> In signing a treaty with the western tribes establishing tribal domains and guaranteeing the borders of Indian country, the U.S. affirmed formally that Indians possessed personal and property rights, including rights in their lands. . . . At a minimum, these recognized tribal rights established a legal benchmark against which the government's actions might be measured in the future, and distinguished Indians from the country's other racial minority, the blacks, to whom the law accorded essentially no right at all.[3]

When gold was found in the Black Hills in 1874, for example, and the Sioux lost the Hills to the westward expansion and "manifest destiny" of White America just as they had lost most of their other lands, they soon began agitating about their loss. Some date the first organized protest to the 1880s, but it was only in the 1920s that the Black Hills case developed as a claim for restitution based on the true value of the seized lands. Over the next sixty years, as the claim made its way through the courts, it evolved into a part of tribal culture, a rallying point and rare source of hope:

2. Ibid., 2.

3. Edward Lazarus, *Black Hills/White Justice: The Sioux Nation Versus The United States 1775 to the Present* (New York: Harper Collins, 1991), 11, 17.

Thirty years after Custer's gold strike, the Black Hills resumed their place at the center of conflict between the U.S. and the Sioux. The land was gone, but in the minds of the Indians, the loss and the injustice were still very much alive. Experience and education had taught them that the white man's world had places to bring their grievances. . . .[4]

As had Nanapush, that is, the Sioux learned from their dealings over the years with the white man that the American democracy provides to the victims of conquest certain remedial legal processes. An instrument of power, the law may work both ways—it may bureaucratize and repress, but it may also provide legitimacy and entitlement to the weaker members of society far beyond what their actual political power could have brought them.

Filing the Black Hills claim along with a number of other claims on behalf of the Sioux nation in 1923, attorney Ralph Case was relying on an emerging language of rights that would become increasingly familiar to the American public as it came to be employed by a number of minority groups. As Morton J. Horwitz puts it,

> Since the late 1930's, the concept of rights has served overwhelmingly to create a legal and political culture that has legitimated the protection of civil liberties for political, religious, and racial minorities and, much more recently, has provided an emancipatory set of ideas or entitlements for cultural minorities, women and homosexuals. Similarly, the marginal and the scorned—the criminally accused, prisoners, aliens, indigents, welfare recipients and illegitimate children—have employed the language of rights in successful legal challenges.[5]

Unlike the Indians, most of the other minority groups, notably blacks, had to overcome a major obstacle before they could embark on a legal journey for equality and empowerment: the lack of legal standing. In *Simple Justice*, Richard Kluger tells of the fight for enactment of black suffrage and for laws to enforce that right. After the period of Radical Reconstruction and the Civil Rights Act of 1875, "the job of reconciling the country's new moral and constitutional commitments to the Negro with its undiluted distaste for him as a human being fell to that es-

---

4. Ibid., 123.

5. Morton J. Horwitz, "Rights," *Harvard Civil Rights–Civil Liberties Law Review* 23 (1988): 393–94.

teemed broker of national disputes, the Supreme Court of the United States." From the very beginning of the fight for civil rights, that is, and especially after the meeting of the National Negro Conference in May 1909, which gave rise to the National Association for the Advancement of Colored People, "the courts were the arena where the black man's fight for equal rights [was to be] most effectively waged."[6]

As the twentieth century is drawing to a close, it is clearer than ever that conditions—social, political, and otherwise—still are far from satisfactory among blacks and other minorities, that, as Derrick Bell puts it, "the salvation of racial equality has eluded us again."[7] The continuing faith in and reliance on litigation has consequently been severely questioned in recent years by lawyers as well as nonlawyers, whites as well as nonwhites. In this chapter, I will look at the debate concerning the role of civil rights litigation in attacking and abolishing the underlying causes of the subordinate status of minority groups. As black Americans may be said to constitute "the paradigm victim group" of American history,[8] I have found it appropriate in my discussion of race and law to draw heavily on the black experience. The focus will be on two black academic writers, Patricia J. Williams and Derrick Bell, who by experimenting with various literary and legal genres have succeeded in their books, *The Alchemy of Race and Rights,* and *And We Are Not Saved* and *Faces at the Bottom of the Well,* respectively, in expressing jurisprudential matters of general importance in a new language and format.

Derrick Bell and Patricia Williams are both among the founding members of the so-called Critical Race Theory (CRT), defined by Bell as "a body of legal scholarship, now about a decade old, a majority of whose members are both existentially people of color and ideologically committed to the struggle against racism, particularly as institutionalized in and by law." CRT writing and lecturing, Bell goes on to say, is characterized by "frequent use of the first person, storytelling, narrative, allegory, interdisciplinary treatment of law, and the unapologetic use of creativity." CRT scholarship will often seem disruptive because "its commitment to anti-racism goes well beyond civil rights, integration,

---

6. Richard J. Kluger, *Simple Justice: The History of Brown v. Board of Education and Black America's Struggle for Equality* (New York: Knopf, 1976), 53, 139.

7. Derrick Bell, *And We Are Not Saved: The Elusive Quest for Racial Justice* (New York: Basic Books, 1987), 3.

8. Mari J. Matsuda, "Looking to the Bottom: Critical Legal Studies and Reparations," *Harvard Civil Rights–Civil Liberties Law Review* 22 (1987): 335.

affirmative action, and other liberal measures."[9] As the definitive example of a legal analysis that makes use of CRT methods, Bell refers to Williams's *The Alchemy of Race and Rights,* and throughout his article he presents his own views and those of Williams and other CRT scholars as fairly identical. As a closer look at Bell's and Williams's work will show, however, there are substantial differences in the way in which the two scholars view the role of law in the fight for black equality.

DERRICK BELL AND THE CRITICISM OF THE USEFULNESS TO THE BLACK CAUSE OF LIBERAL RIGHTS DISCOURSE

> Principles, hell! What I do not understand—and this is what I really want to get clear—is what principle is so compelling as to justify continued allegiance to obsolete civil rights strategies that have done little to prevent—and may have contributed to—the contemporary statistics regarding black crime, broken families, devastated neighborhoods, alcohol and drug abuse, out-of-wedlock births, illiteracy, unemployment, and welfare dependency?[10]

To Geneva Crenshaw, the lawyer-prophet and heroine of both *And We Are Not Saved* and *Faces at the Bottom of the Well,* as to her author, racial symbols—especially those of a legal kind—constitute a limited legacy.[11] In a series of allegorical stories and encounters with fictional characters, Derrick Bell attempts to convey the "need to be realistic about our present and future civil rights activities" and "to provoke blacks and their white allies to look beyond traditional civil rights views."[12] However reassuring and comforting these views are, they tend to obscure the harsh racial reality of contemporary American society. Only when civil rights advocates see the racial world as it really is and structure their strategies and responses accordingly may the burdens of racism be alleviated, Bell argues.

9. Derrick Bell, "Who's Afraid of Critical Race Theory?" *University of Illinois Law Review* (1995), no. 4, 898–99. The other founding members include Richard Delgado, Charles Lawrence, and Mari Matsuda.

10. Derrick Bell, *Faces at the Bottom of the Well: The Permanence of Racism* (New York: Basic Books, 1992), 59–60.

11. Cf. the title of chap. 1 of *Faces at the Bottom of the Well,* "Racial Symbols: A Limited Legacy."

12. Bell, *Faces at the Bottom of the Well,* 60–61.

The picture Bell paints of race relations in contemporary America is not a happy one. Whereas in *And We Are Not Saved,* he "still sees reason for a hopeful future," challenging Geneva Crenshaw to "come up with a more effective technique" lest he "stay with litigation,"[13] Bell does not leave the reader with much hope in his second book of Geneva Crenshaw stories. Realizing that the dire message of *Faces at the Bottom of the Well* may alienate, even disgust and anger, he outlines in his preface to the book how "the challenge throughout has been to tell what I view as the truth about racism without causing disabling despair."[14] As we shall see later, some of his readers think he has failed or not lived up to this challenge and have taken him to task for what they see as a fatal loss of faith in future black efforts to win freedom and equality.

Of all the tales of defeat for blacks that make up Bell's version of the story of race relations in the United States, none is more depressing than the allegory of "The Space Traders." The last of nine chapters, this allegory forms a powerful and highly effective finale to *Faces at the Bottom of the Well.* Bell's attempt in the epilogue to go "beyond despair" notwithstanding, it is the story of "The Space Traders" that the reader remembers when he or she puts down the book. On January 1, 2000, Americans witness the landing along the Atlantic coast of one thousand ships from a star far out in space. Unlike "that earlier one of three small ships, one October over more than five hundred years before," which had carried trinkets and other cheap pieces of jewelry to the Indians of the island of Santo Domingo in the Caribbean, the huge vessels of the Space Traders carry

> treasure of which the U.S. was in most desperate need: gold, to bail out the almost bankrupt federal, state, and local governments; special chemicals capable of unpolluting the environment, which was becoming daily more toxic, and restoring it to the pristine state it had before Western explorers set foot on it; and a totally safe nuclear engine and fuel, to relieve the nation's all-but-depleted supply of fossil fuel.

In exchange for their valuable treasure, the Space Traders want to take back with them all African Americans now living in the United States. Revealing nothing about why they are interested only in black people or

13. Bell, *And We Are Not Saved,* 93.
14. Bell, *Faces at the Bottom of the Well,* ix.

what fate will await the African Americans, the Traders give the government sixteen days to consider their proposal. On January 17—"the day when in that year the birthday of Martin Luther King, Jr., was to be observed"—they will come back for an answer.[15]

Predictably enough, the discussion that follows as a result of the Space Traders' offer is a highly animated one. During the sixteen days at their disposal, the various segments of the American population meet to figure out how best to cope with this puzzling new situation. Much is at stake—for some, the deportation of every black American will mean the ultimate solution to the most persistent of American problems; for others, every sacred principle upon which the United States was built will be violated should the government decide to go along with the Traders' proposal. Bell's description of the often shockingly cynical motives and rationalizations behind the decisions finally made by the various groups is a masterful indictment of the American political and legal process, as well as a living illustration of his message that blacks will forever be confined by white racism to the bottom of American society. When, at the end, "heads bowed, arms now linked by slender chains, black people left the New World as their forebears had arrived" to bound the Space Traders' ships, it seems inevitable, unavoidable.[16]

Awaiting his deportation along with his black brethren, Professor Golightly ponders what went wrong. As the only unofficial black cabinet member, Golightly has been able behind the scenes and under cover of lending his support to the president's conservative policies to do "more for black people than had a dozen of the loud-mouthed leaders." He is not surprised that events have turned out the way they have. What distresses him is "his failure to convince the black leaders of the Anti-Trade Coalition to heed their own rhetoric: namely that whites in power would, given the chance, do to privileged blacks what, in fact, they had done to all blacks." At the conference of the so-called Anti-Trade Coalition, a gathering of black and liberal white politicians, civil rights representatives, and progressive academics, Golightly had appeared despite the protest of many participants who considered him a traitor because of his opposition in the past to various civil rights initiatives. Rather than resist the Traders' offer, he had urged, blacks ought to accept it and work to make whites jealous by spreading the rumor that a "virtual paradise"

15. Ibid., 158, 159–60.
16. Ibid., 194.

has been promised to and is awaiting blacks on the Space Traders' star." Refusing to "stoop to this bit of trickery that might have saved them," his "high-minded brothers at the conference" had decided "to fail with integrity."[17]

Along with a number of other fictional characters in *And We Are Not Saved* and *Faces at the Bottom of the Well*, notably Geneva Crenshaw, Professor Golightly gives voice to Bell's criticism of highfalutin and hollow civil rights rhetoric and corresponding calls for common-sense realpolitik. "Realist[s] in an idealist world,"[18] unflinching pragmatists, these characters emphasize time and again how "all . . . the fancy juris-prudential ideas in the world won't stop them. Racism isn't about so-phistication. Combating it isn't about finesse, except in the most vulgar sense of making a shameless appeal to the predictable self-interest of whites."[19] Having for years taught civil rights law and having believed as a civil rights attorney that the law might solve the problem of race, Bell has by now become convinced that racism is a permanent feature of American society and that "a realistic appraisal of racism's crucial role in the society, far from being capitulation, would enable us to recognize the potential for effecting reform in even what appear to be setbacks."[20]

Stubbornly holding on to the view that racism can be effectively fought with the enactment and subsequent enforcement of civil rights laws, numerous indications to the contrary notwithstanding, civil rights advocates have never gotten to the real question, the real nature of racism. Ever since the first slaves were brought to the New World, racism has been an integral part of the American experience. To this day,

---

17. Ibid., 171, 193, 175, 193.

18. Bell, *And We Are Not Saved*, 42.

19. Bell, *Faces at the Bottom of the Well*, 107. In his preface to the book, Bell writes that "The Space Traders" originated in a 1989 lecture he gave, which was subsequently published in a law journal. The striking similarity between the character of Professor Golightly and Clarence Thomas must therefore be a coincidence; or rather, a clever presentiment on Bell's part as to what was to come. About Thomas's nomination to the Supreme Court, Bell writes in his contribution to *Court of Appeal* (New York: Ballantine, 1992): "I am tempted to support his nomination . . . I have concluded that Judge Thomas is not really a conservative, but, rather, a committed black revolutionary. . . . An all-white Supreme Court hostile to racial issues is one thing. But a court with its lone black Justice joining the majority in its anti–civil rights decisions will send a clear message: It is useless to continue seeking relief through law for America's still rampant racism" (36–37).

20. Ibid., 92.

"Americans achieve a measure of social stability through their unspoken pact to keep blacks on the bottom." Most Americans—whites as well as blacks—know but refuse openly to admit that whites are "bonded" by racism, and that "racism is in a state of symbiosis with liberal democracy in this country." Racism is, in other words, here to stay, and the sooner civil rights advocates face facts, the better. "Old formulas" and long-held beliefs such as the belief in education as the key to the race problem— once whites can be brought to understand the true evils of racial discrimination, they will be willing to give it up—or the belief in the possibility of achieving full integration of blacks into white society, have by now become not only obsolete, but indeed counterproductive. Unless discarded, such beliefs may serve as a pacifying opiate to blacks, keeping up hope in reform that will never come and misdirecting black efforts.

> My position is that the legal rules regarding racial discrimination have become not only *reified* (that is, ascribing material existence and power to what are really just ideas)—as the modern inheritor of realism, critical legal studies, would say—but *deified*. The worship of equality rules as having absolute power benefits whites by preserving a benevolent but fictional self-image, and such worship benefits blacks by preserving hope. But I think we've arrived at a place in history where the harms of such worship outweigh its benefits.[21]

The search for progress in American race relations via the courts is furthermore impeded by the fact that the very Constitution on whose fundamental principles of freedom and equality civil rights litigation is based is itself inherently racist. The ten provisions in the Constitution directly or indirectly providing for slavery and protecting slave owners[22] gave priority to property over human rights. The fundamental contradiction between slavery and equality that was written into the Constitution has remained, and has led to a certain unwillingness on the part of the Supreme Court to provide relief for the real economic-political disadvantages of blacks set in motion by the Framers. If "the real problem of race in America is the unresolved contradiction embedded in the Constitution and never openly examined, owing to the self-interested attachment of some citizens of this nation to certain myths," and "if this

---

21. Ibid., 152, 155, 152, 101.
22. See note, p. 3, *Faces at the Bottom of the Well.*

situation is part of the nation's basic law," Geneva asks Bell in one of their dialogues, then "how are we to reach the whites in power today and gain redress?"[23]

The two alternatives to litigation as means to end racial discrimination that have been advocated down through black history, violent revolution and black exodus, are no longer viable either. In *And We Are Not Saved,* Geneva—and her author—still hopes that it may be possible to "evolve a new vision for achieving racial justice—one that would not rely on violent revolution nor require a black exodus."[24] In Bell's second book of Geneva Crenshaw stories, however, the word "vision" is no longer to be found. A strange paradox is all he leaves his reader with: a realization and in a sense silent acceptance of the fact that racism is permanent, coupled with an attempt to defy and resist this racism. "Making something out of nothing" is what blacks have always been good at:

> It is a question of *both, and. Both* the recognition of the futility of action—where action is more civil rights strategies destined to fail—*and* the unalterable conviction that something must be done, that action must be taken.[25]

Bell's obvious disillusion with the achievements of civil rights litigation and his lack of vision and hope for the future have, as briefly mentioned above, elicited certain rather sharp responses. Thus, his former colleague at the Harvard Law School, Randall L. Kennedy, has charged that *Faces at the Bottom of the Well* "yields only meager intellectual nourishment." Bell is right to point out the extent to which racism has penetrated into virtually every corner of social life, Kennedy acknowledges. Yet, his

> one-dimensional assertion of unrelieved gloom is remarkably weak, a condition that stems to a large extent from his failure to attend properly to the difficult task of persuasion. One would have thought, for instance, that in making his sweeping assertion, Professor Bell might at least have alluded to the conditions that make possible Douglas Wilder's election as governor of Virginia, or General Powell's appointment to lead the na-

23. Bell, *And We Are Not Saved,* 49–50.
24. Ibid., 100.
25. Bell, *Faces at the Bottom of the Well,* 199.

tion's military, or the re-enactment and strengthening of the Voting Rights Act against the high-tide of Reaganism, or the popularization of "diversity" movements in practically all spheres of American life notwithstanding resistance to them, or the fact that, among the employed, the wage gap between white and black workers has steadily been lessening, or the enactment of the Civil Rights Act of 1991 even in the teeth of President Bush's recalcitrance.[26]

Things are more complex than Bell makes them out to be, Kennedy claims. Blacks do in fact already exercise a good deal more power than they used to, and there is good reason to believe that they will in the future attain additional positions of authority and respect.[27]

Unfair as he may have considered this kind of criticism to be, it seems to have had an effect on Bell. In his third book of Geneva Crenshaw stories, *Gospel Choirs,* from 1996, he allows Gleason Golightly to get his revenge. In chapter one, "Redemption Deferred: Back to the Space Traders," we get to know what happens to all America's blacks after they have disappeared into the Space Traders' ship. The Space Traders want to make absolutely sure that the black people really *want* to go with them, so they ask everybody to vote on whether they want to con-

26. Randall L. Kennedy, "Derrick Bell's Apologia for Minister Farrakhan: An Intellectual and Moral Disaster," *Reconstruction* 2.1 (1992): 92. See also Leroy D. Clark's "Critique of Professor Derrick A. Bell's Thesis of the Permanence of Racism and His Strategy of Confrontation" (*Denver University Law Review* 73.1 [1995]): "Despite Professor Bell's prophecy of doom, I believe he would like to have his analysis proven wrong. However, he desperately leans on a tactic from the past—laying out the disabilities of the black condition and accusing whites of not having the moral strength to act fairly . . . At some point it becomes dysfunctional to refuse giving any credit to the very positive abatements of racism that occurred with white support, and on occasion, white leadership. . . . Professor Bell's 'analysis' is really only accusation and 'harassing white folks,' and is undermining and destructive. . . . There is only rage and perplexity. No bridges are built—only righteousness is being sold" (49–50).

27. Bell seems to be especially frustrated with Randall Kennedy's criticism. In "Who's Afraid of Critical Race Theory?" Bell calls Kennedy CRTs "most politically damaging critic": "When a black scholar at a prominent law school tells anyone who will listen that other folks of color are deluded about being excluded on the basis of their race; when a black scholar argues against race-conscious legal remedies or hiring policies; when a black scholar contends that there is no hidden 'white' normativity or perspective but rather a meritocratic normativity (the companion claim to the claim that there is no minority perspective); when a black scholar says all these things, all who rarely listen to scholars of color sit up and take notice" (908).

tinue or to go home. Golightly pleads with his brethren—successfully this time:

> Yes, we all know from our own experiences in the last forty years that promises have not been kept. Yet is it not through struggling against evil that we achieve our salvation? Do we not owe it to our forebears, to our children, to ourselves to return to America, not as a further gift to an uncaring nation, but as a proof that we can—by the example our ancestors set us—wring out of present danger a life of commitment and service to one another and our brother and sister Americans of any color?[28]

Given the highly cynical and disillusioned mode of Bell's two earlier books, the mere fact that Golightly's conciliatory attitude toward America carries the day is remarkable and perhaps indicative of a change of heart on Bell's part.[29]

Other parts of legal academia have taken more kindly to Bell and his work. In calling for economic and political, in addition to legal, action, Bell reiterates conclusions reached by other members of legal academia, notably members of the Critical Legal Studies (CLS) movement, as well as members of other disciplines. In *The Truly Disadvantaged,* for instance, sociologist William Julius Wilson examines what he considers to be the shortcomings of legally based policies such as affirmative action

---

28. Derrick Bell, *Gospel Choirs: Psalms of Survival for an Alien Land Called Home* (New York: Basic Books, 1996), 24.

29. It should be noted, however, that if Bell is more optimistic in *Gospel Choirs* than in his two previous novels, it is not because he has changed his mind about the law. It is toward the traditions of the black community, and in particular black music, that his optimism is directed in his third book of Geneva Crenshaw stories. Gospel music, he says, "speaks to the unavoidable fact that, at bottom, we are all in the same boat. There is potential in this music to touch and unite across barriers of race and class" (*Gospel Choirs,* 3–4). As for the law, Bell is as negative in his assessment of its ideal and potential in *Gospel Choirs* as he was in his previous two books. "The civil rights lawyers with whom I worked in the early 1960s," he writes, "were well trained and practiced the law with great skill and commitment to their clients and the whole black race. They were heroic figures who, I was convinced, would lead us away from the old world of racial segregation and, through law, carve out a new road toward equal opportunity and racial integration. They are still my heroes, but much of what they, and we who emulated them, accomplished was all too soon subverted. . . . In urging the use of law and litigation as the major means to end racial discrimination, we acted in good faith. We failed, however, to recognize that even the most clearly stated protections in law can be undermined when a substantial portion of the population determines to ignore them" (53).

in addressing the problems of the ghetto underclass. After 1970, for a period of several years, Wilson asserts, the liberal community, policy makers, and civil rights leaders were too "preoccupied with the affirmative action agenda of the black middle class" to do something about "the deteriorating social and economic conditions of the ghetto underclass."[30] The disillusioned attitude toward rights displayed by CLS scholars was never better expressed than by Mark Tushnet in "An Essay on Rights" from 1984. In this essay, Tushnet states that "it's not just that rights-talk does not do much good. In the contemporary United States, it is positively harmful." The language of rights may describe important aspects of human experience, but often the very treatment of those experiences as instances of abstract rights tends to mischaracterize or reify them. "The experiences become desiccated when described in that way. We must insist on preserving real experiences rather than abstracting general rights from those experiences."[31]

In talking about legal rules regarding racial discrimination as "reified," even "deified," Bell acknowledges his affinity with CLS. He is not the only minority scholar to do so. For some of these scholars, however, CLS has come to hold not only "promise," but also "frustration," as José A. Bracamonte puts it in his foreword to a special issue of *Harvard Civil Rights–Civil Liberties Law Review* from 1987, entitled "Minority Critiques of the Critical Legal Studies Movement." It is this frustration that has given rise to Critical Race Theory.

PATRICIA WILLIAMS AND THE DEFENSE OF RIGHTS TALK

The frustration with CLS experienced by Patricia Williams and other CRT scholars is related to the topic of rights. Agreeing that CLS offers a progressive agenda which in many ways makes it a natural ally of minority groups, these scholars are uncomfortable with what they consider the failure of the CLS movement—most of whose founding members are white males in secure academic positions—to understand and incorporate the reality of racial discrimination in American society. One of the most important messages of CLS—that rights discourse is alienating, indeterminate, and legitimates hierarchy—may be consistent with the

---

30. William Julius Wilson, *The Truly Disadvantaged: The Inner City, the Underclass, and Public Policy* (Chicago and London: University of Chicago Press, 1990), 15.

31. Mark Tushnet, "An Essay on Rights," *Texas Law Review* 62.8 (May 1984): 1386, 1382.

experience of minority communities, but it dismisses a little too high-handedly and patronizingly the value of that discourse to people of color. Patricia Williams puts it in this way:

> In a semantic as well as a substantive sense, then, I think that CLS has ignored the degree to which rights-assertion and the benefits of rights have helped blacks, other minorities, and the poor. . . . It is very hard to watch the idealistic or symbolic importance of rights being diminished with reference to the disenfranchised, who experience and express their disempowerment as nothing more or less than the denial of rights.[32]

On the issue of the utility of a rights-based fight for racial equality, that is, Patricia Williams parts ways with CLS as well as, by implication, with her "teacher, friend, and inspiration," Derrick Bell.[33] Unlike the "white male heavies" of the CLS movement, Bell is obviously very much aware of the importance of racism to the American experiment, and Williams wholeheartedly agrees with his call to arms here and now. It is to the cynical and pessimistic conclusion Bell draws from his assessment of the dire straits under which many, if not most, blacks still live after decades of civil rights litigation, that she objects. Bell fails to acknowledge[34]—as do his white colleagues in as well as outside of CLS—the extent to which blacks have given rights "life where there was none before. . . . And this was not the dry process of reification . . . but its opposite. This was the resurrection of life from ashes four hundred years old."[35] For blacks, the prospect of attaining full rights under the law has always been a highly motivational, semireligious source of hope, and some of the worst moments in the history of the United States occurred, not because people asserted their rights, but because they failed to commit themselves to a fight for rights.

32. Patricia J. Williams, "Alchemical Notes: Reconstructing Ideals from Deconstructed Rights," *Harvard Civil Rights–Civil Liberties Review* 22 (1987): 405.

33. Ibid., note of acknowledgment, 401.

34. Williams never directly criticizes Bell. As Randall Kennedy has pointed out, it is interesting that Bell seems to be forgiven for "sins" with which white scholars are charged. "Bell's work receives none of the criticism aimed at CLS work, even though it displays several of the same features for which white CLS scholars are chided" ("Racial Critiques of Legal Academia," *Harvard Law Review* 102 (1989): 1786.

35. Patricia J. Williams, *The Alchemy of Race and Rights: Diary of a Law Professor* (Cambridge, Mass.: Harvard University Press, 1991), 163.

"Rights" feels new in the mouths of most black people. It is still deliciously empowering to say. It is the magic wand of visibility and invisibility, of inclusion and exclusion, of power and no power. The concept of rights, both positive and negative, is the marker of our citizenship, our relation to others . . . In discarding rights altogether, one discards a symbol too deeply enmeshed in the psyche of the oppressed to lose without trauma and much resistance.[36]

The making of something out of nothing has taken immense alchemical fire. Without this fire, without this familiar alchemy of race and rights, Williams asks, what hope will there be for the future?

Differences in opinion as to whether or not rights rhetoric has been and continues to be an effective discourse for blacks may be racially motivated, Williams suggests. Whereas blacks will experience this discourse as empowering, it tends to be perceived as disempowering by whites—or at least by whites who are so well situated that they no longer need such rights discourse. Whites can "afford," so to speak, to dispense with the formality of rights. To blacks, however, it is precisely the formal structure of the law that decreases the likelihood of prejudice and racism. When white critics dream of informal, small-scale politics relying on goodwill and a sense of community, they forget or ignore the historical truth that there is a certain "interaction among rules, conduct, and character." As Richard Delgado puts it, the focus on informality on the part of certain white intellectuals, especially members of CLS,

> ignores the influence that rules have on an individual's character and action. A society that enacts rules and provides structures to curb racism announces that racism is unacceptable behavior . . . The bottom line is that formal public settings are relatively safe for minorities while informal private settings present risks. To minimize racism, one should structure settings so that public norms are enforced, and prejudice openly confronted and discouraged.[37]

To Patricia Williams as to Richard Delgado, a firm commitment to formal norms of fairness and behavior is needed to prevent the loss of gains already made in battling racism. The story of how she and her col-

36. Ibid., 164–65.
37. Richard Delgado, "The Ethereal Scholar: Does CLS Have What Minorities Want?" *Harvard Civil Rights–Civil Liberties Review* 22 (1987): 315, 318.

league, Peter Gabel, a contributor to CLS scholarship, went about leasing an apartment in New York in completely different ways, illustrates this point. When Gabel found an apartment he liked, he handed over to the owners a substantial deposit in cash without ever asking for a lease or a receipt. Trusting his lessors after but a brief conversation, Gabel felt that a formal, signed lease would put an unnecessarily formal barrier to what he hoped would develop into an enduring relationship with these lessors. To Gabel, "the logical ways of establishing some measure of trust between strangers were an avoidance of power and a preference for informal processes generally." Williams, raised in a neighborhood where white landlords systematically refused to sign any formal contracts with their black tenants—"such informality in most white-on-black situations signal[ling] distrust, not trust"—was highly surprised to hear that Gabel's lessors showed up as promised, that his faith had paid off.[38]

When Williams herself finally located an apartment in a house owned by some friends, she made sure to sign "a detailed, lengthily negotiated, finely printed lease firmly establishing me as the ideal arm's length transactor." Though hoping like Peter Gabel to be able to form a warm relationship with the people in whose house she would live, Williams feared that the lack of some formal structure to that relationship would leave her estranged and powerless, without "sufficient *rights* to manipulate commerce." What this little story of the different approaches to leasing an apartment shows, she explains, is that

> one's sense of empowerment defines one's relation to the law, in terms of trust, distrust, formality/informality, or rights/no-rights . . . On a semantic level, Peter's language of circumstantially defined need, of informality, solidarity, overcoming distance, sounded dangerously like the language of oppression to someone like me who was looking for freedom through the establishment of identity, the formulation of an autonomous social self.

However alienating and distance-creating it is to enter into a contractual relationship with another person, such a relationship is one between equals. Slaves and oppressed people are not permitted to engage in commerce. Transactions at arm's length are after all an improvement

38. Williams, *Alchemy of Race and Rights,* 147, 148.

over no transactions at all, or transactions in which one is the object of purchase: "stranger-stranger relations are better than stranger-chattel."[39]

Contractual relationships are at the core of Williams's interest and concern in the law. She teaches contracts, and the bulk of her writing deals with "contract and something like communion":

> Most of my work is concerned with the division between the commercial and the communitarian, or the legal and the illegal, the righted and the outlawed, the legitimate and the illegitimate, the propertied and the dispossessed.

The interplay of notions of public and private, market and family are especially interesting in a society such as the American in which property has always been valued and trusted, and in which basic rights historically have been defined as rights to property and ownership. In such a society, ownership constitutes the basic framework within which human relationships are formed and carried on, and being power- or rightless often means ending up as someone else's property. Until the rightless person gains access to basic rights, he or she will be seen by those holding rights as nothing but an object to be used. Williams therefore sees it as a major obligation in her own writing "to give voice to those people or things that, by virtue of their object relation to a contract historically have had no voice."[40]

What first made Williams interested in this crucial connection between contractual relationships and constitutional rights was her family history. Some years before, her sister had found an old document that looked like a contract of sale for their great-great-grandmother. "It is a very simple but lawyerly document, describing her as 'one female' and revealing her age as eleven; no price is specified, merely 'value exchanged'." What could it possibly have been like, Williams often wonders, at the age of eleven to become the forced mate of a white man twice her age—a man who would practice his sexual prowess on her in order a few years later to marry a "respectable" white woman; a man to whom her children, having been taken from her as she had been taken from her mother, would grow up reverent and obedient? The contract of

39. Ibid.
40. Ibid., 15, 160.

sale of her great-great-grandmother has forever personalized, Williams tells us, her analysis of the law of contracts and of the effects on its inhabitants of a society in which money and ownership are used to express appreciation and valuation. The personal property of a wealthy white man, never "owning" her own fate, Williams's great-great-grandmother was fair game from the perspective of those who had rights. "The body of private laws epitomized by contract, including slave contract, is problematic because it denies the object of contract any rights at all."[41]

Personal "anecdotes"[42] and experiences such as the story about her great-great-grandmother form an important part of *The Alchemy of Race and Rights*. As we shall see, Williams—like Bell—is highly conscious about having created with her "diary of a law professor" a whole new genre of legal writing. All these anecdotes tell of the exclusion of the powerless—most often blacks—by the powerful—most often whites. They urge us to listen to the voices of America's dispossessed and to include them in our discourse of rights so that they may one day be full-fledged members of our society. As the law and legal writing traditionally have valued neutral and objective principles and formalized, color-blind liberal ideals, the actual experience, history, culture, and intellectual tradition of people of color have been misrepresented, even excluded. "Neutrality is the standard for assuring these ideals; yet the adherence to it is often determined by reference to an aesthetic of uniformity, in which difference is simply omitted."[43] To make audible the voices of the excluded, our concept of rights needs to be expanded, therefore, beyond the rules of process and formal equality sanctified in mainstream liberal theory. Those who have experienced discrimination speak with a special voice to which we should listen, and as another CRT scholar, Mari J. Matsuda, has suggested, "the method of looking to the bottom can lead to concepts of law radically different from those generated at the top."[44] The diversity needed in the law and legal writing may be provided by storytelling—by "anecdotes" or "chronicles," for instance—telling of personal and subjective experiences, rather than of objective and neutral principles. Storytelling may include what the law traditionally excludes.

41. Ibid., 17, 159.
42. Ibid., 42.
43. Ibid., 48.
44. Matsuda, "Looking to the Bottom," 326.

In following up her defense of the formality of civil rights discourse with a wish to include in this discourse the excluded voices of minority groups, Williams runs into a problem with which Bell did not have to contend. At one and the same time, she emphasizes the importance, yet condemns the formality, of the law. Is she reconstructing in her alchemy of race and rights the ideology of liberalism, exemplified by individual rights, procedural fairness, equality, and liberty, her reader cannot help wondering, only in order later to deconstruct it in her call for diversity and multivoicedness? Or may her ambiguous attitude toward law's formality be accounted for as an example of the tension inherent in CRT between a "modernist" commitment to radical emancipation by the law and a "postmodernist" commitment to radical critique of the law? Angela P. Harris, who does not see this tension as a problem but rather as a source of strength, explains the uneasy coexistence of deconstructionist and reconstructionist views of law in CRT scholarship in this way:

> CRT is the heir to both CLS and traditional civil rights scholarship. CRT inherits from CLS a commitment to being "critical," which in this sense means also to be "radical" [while] . . . [a]t the same time, CRT inherits from traditional civil rights scholarship a commitment to a vision of liberation from racism through right reason. Despite the difficulty of separating legal reasoning and institutions from their racist roots, CRT's ultimate vision is redemptive, not deconstructive.[45]

In showing a certain reluctance to part with the key concepts of liberal jurisprudence as well as in talking about a re- rather than a deconstruction of such concepts, Williams places herself squarely in the tradition not only of CRT, but also of American feminism. As we shall see in the following chapter, most American feminists, though often identifying postmodern ways of thinking with women, are not interested in following the call of their French sisters for a complete deconstruction of the concept of gender. Such a deconstruction would mean leaving behind the male language of rights discourse, a step American feminists are not prepared to take. What they urge instead is anchoring male rights talk to female notions of caring and relationships in such a way that a synthesis of male and female is created.

45. Angela P. Harris, "Foreword: The Jurisprudence of Reconstruction," *California Law Review* 82 (1994). Quoted in Bell, "Who's Afraid of Critical Race Theory?" 899.

Whatever her intentions, Williams's reflections on the important topic of legal formality do at times seem somewhat inconsistent. This inconsistency is visible at the level of her linguistic performance as well. Reading through *The Alchemy of Race and Rights,* one cannot help but be puzzled at times by the stylistic maneuvers of its author. Straightforwardly told and very accessible passages alternate with highly complex and difficult ones. Thus, Williams's anecdotes are delightfully uncomplicated, whereas her thoughts on more abstract jurisprudential matters are more difficult to follow. Expressions scattered throughout the more theoretical parts, such as "a mere floating signifier, a deconstructive polymorph par excellence," or "if our laws are thus piano-wired on the exclusive validity of literalism,"[46] remind one of Mark Tushnet's—and Derrick Bell's—observations on the reifying tendency of rights discourse. True, we are told in chapter one that Williams wants to "bridge the traditional gap between theory and praxis" by means of creating "a text that is multilayered—that encompasses the straightforwardness of real life *and* reveals complexity of meaning."[47] Yet it seems—at least to this reader—that the stylistic gap between theory and praxis is never successfully bridged, but remains unnecessarily wide.

BELL, WILLIAMS, AND THE CREATION OF A NEW LEGAL-LITERARY GENRE

I am not sure who coined the phrase "critical race theory" to describe this form of writing, and I have received more credit than I deserve for the movement's origins. I rather think that this writing is the response to a need for expressing views that cannot be communicated effectively through existing techniques. In my case, I prefer using stories as a means of communicating views to those who hold very different views on the emotionally charged subject of race. People enjoy stories and will often suspend their beliefs, listen to the story, and then compare their views, not with mine, but with those expressed in the story. (Derrick Bell)[48]

Both Bell and Williams are, as briefly mentioned above, very conscious about the form of their writing. To both, the scope of traditional legal writing is too narrow. In order to be able to say something new, some-

---

46. Williams, *Alchemy of Race and Rights,* 123, 140.
47. Ibid., 6.
48. Bell, "Who's Afraid of Critical Race Theory?" 902.

thing different and challenging on a topic on which "most of what can be said . . . has been said, and likely more than once," they have chosen, as Bell puts it, "the tools not only of reason but of unreason." For Bell, that tool is "fantasy," a combination of fairy tale and its modern equivalent, science fiction, and Socratic dialogue. Thus, the chapters of *And We Are Not Saved* open with one of Geneva Crenshaw's chronicles—found by Bell, "handsomely bound," on his desk one day—and close with a discussion between Bell and Geneva in which the latter attempts to explain to the former the real significance of the chronicle just related.[49] In *Faces at the Bottom of the Well*, we again meet Geneva and her allegorical stories, but we are also introduced to a number of other colorful personalities with whom Bell conducts serious conversations in his "continuing quest for new directions in our struggle for racial justice."[50]

As indicated by the subtitle of *The Alchemy of Race and Rights*, "Diary of a Law Professor," Patricia Williams employs literary devices of a more personal kind. Several of her "anecdotes" are autobiographical, and the incidents related in those that are not have happened to people she knows well. Her inclusion of "parody, parable, and poetry," as well as her borrowings from other nonlegal academic disciplines, moreover, makes for a highly varied and entertaining reading experience. With its "intentional departure" from traditional legal language, which "flattens and confines in absolutes the complexity of meaning inherent in any given problem," *The Alchemy of Race and Rights* constitutes an attempt to "create a genre of legal writing to fill the gaps of traditional legal scholarship."[51] The reader is invited to participate actively both in Williams's more theoretical musings on the jurisprudence of rights or the rhetoric of power relations and in her personal stories of exclusion and prejudice—finding it hard at times, as already mentioned, to stay afloat amid all this complexity and multilayeredness of meaning.[52]

The effect these "tools of unreason" are meant to have on the reader is

---

49. Bell, *And We Are Not Saved*, 4, 5, 21.

50. Bell, *Faces at the Bottom of the Well*, ix.

51. Williams, *Alchemy of Race and Rights*, 8, 7, 6, 7.

52. In a later book, *The Rooster's Egg: On the Persistence of Prejudice* (Cambridge, Mass.: Harvard University Press, 1995), Williams again mixes law and personal narrative. Her focus this time is somewhat broader. She claims that "the debate about equality has shifted to one of free speech" (19), and that "the judicial responsibility to check the tyranny of any majority is abdicated out of a hypothesized fear of advancing or benefiting special groups" (103).

an emotional one. Bell and Williams hope to be able to make their readers *feel,* not just intellectually grasp, the impact of laws and legal decisions: how laws and decisions made by people in power affect other people as *subjects,* not just as objects. If the reader can be prodded into gaining at least some understanding of what it feels like to lead a life of oppression, to be as Williams calls it "an object of property," then he or she may finally see the immoral nature of slavery and racism. Bell and Williams would agree with Robin West when she explains that

> The "story" of the law of slavery and racism is not just the story of the evolution of the texts of the Dred Scott *decision,* the Fourteenth *Amendment,* the Civil Rights *Act,* or the Equal Employment *law.* Slavery was the lives and stories of Dred Scott, of the "sixty million and more" who died on the slave ships and to whom [Toni] Morrison dedicates [*Beloved*], of Morrison's Sethe, of Twain's Jim, of Patricia Williams' great-great-grandmother, and of their families and ancestors and descendants . . . Laws have a profound impact upon the subjectivity of people, children, slaves, women, and other living things who either might or might not participate in their textual production, interpretation, or critique. Until we learn to feel, to empathize with, and to assume those effects, we will not achieve even a decent understanding of the legal texts themselves.

When the "textually excluded—those robbed of subjectivity and speech—speak, they speak of the subjective experience of objecthood,"[53] and it is only by listening to these excluded voices that we may realize how what in theory and principle may look like a promising, fair law or doctrine may in fact come to operate as an instrument of oppression upon the textually excluded.

In using storytelling as an instrument in the fight for racial equality, Bell and Williams draw on a centuries-long tradition in the black community. Thus, Henry Louis Gates has suggested, for example, that blacks have learned as a result of their oppression to appropriate traditional forms of art in order then creatively and subversively to turn them into new artistic forms.[54] Likewise, Erlene Stetson, in a study of American black women's poetry, claims that "creativity has often been a sur-

53. Robin West, "Communities, Texts, and Law: Reflections on the Law and Literature Movement," *Yale Journal of Law and the Humanities* 1.1 (1988): 146, 155, 143.

54. See Henry Louis Gates Jr., *The Signifying Monkey: A Theory of African-American Literary Criticism* (New York: Oxford University Press, 1988).

vival tactic." Considering words a major means of criticizing the status quo, black women have traditionally used as creative strategies "a compelling quest for identity, a subversive perception of reality, and subterfuge and ambivalence."[55] For legal theorists such as Bell and Williams,

> the relevance of the black artists' fight to establish progressive language and music is that the fight over the body and soul of American law is part of the same struggle. The law, as critical scholars recognize, consists of language, ideas, signs, and structures that have material and moral consequences.[56]

On the contemporary American cultural scene, one strand of this black tradition of subversive storytelling, to which Bell's and Williams's books form an interesting and innovative contribution, has developed into what Toni Morrison has called "American Africanism." An effort "to avert the critical gaze from the racial object to the racial subject," Morrison's Africanist project in *Playing in the Dark* is to show how what have always been considered the central characteristics of American identity—individualism, masculinity, autonomy, and innocence, coupled to an obsession with death and hell—are in fact responses to a dark and abiding Africanist presence, an African "other."

> Africanism is the vehicle by which the American self knows itself as not enslaved, but free; not repulsive, but desirable; not helpless, but licensed and powerful; not history-less, but historical; not damned, but innocent; not a blind accident of evolution, but a progressive fulfillment of destiny . . . It was this Africanism, deployed as rawness and savagery, that provided the staging ground and arena for the elaboration of the quintessential American identity.[57]

For Morrison, that is, the word "American" can only be understood in association with race.

And for lawyers and writers like Bell and Williams, one may add, American racism can only be understood in association with the law. Indeed, it is this link between American identity, race, and the law that

55. Erlene Stetson, quoted in Matsuda, "Looking to the Bottom," 336.
56. Matsuda, "Looking to the Bottom," 337.
57. Toni Morrison, *Playing in the Dark: Whiteness and the Literary Imagination* (Cambridge, Mass.: Harvard University Press, 1992), 6, 90, 52, 44.

makes *And We Are Not Saved, Faces at the Bottom of the Well,* and *The Alchemy of Race and Rights* so provocative and interesting. Modern versions of the lawyer and man-of-letters of old, described by Robert A. Ferguson in *Law and Letters in American Culture,*[58] Bell and Williams use their knowledge about the law as a starting point as well as a point of reference in a critical assessment of American culture. Holding up as a torch the promise of freedom and equality for all outlined in the Constitution and comparing this (legal) promise to the harsh racial reality of contemporary America, these two writers demonstrate how the American experiment has come to fail, primarily on account of race.

In a dream toward the end of *The Alchemy of Race and Rights,* Patricia Williams speaks of the law and her relationship with it thus:

> The Law. The law says, the law is. My life, my tissue, my membrane. Connection, suspicion, privacy, the secret wedged in the void. The corrupt entrenchment of my thirst and loneliness. I am a tiny fragment, a gear and linchpin to the law.[59]

To Bell as well as to Williams, the law is much more than just a collection of texts. For better or for worse, they argue, in modern America the law has come to constitute one of the most important ways in which people define themselves and their relationship to each other. Whether viewed as an alchemical reaction or a trap, race and the law seem inseparable—one is hardly conceivable without the other.

CONCLUDING REMARKS

From the very beginning, the black fight has been a fight for civil rights. Relegated to the role of outsider or misfit, blacks have believed that the most effective path toward participation in America's public life as equal members is the path of the law. Unlike Native Americans, whose treaties with the American government formalized at least some measure of legal rights, blacks had to start completely from scratch in securing for themselves legal standing. As it has become embarrassingly clear within the past couple of decades that the black fight for civil rights and freedoms has not resulted in the hoped-for integration of blacks into American

58. Robert A. Ferguson, *Law and Letters in American Culture* (Cambridge, Mass.: Harvard University Press, 1984).

59. Williams, *The Alchemy of Race and Rights,* 208.

society, critical voices have been raised as to whether the structuring of the black fight around civil rights has been a wise one.

Derrick Bell's is one such critical voice. Unless black leaders and civil rights advocates start looking beyond traditional civil rights views toward more pragmatic political solutions, Bell warns, the problems blacks are facing now will only get worse. Patricia Williams strongly disagrees. She defends the rights-based fight for racial equality on the grounds that to the black community, the possibility of gaining important legal rights has always served an important motivational function. Without the commitment to the fight for rights, blacks would have very little hope left for the future. What to Bell is not only a *reified,* but a *deified* worship of "rights," Williams sees as a semireligious source of hope for the oppressed.

An important part of Williams's thoughts and writings on the law concerns the claim to neutrality and objectivity made by liberal legal discourse. Much like the majority of American feminists, she sees in this claim an effort to obscure the fact that neutral equals male, the concrete result of which is an exclusion of those who are different, that is, nonwhite and nonmale. In order that the voices of the excluded may be heard, she argues, it is necessary to open up the genre of legal writing. *The Alchemy of Race and Rights* constitutes her vision of what such expanded legal writing might look like. Personal anecdotes and borrowings from nonlegal academic disciplines such as literature tell of the personal effects of the law on America's dispossessed.

How can Williams's insistence on the continued importance of formal rights talk for the black fight be reconciled with her wish to add to the "neutrality" and "objectivity" of formalized liberal ideals a multivoiced or multicultural perspective? There is clearly a problem here. What Williams seems to be doing, however, is akin to what other feminists are attempting to do: to take the best of the liberal tradition and combine it with the best of contemporary postmodern theories of multiculturalism and gender. To this embedding of a male ethic of rights within a female ethic of care, chapter six is devoted.

VI

"Embedding Rights within Relationships"
Gender, Law, and Sara Paretsky

My work was not done from a legal perspective, although the law was very present at the beginning stages of my work and raised a question for me which has persisted throughout it.

Carol Gilligan, "Feminist Discourse, Moral Values, and the Law"

Although Gilligan's claims about sex difference are presented in the context of her challenge to psychological moral development discourse, the dominant standard Gilligan challenges, the ethic of rights, is familiar to lawyers from the rhetoric of liberal jurisprudence.

Mary Joe Frug, *Postmodern Legal Feminism*

With the publication in 1982 of *In a Different Voice,* Carol Gilligan set the stage for a renewed and intensified discussion about the differences between men and women. Drawing from psychological theory and empirical research on moral reasoning, Gilligan claims that women tend to use a "different voice," that is, a voice unlike the male voice and one that prominent theorists have generally associated with the highest stage of ethical development. What this different, predominantly female voice stresses is concrete respon-

The title of this chapter is taken from Martha Minow, *Making All the Difference: Inclusion, Exclusion, and American Law* (Ithaca, N.Y.: Cornell University Press, 1990), 15.

sibilities and relationships rather than more abstract principles of rights and justice. Concluding that conventional approaches focus on and value rights at the cost of relationships, Gilligan insists that issues and norms associated with women be paid attention to and that existing structures be altered so as to accommodate caretaking interests.

In a Different Voice became an immediate hit. For feminists in a wide spectrum of disciplines who were participating in what has often been referred to as the "sameness versus difference" debate, Gilligan's work came to provide the theoretical foundation for the belief that differences, biological or cultural, ought to be taken into account in order to achieve real or substantial equality. The model of equality and treatment based on an assumption of sameness between men and women, upon which feminist theory had concentrated since the rebirth of the dormant feminist movement in the United States in the 1960s, had come to be seriously questioned by the early 1980s. Equality, or "equal protection" under the Fourteenth Amendment, it seemed, did not always result in equal treatment of women; " 'equality' could be formal (that is, men and women could be treated alike) but hollow (because they were not equal in fact, or substantively equal)."[1] Unless it was repeatedly affirmed and drawn attention to, feminists now claimed, that different, female voice would not stand a chance competing against the male voice, which formed the basis for the (neutral) standard women were supposed to equal.

To the legal establishment, perhaps more than to any other profession, Gilligan's criticism of the ethic of rights was, as Mary Joe Frug pointed out, "familiar . . . from the rhetoric of liberal jurisprudence." Developing out of and along with the civil rights movement, the women's movement was from the very beginning committed to the use of law to bring about social change. Several of the women prominent in the movement had gone to law school, and in the early days in the 1960s and '70s they had begun to develop feminist legal theories that confronted the theoretical legal frameworks created by men. Even when, much later, legal feminists along with other feminists joined in the discussion carried out by minority and critical legal scholars, outlined in chapter five, as to whether rights talk promotes wide political change or leads to

1. Carrie Menkel-Meadow, "Feminist Legal Theory, Critical Legal Studies, and Legal Education or 'The Fem-Crits Go to Law School,'" *Journal of Legal Education* 38 (1985): 72.

an empowerment of largely symbolic and therefore dubious value, they never fundamentally questioned the usefulness for the women's cause of the legal vernacular and the legal arena. As Martha Minow puts it, "there is something too valuable in the aspiration of rights, and something too neglectful of the power embedded in assertions of another's need, to abandon the rhetoric of rights."[2] The inherent categorizations and the tendency to construe the world as a series of binary oppositions—normal, abnormal; independent, dependent; male, female—of the law notwithstanding, American feminists, lawyers as well as non-lawyers, with rare exceptions, have kept returning to the law for ammunition in their fight for equality.

That Gilligan's work, though not consciously done, as we saw, "from a legal perspective," raised questions that have obvious implications for legal analysis, need not surprise us. In today's law-permeated America, any work whose subject touches upon identity—especially race-, gender-, or class-related identity—tends invariably to use a legal vernacular. What may perhaps be somewhat more puzzling is the unwillingness on the part of most American feminists to leave behind the fixed, hierarchical concepts and terminology of the existing legal order. Unlike French feminists such as Julia Kristeva, Luce Irigaray, and Hélène Cixous, who are engaged in attempts to deconstruct the duality or binary opposition of masculinity and femininity altogether, American feminists by and large remain committed to a discussion along sameness versus difference lines or, in legal terms, equal treatment versus special treatment lines. The change advocated typically involves, not a *de-,* but a *re*construction or synthesis of the old, familiar liberal and radical notions of sameness and difference. And when the argument advanced partakes of deconstructive moves (such as a recognition that the debate over sameness and difference reflects the displacement onto women of the human choices already made in the construction of social and cultural worlds), it tends to display not only certain materialist concerns, but also a commitment to rendering social constructions of gender more visible and hopefully thereby more mutable. Thus, Martha Minow suggests "embedding rights within relationships," a "dialectical approach connecting a renewed interest in relationships to the prior frameworks that emphasized rights and distinctions between people,"[3] just as Carol Gilligan asserts

2. Minow, *Making All the Difference,* 307.
3. Ibid., 15.

that, "it's no longer simply about justice or simply about caring; rather, it is about bringing them together to transform the domain."[4]

This chapter will argue that the legal framework and vocabulary within which so much of American feminist thinking operates neither allow for nor make desirable a deconstruction of duality. The adversarial nature of American law—and especially American common law—lends itself well to and perpetuates the sort of oppositional logic implied by the binary terminology of male versus female. The common law, it may be recalled from chapter one, is dualistic in more than one sense. It originates in the actual customs and practices of communities and works from the bottom up as well as from the top down, containing elements of both practice and theory. When feminists such as Carrie Menkel-Meadow and Carol Gilligan claim that the feminine perspective "includes a real, concretized, contextualized, and experiential dimension," and that the female "ethic of responsibility relies on the concept of equity, the recognition of difference in need,"[5] they are, in effect, relying on a common-law vocabulary to make a philosophical point. And precisely because the common law, as it was originally and ideally conceived, combines practice and theory, equity and equality, feminine and masculine, it holds out a promise of incorporation and synthesis—a promise potentially so rewarding that most American feminists have never felt the need fundamentally to deconstruct it.

Holding on to the rhetoric of rights, but making sure that it is firmly fixed within an ethic of care and relationships, is easier said than done, however. Often the tension between individual rights and a morality of care and responsibility builds up to such an extent that no compromise is possible. Up through the 1980s and '90s, one of the most interesting arenas in which this tension and a possible reconciliation between male and female has been discussed has been feminist detective fiction. For writers such as Sara Paretsky, Sue Grafton, Amanda Cross, and Antonia Fraser, just to mention some of the more well known, the reinvention or reworking of the "hard-boiled" school of detective fiction has made it possible to raise and explore, in innovative, sensitive, and surprising

---

4. Gilligan, in "Feminist Discourse, Moral Values, and the Law: A Conversation," *Buffalo Law Review* 34 (1985): 45.

5. Menkel-Meadow, "Feminist Legal Theory," 80, and Gilligan, *In a Different Voice: Psychological Theory and Women's Development* (Cambridge, Mass.: Harvard University Press, 1981), 164.

ways, issues affecting women—violence, sexual violence, victimization, conflict between individuals and authority, and conflict between men and women.

The politically satisfying plots of many of the female detective novels notwithstanding, various aspects of these novels are both problematic and embarrassing to feminist ways of thinking. Thus, private eye V. I. Warshawski, the heroine of Sara Paretsky's novels and the focus of this chapter, invokes the concerns of contemporary feminism, while simultaneously adopting and uncritically accepting the aggressive, gun-slinging attitudes of her male predecessors. Having her heroine oscillate between manifestations of extreme independence and autonomy and yearnings for connection and relationships, Paretsky successfully lays bare the difficulties inherent in embedding rights within relationships. V.I. or Vic's personal contradictions are made part of the novels' ten-sions, and taken together, Paretsky's eight "V. I. Warshawski Mysteries"[6] to date may be seen as a kind of female bildungsroman, tracing the progress of a woman from fear of being abandoned through feelings of annihilation, loss, and despair to active involvement and reconciliation with other people. Throughout, the personal is discussed against the background of the law and the conventions of the detective novel, and thereby made political or public.

In the first part of this chapter, the focus will be on the more theoret-ical aspects of gender and feminism. In the second part, these aspects will be applied to an analysis of Sara Paretsky's novels in an attempt to illuminate main character V. I. Warshawski's development from autono-mous selfhood to a selfhood embedded within relationships.

AMERICAN VERSUS FRENCH FEMINISM; AMERICAN FEMINISM AND THE COMMON LAW

In recent years, a complicated debate has taken place between Anglo-American and French feminisms.[7] At the center of this debate have been

6. Sara Paretsky's collection of short stories, *Windy City Blues* (New York: Delacorte Press, 1995), will not be discussed in this chapter. While these stories concern V. I. Warshawski (cf. the subtitle, "V. I. Warshawski Stories"), they add nothing new to Paretsky's portrayal of V. I. in her eight novels.

7. In the following, I will be relying on Mary Eagleton's introduction to *Feminist Literary Criticism* (London: Longman, 1991). Like Eagleton and Moi, I wish to empha-size that "not all Anglo-American writers expound Anglo-American criticism, nor all

issues concerning subjectivity, identity, theory, and practice, and what the participants in the debate have tried to grapple with is the political meaning of feminism: what is and ought to be the point of feminist studies if they do not succeed in bringing about political change? What follows is a comparison between Anglo-American and French feminisms as these have come to be expressed in the writings of Elaine Showalter and Toril Moi, respectively. Such a comparison brings to light the key problematics of current feminism, just as it helps to isolate concerns of specific importance to Anglo-American feminist critics.

More than perhaps anywhere else, it is in their discussion of Virginia Woolf's masterpiece *A Room of One's Own* that Showalter's (Anglo-American) and Moi's (French) approaches to feminism are revealed. In her chapter on Woolf in *A Literature of Their Own,* Showalter wants "to demystify the legend of Virginia Woolf." The emphasis in recent feminist criticism on Woolf as "the apotheosis of a new literary sensibility—not feminine but androgynous"—is misplaced, even dangerous. Androgyny and the retreat into "a room of one's own" may look attractive as abstract ideals, but they do not go very far toward solving the concrete problems of everyday life.[8]

Its claim to be spontaneous and intimate notwithstanding, *A Room of One's Own* is "an extremely impersonal and defensive book," according to Showalter.[9] Woolf comes across as depersonalized, even desexed. Her distance and lack of involvement are especially noticeable in her multiple points of view. These playful shifts and changes of perspective are treacherous in that they make it virtually impossible to pin down Woolf's individual self and gender identity. In the midst of these multiple perspectives, it is not clear to the reader what sort of message—if indeed any at all—Woolf intends to convey.

French feminists French criticism; the generalized terms disguise the multiplicity of critical practices coexisting within each tradition . . . The terms 'Anglo-American' and 'French' must not be taken to represent purely national demarcations: they do not signal the critics' birthplace but the intellectual tradition within which they work" (4). See also Drucilla Cornell, "The Double-Prized World: Myth, Allegory, and the Feminine" (*Cornell Law Review* 75 [1990]), for an interesting discussion about the difference between Robin West and Kristeva—a difference that is not unlike that between Showalter and Moi.

8. Elaine Showalter, *A Literature of Their Own: British Women Novelists from Brontë to Lessing* (Princeton, N.J.: Princeton University Press, 1977), 265, 263.

9. Ibid., 282.

Within the literary criticism of Elaine Showalter, claims Toril Moi, there is detectable "a strong, unquestioned belief in the values . . . of traditional bourgeois humanism of a liberal-individualist kind." Behind Showalter's dislike of Woolf is the latter's rejection of "the fundamental need for the individual to adopt a unified, integrated self-identity. Both Woolf and Lessing radically undermine the notion of the unitary self, the central concept of Western male humanism and one crucial to Showalter's feminism." What Showalter sees as evasion and fear of confronting real-life issues on Woolf's part is in fact, says Moi, a recognition of and attempt to subvert rigid gender identities. Throughout her life, Woolf steadfastly refused to conform to definitions of sexual identity officially condoned by society and did her best in her writing by means, for instance, of multiple points of view "to deconstruct the death-dealing binary oppositions of masculinity and femininity." In her rejection of traditional humanist desires for unity of thought and vision, Woolf may be seen as a precursor of modern French feminism. She grasped what Anglo-American feminists such as Elaine Showalter have failed to grasp, namely that the traditional humanism represented by Anglo-American feminism

> is in effect part of patriarchal ideology. At its center is the seamlessly unified self—either individual or collective—which is commonly called 'Man'. As Luce Irigaray or Hélène Cixous would argue, this integrated self is in fact a phallic self, constructed on the model of the self-contained, powerful, phallus. Gloriously autonomous, it banishes from itself all conflict, contradiction and ambiguity.[10]

In Moi's opinion, Showalter, like most Anglo-American feminists, lacks an adequate *theoretical* apparatus to understand fully what Woolf was all about. Searching for a unified individual self and valuing the experiential over the theoretical, Showalter et al. run the risk not only of reducing, but also of entirely missing the point of works of a nonrealist kind. Rather than looking toward the past and the by now obsolete (in Moi's opinion) writings of the Marxist critic Georg Lukács, to whose theories about the realist novel representing the totality of human life in a social framework we shall return later, Showalter would be better off letting herself be inspired by contemporary French feminist writing.

10. Toril Moi, as quoted in Eagleton, ed., *Feminist Literary Criticism,* 42, 47, 43.

It is in the work of Julia Kristeva, asserts Moi, that we may reach a new and radically transformed awareness of the nature of the feminist struggle. According to Kristeva, the feminist struggle may be divided into three historical-political stages. These stages Moi summarizes as follows:

(1) Women demand equal access to the symbolic order. Liberal feminism. Equality.
(2) Women reject the male symbolic order in the name of differences. Radical feminism. Femininity extolled.
(3) (This is Kristeva's own position) Women reject the dichotomy between masculine and feminine as metaphysical.[11]

Showalter and her fellow Anglo-American feminists recoil from the challenge of the very notion of a unified identity that is implied by the deconstruction of the opposition between masculinity and femininity at Kristeva's third stage. Persisting in defending women *as* women, says Moi, these feminists fail to grasp the underlying metaphysical nature of constructed gender identities.

A quick survey of American feminism—and in the following I shall concentrate on the *American* part of Anglo-American feminism—bears out Moi's contention. The American debate has remained loyal to the issue of sameness versus difference. There have been but few attempts to move beyond the male-female dichotomy.[12] Here, I will briefly look at a couple of these attempts before moving on to the bulk of American feminist writing, which has largely preoccupied itself with questions relating to liberal or radical feminisms, searching for answers, that is, within a binary oppositional framework.[13]

11. Ibid., 46.
12. Of other critics who identify with aspects of postmodern activity may be mentioned Drucilla Cornell (see e.g., "The Double-Prized World: Myth, Allegory, and the Feminine," mentioned above) and Tracy E. Higgins (see e.g., "By Reason of Their Sex: Feminist Theory, Postmodernism, and Justice," *Cornell Law Review* 80 [1995]).
13. In what follows, I am offering a necessarily abbreviated and greatly simplified survey of American feminism. My intention is merely to suggest a certain tendency. I am aware that I risk grouping together as either sameness or difference proponents feminists whose approach, upon a closer inspection than I can offer here, is influenced by the arguments of both camps. I do not mean to suggest that U.S. feminists simply or uncritically embrace sameness or difference, but merely that upon considering the various arguments advanced in the debate, most of these feminists end up rejecting

One American feminist who has been involved in promoting what she calls a "postmodern legal feminism" is the late professor of law Mary Joe Frug.[14] Her objective being "to demonstrate in a concrete situation how sexual differences can be discussed without resorting to dichotomized description in which maleness and femaleness are presented as rigidly opposite characteristics," Frug draws on postmodern insights from a variety of disciplines. In her version, postmodern feminism focuses on particular doctrinal issues, claims that sexual differences are complex, ever-shifting practices, and contests conventional and stalemated understandings of gender in deliberately invoking *differences.* By privileging differences *within* the sexes—differences within maleness or femaleness relating to race, class, sexual orientation, and other realities of experience—rather than privileging differences *between* the sexes, "postmodern feminists are thus able to treat women as historically situated individuals with commonalities *at the same time* that they are challenging the link between femininity and biological femaleness."[15]

For Catharine A. MacKinnon, too, the future of gender studies lies in a repudiation of the male-female dichotomy. As long as issues of gender turn on whether women can be the same as or different from men, the perspective taken will inevitably be a masculine one in that men are set up as the standard. We should forget about the question of difference and focus directly on dominance and political hierarchy: "gender is an inequality of power, a social status based on who is permitted to do what to whom. Only derivatively is it a difference."[16] Women are a subordinate group, the victims on a day-to-day basis of patterns of abuse such as rape, battery, and incest. This abuse often remains unacknowledged, tacitly accepted from a male point of view as the eroticization of dominance and submission. "Dominance and submission made into sex, made into the gender difference, constitute the suppressed social content of the gender definitions of men and women."[17] Indeed, "to be rap*able,* a position which is social, not biological, defines what a woman

---

postmodern ways of looking at the world as not offering a viable alternative to either sameness or difference.

14. Mary Joe Frug, *Postmodern Legal Feminism* (New York: Routledge, 1992).

15. Ibid., 13, 123.

16. Catharine A. MacKinnon, *Feminism Unmodified: Discourses on Life and Law* (Cambridge, Mass.: Harvard University Press, 1987), 8.

17. MacKinnon, in "Feminist Discourse, Moral Values, and the Law: A Conversation," 27.

is."[18] The fight against male dominance is consequently a very concrete and a very sexual-political one. It is no coincidence that MacKinnon has concentrated her political efforts over the past decade on issues such as pornography, sexual harassment, and abortion.[19]

Beyond questioning the binary oppositional framework of male and female, Frug and MacKinnon do not seem to have much in common. Yet they both present in their writings "domesticated" or Americanized versions of postmodern theories of discourse, deconstruction, and hierarchical patterns. Frug's emphasis on differences within the sexes, no less than MacKinnon's focus on sexual dominance and submission, takes as its point of departure the concrete, real, and experiential dimension of women's lives. For both, it is in the realm of practice, of the historical and political world, that the fight might be fought. Theory and ideology count, but textuality and discourse analysis are never favored over the specificity of history and culture. This no doubt reflects the fact that Frug and MacKinnon, like many other feminist legal theorists, are also activists who believe they can influence the existing legal and political framework.[20] What we see here is a shift of perspective within rather than a radical subversion of existing modes of thought.[21]

The rootedness of Frug and MacKinnon in practice makes the difference between their work and that of other American feminists one of degree rather than kind. The latter may—very roughly speaking—be divided into two categories: feminist work that critically analyzes and

18. MacKinnon, "Feminism, Marxism, Method, and the State: Toward a Feminist Jurisprudence," *Signs* 8.4 (1983): 651.

19. See e.g., MacKinnon, *Only Words* (Cambridge, Mass.: Harvard University Press, 1993).

20. I thank Martha Minow for drawing my attention to this fact.

21. MacKinnon herself talks about a "shift in perspective from gender as difference to gender as dominance," in "Difference and Dominance: On Sex Discrimination," *Feminist Legal Theory*, ed. Katharine T. Bartlett and Rosanne Kennedy (Boulder, Colo.: Westview Press, 1991), 90. See also Drucilla Cornell and Tracy Higgins (see note 12 above), who both criticize MacKinnon for advocating a "masculine" ideal of autonomy and selfhood. For Cynthia Ward, too, MacKinnon is a closet liberalist: "Neither MacKinnon's critique of male domination nor her advocacy of consciousness-raising as the best feminist methodology are at all incompatible with liberal visions of autonomy and selfhood" (Cynthia Ward, "The Radical Feminist Defense of Individualism," *Northwestern University Law Review* 89 [1995]: 893). Ward furthermore takes MacKinnon to task for wishing to speak for all women—a wish that "necessarily involves the suppression of diversity among women" (888).

then proceeds to affirm sameness or equality between the sexes; and feminist work that rejects sameness altogether and extols femininity. The key question for both sameness and difference feminists is whether "feminists' traditional focus on gender-neutrality is a bankrupt ideal," as Joan C. Williams puts it.[22] As feminists have increasingly become aware, deep-seated social differences continue to encourage men and women to make very different choices in relation both to work and to family. Do these choices merely reflect the oppressive realities of the current gender system or are they the expression of basic and very real gender differences? And, on a more theoretical level, are feminist notions of the self, knowledge, and truth still compatible with the categories of Enlightenment thinking, or should postmodernism be adopted by feminism as a theoretical ally?

Joan Williams and Sabina Lovibond belong to the group of feminists who still believe that the Enlightenment way of thinking contains a promise of social reconstruction and emancipation from traditional ways of life. The difference between Enlightenment and postmodern views, writes Lovibond, is that

> the Enlightenment pictured the human race as engaged in an effort towards universal, moral and intellectual self-realization, and so as the subject of a universal historical experience; it also postulated a universal human *reason* in terms of which social and political tendencies could be assessed as "progressive" or otherwise (the goal of politics being defined as the realization of reason in practice). Postmodernism rejects this picture: that is to say, it rejects the unity of reason. It refuses to conceive of humanity as a unitary subject striving towards the goal of perfect coherence (in its common stock of beliefs) or of perfect cohesion and stability (in its political practice).[23]

The Enlightenment way of thinking contains a promise of social reconstruction and emancipation from traditional ways of life—a promise that "sooner or later, arbitrary authority will cease to exist." Postmodernism, by contrast, offers no such promise, but "would have us plunge, romantically, into the maelstrom without making it our goal to emerge

22. Joan C. Williams, "Deconstructing Gender," in Bartlett and Kennedy, eds., *Feminist Legal Theory*, 95.
23. Sabina Lovibond, "Feminism and Postmodernism," *New Left Review* 178 (1989): 6.

on *terra firma.*"[24] The claim made for women of the central critiques of postmodernism and the identification of those critiques with the female, different voice are far from constructive. Not only do they effectively kill any aspiration feminists may have had about ending the battle between the sexes and replacing it with communication and truth; they also expose women to a power game of unprecedented viciousness. If there is no rational basis for distinguishing between true and false beliefs, then it seems that power alone will be the determining factor in the competition between different truth claims. This is a frightening prospect to those who are oppressed by or in general lack the power of others. The postmodern epistemology's view of truths as necessarily partial and contextual is consequently "not in any meaningful way 'women's voice,'" says Joan Williams.[25] Indeed, asks Lovibond, "how can anyone ask me to say good-bye to 'emancipatory metanarratives' when my own emancipation is still such a patchy, hit-and-miss affair?"[26]

The most widely influential description of gender from the difference side of the spectrum is Carol Gilligan's *In a Different Voice,* whose core claim that women are focused on relationships, responsibility, and caring rather than on separation, autonomy, and hierarchy has inspired, as we saw, a large number of feminists. Among these is Christine Littleton, who sums up difference attacks on sameness theories in this way: "equality analysis defines as beyond its scope precisely those issues that women find crucial to their concrete experience as women." First of all, equality analysis is not very useful when it encounters real differences. Second, it locates difference in women rather than in relationships between the sexes, and last, but not least, it uncritically takes for granted that social institutions are gender-neutral. Consequently, "equality models, with their insistence that difference be ignored, eradicated or dissolved are not responsive to the feminist critique of equality."[27]

Feminists of difference often identify postmodern ways of thinking with women, noting that women traditionally have been thought to prefer sensitivity to context and a faith in emotions and intuition as modes of thought to abstract and logical thinking. Feminism and post-

---

24. Ibid., 11, 15.

25. Williams, in Bartlett and Kennedy, eds., *Feminist Legal Theory,* 98.

26. Lovibond, "Feminism and Postmodernism," 12.

27. Christine Littleton, "Reconstructing Sexual Equality," in Bartlett and Kennedy, eds., *Feminist Legal Theory,* 43, 44.

modernism do share a faith in contextual thinking and a wish to understand and reconstitute the self, gender, knowledge, social relations, and culture without resorting to linear, teleological, hierarchical, and holistic ways of thinking and being. Yet a reluctance on the part of American feminists to go all the way, as it were, to welcome the conflicts and ambiguities that result from a deconstruction of the duality of gender and unitary self along French feminist lines, is noticeable in many of the solutions proposed to the dilemmas of gender.

> Postmodernism is at once promising and threatening for feminism. Divisions within feminism over descriptions of women's experience, coupled with the risk of reinforcing traditional gender roles, have continued to draw feminists away from broad theories of gender difference and towards a recognition of the contingency and partiality of any particular account of gender. By questioning the possibility of true accounts and emphasizing the constitutive role of language, postmodernism resonates with feminist critiques of legal accounts of womanhood.
>
> At the same time, if postmodernism disables truth claims feminists themselves cannot claim to tell true stories of women's experience . . . Feminists, along with other groups on the margin of power, are reluctant to relinquish the hope that resort to some standard independent of politics and culture will strengthen their claim.[28]

For Minow and Gilligan, as we saw, the proper response is one of reconciliation and integration of masculinity and femininity, one of "embedding rights within relationships" and bringing together justice and caring "to transform the domain." Indeed, in Gilligan's conception of female moral development, progress toward a moral maturity of responsibility and care in social relationships is depicted as leading through and incorporating a discovery of the worth of self and individual rights. "Development for both sexes," she writes, "would therefore seem to entail an integration of rights and responsibilities through the discovery of the complementarity of these disparate views."[29]

Suzanna Sherry also talks about integration. Observing, in an interesting article called "Civic Virtue and the Feminine Voice in Constitu-

---

28. Higgins, "By Reason of Their Sex," 1570–71.
29. Gilligan, *In a Different Voice*, 100.

tional Adjudication,"[30] that men and women in general think differently about the world, Sherry contends that the masculine perspective reflects liberal theory, whereas the feminine counterpart more closely parallels classical republican theory as it is expressed in the works of Aristotle, Machiavelli, and Jefferson. The path so often taken in response to this dichotomy, dismissal of one's opponents and their viewpoints, she finds unproductive and instead advocates and ascribes to a feminine perspective an integration and reconciliation of the two paradigms. The injection of such a feminine emphasis on reconciliation may, she hopes, significantly alter the current, somewhat stalemated debate on gender—"to avoid the Scylla of liberalism's overemphasis on autonomy and the Charybdis of the neoclassical tendency to romanticize the community and subsume the individual, we must reconcile the modern and classical traditions, not simply replace the former with the latter."[31]

The truly feminine and feminist response for many American feminists, it would thus seem, is one of integration and synthesis rather than one of deconstruction. Believing that it is possible, even desirable, to work from within a binary oppositional framework, these feminists are still, to a significant extent, within what Lovibond calls "the Enlightenment habit of thought."[32] And within such a habit of thought, the law—and especially the common law—provides a useful arena and a handy vernacular in which to fight. The common law, as we saw in chapter one, is in its very nature both material and ideological, its foremost principle a reliance on prevailing community standards, or law as custom transformed. Emphasizing continuity and peaceful incorporation of change rather than sudden and violent reform, it has always attempted to reconcile and create a usable synthesis out of new principles and ideas added by historical events and transformations into the older tradition in a comprehensive and meaningful way. For the partiality to the experiential rather than the theoretical and the attempt to reconcile masculinity and femininity on the part of many American feminists, common-law thinking therefore provides a framework that is flexible enough to make ventures into deconstruction unnecessary. Like

30. Suzanna Sherry, "Civic Virtue, and the Feminine Voice in Constitutional Adjudication," *Virginia Law Review* 72 (1986): 543–616.

31. Ibid., 578.

32. Lovibond, "Feminism and Postmodernism," 11.

the rest of American culture of which they form an important part, American feminists, to make a political, cultural, or philosophical point, therefore rely on—feminists of the French postmodern school would probably say, are trapped by—rights talk.

REALISM, DETECTIVE FICTION, AND SARA PARETSKY

Vic as a Female Lukácsian Type

One of the literary theoreticians Elaine Showalter mentions in her discussion of Virginia Woolf is the Marxist critic Georg Lukács. What Showalter and other Anglo-American feminists find attractive about Lukács's aesthetics is his reading of great art as that which sustains an ideal of the total human being, the human being both as a private individual and a public citizen.[33] The realist novel is for Lukács the supreme narrative form in that it attempts, as objectively as possible, to portray "types." A type is "a peculiar synthesis which organically binds together the general and the particular both in characters and situations," and "true great realism . . . depicts man and society as complete entities, instead of showing merely one or the other of their aspects."[34] Transferred to the realm of feminist writing, a Lukácsian type would be a truthful or true-to-life portrayal of a (strong) woman with whom the reader may identify, a portrayal that would include equal emphasis on the private and the public.

In a certain sense, Sara Paretsky's main character, V. I. Warshawski, may be seen as such a female Lukácsian type; and Paretsky's medium, the detective novel, as a realistic piece of art along Lukácsian lines. Medium and contents, form and substance go hand in hand in Paretsky's writing. As for the former, the choice of the detective novel as the forum in which to pursue issues of relevance to women is itself significant. Unlike almost any other literary genre, the detective story owes its origin to one author alone: Edgar Allan Poe. With the publication in 1841 of "The Murders in the Rue Morgue," featuring as its central character the Chevalier C. Auguste Dupin, Poe created the prototype of the great detective. What chiefly characterizes Dupin are his impressive reasoning powers and intellectual brilliance. With this brilliance, Dupin

33. This is Moi's speculation. See Toril Moi, in Eagleton, ed., *Feminist Literary Criticism,* 40–41.

34. Lukács, as quoted by Moi, in ibid., 41.

sets out to impose order and stability on a world that all too often seems impervious to reason, thereby becoming, as Michael Holquist puts it, "the essential metaphor for order":

> The detective, the instrument of pure logic, able to triumph because he alone in a world of credulous men, holds to the Scholastic principle of *adequatio rei et intellectus,* the adequation of mind to things, the belief that the mind, given enough time, can understand everything. There are no mysteries, there is only incorrect reasoning. This is the enabling discovery Poe makes for later authors: he is the Columbus who lays open the world of radical rationality which is where detectives have lived ever since.[35]

During the 1920s and '30s, a new type of fictional detective came into being in the United States: the private investigator, private eye, or colloquially, hard-boiled dick. Unlike his English predecessors, this new type is, in the words of T. J. Binyon, "the product of American reality." At times belonging to a detective agency, and at other times a lone individual fighting for the helpless and oppressed, he reflects, along with the gangsters, the violence, and the gunplay, "American life during and after Prohibition."[36] In the hard-boiled American school, "you get . . . something like real blood, actual corpses instead of mere excuses for yet another demonstration of the detective's superhuman skills."[37] The differences between the private eye and the traditional private detective are considerable. John C. Cawelti mentions two as particularly important: "The substitution of the drama of solution to the detective's quest for the discovery and accomplishment of justice; and the substitution of a pattern of intimidation and temptation of the hero for the elaborate development in the classical story of what Northrop Frye calls 'the wavering finger of suspicion' passing across a series of potential suspects."[38] Behind the façade of toughness and cynicism of the private eye lies a highly moral stance. In an urban world where the police are all too

---

35. Michael Holquist, "Whodunit and Other Questions: Metaphysical Detective Stories in Post-War Fiction," *New Literary History* 3.1 (Autumn 1971): 141.

36. T. J. Binyon, *Murder Will Out: The Detective in Fiction* (Oxford: Oxford University Press, 1989), 31–32.

37. Holquist, "Whodunit and Other Questions," 146.

38. John C. Cawelti, *Adventure, Mystery, and Romance: Formula Stories as Art and Popular Culture* (Chicago: University of Chicago Press, 1976), 142.

often corrupt and cannot be trusted and where those forming the social elite are too selfishly occupied with pursuing wealth and fame to care about the helpless and innocent, basic moral functions of exposure and protection fall to the private eye, whose investigation thereby becomes a matter not simply of locating the guilty but also of defining his own moral position.

The protagonists created by Raymond Chandler and Dashiell Hammett are more human, more fully rounded; their skills and powers of mind not as superhuman as those of their predecessors. Even so, within the microcosm of the detective novel, their function remains essentially the same: to investigate, detect, and expose the criminal. The hard-boiled detective novel may not provide its readers with the sense of relief and reassurance at a world put back in order so effectively conveyed by the classical story of detection. Yet its readers cannot help being cheered by the mere attempt undertaken by the detective to set straight just one small corner of the amoral and corrupt world in which we all live. What makes the genre of hard-boiled fiction so popular, one may speculate, is similar to what lies behind the success of a show like *The People's Court:* the reassurance that something is *done,* a problem—however inferior—solved. The background, in both cases, against which some sort of "happy end" is reached, is the law; the method used to get that far, argumentation and deduction.

Though exploiting for her own (feminist) use the hard-boiled detective story by expanding and changing certain possibilities within it, Sara Paretsky, in her eight "V. I. Warshawski Mysteries," by and large stays within its parameters.[39] Bringing distinctly female characteristics to the role of detective, V.I. or Vic never compromises the conventions of the genre. The urban setting, the antagonism between Vic and the police, the nature of the investigation, the presence of organized crime, the violent action throughout, Vic's intake of alcohol and sexual encounters, the first-person narration, the pattern of action (from a presentation of the crime, through the investigation, to a solution and apprehension of the criminal)[40]—it is all still there. What Paretsky does, that is, is to

---

39. The eight detective novels are: *Indemnity Only* (1982), *Deadlock* (1984), *Killing Orders* (1985), *Bitter Medicine* (1987), *Blood Shot* (1988), *Burn Marks* (1990), *Guardian Angel* (1992), and *Tunnel Vision* (1993).

40. See Binyon's schematic illustration of the main differences between private detective and private eye in *Murder Will Out,* 32.

work or transform *from within* a traditional genre. Her choice of arguably the most masculine of genres—a genre, moreover, which is noto-
rious for its problematic representation of women[41]—in which to convey her feminist message is a perfect one. It signals a wish to rework that
which already exists, so as to peacefully incorporate new elements, new
concerns. "Provisionally radical"[42] rather than subversive, the choice of
form underscores Paretsky's message, which, as we shall see, is one of
reconciling the ethics of rights and care or "embedding rights within
relationships."

In *Burn Marks,* police officer Bob Mallory calls into question Vic's
reasoning powers. "You don't know how to reason, how to follow a chain
of evidence to a conclusion, so you start making up paranoid fantasies."[43] Considering Mallory's opinion that Vic ought to marry and
settle down rather than play the detective and obstruct the work of
"Chicago's Finest," and that Vic's "paranoid fantasies" turn out more
often than Mallory cares to admit to be everything but paranoid, this
comment of Mallory's is intended less as a statement of fact than as yet
another reminder to Vic that she happens to be in the wrong line of
work. Vic is, in fact, pretty good at putting two and two together. When
asked about how she proceeds with an investigation, she explains: "Oh,
I talk to people. If they get angry, then I think they know something. So
I poke around and talk to more people. And after a while I've learned a
whole lot of stuff and some of it starts fitting into a pattern."[44] Why she
should apologetically add, "not very scientific, I'm afraid," is not at all
obvious; Sherlock Holmes himself could not have come up with a better
answer had anyone inquired about his investigative method.

As Vic goes about her investigations, her life is described for the
reader in painstaking detail. Of the way she dresses, when and how she
cleans her apartment, what she eats, and what she thinks about as she is
eating, we are given detailed accounts. One day for lunch, we hear, Vic
"ate a salad made of iceberg lettuce and an old tomato and a frittata that
was surprisingly light and carefully seasoned. In the little ladies' room at
the back I got the most noticeable chunks of dirt off my shirt. I didn't

41. See Cawelti, *Adventure, Mystery, and Romance,* 147.
42. The phrase is Anne Cranny-Francis's. It is used derogatorily in *Feminist Fiction:
Feminist Uses of Generic Fiction* (Cambridge: Polity Press, 1990), 176.
43. Sara Paretsky, *Burn Marks* (New York: Dell, 1990), 297.
44. Paretsky, *Bitter Medicine* (New York: Penguin, 1988), 119.

look fabulous, but maybe that suited the neighborhood better . . . All during lunch I'd turned over various approaches to Pankowski and Ferraro in my mind . . ."[45] Personal is mixed with professional, each serving to underscore and illuminate the other.

Her professional specialty being financial crime, especially insurance fraud, Vic is at her best and most sincere when fighting for the defenseless and victimized, those who are unable to fight back—"I don't want innocent bystanders screwed out of their rights," as she puts it at one point.[46] Yet her involvement often begins as a favor to a friend or a member of her family. *Bitter Medicine,* for example, opens with the Alvaredo family asking her to chauffeur a member of their family and her husband to a job interview. The Alvaredos have on numerous occasions given of themselves freely. So, "I had no choice," Vic explains, "I agreed to pick them up at Lotty's clinic at noon."[47] In Lukácsian realistic fashion, that is, Paretsky "depicts man [in this case woman] and society as complete entities, instead of showing merely one or the other of their aspects."[48]

Vic's Moral Development

When we first encounter V. I. Warshawski, private investigator, in *Indemnity Only* (1982), she has been in business for herself for about four years. Within the first pages of the novel, the essentials are laid out. The setting is Chicago; Vic is poor but coping, messy but no slob, brainy, pretty, formerly married but now on her own, exercises in order to keep herself fit for the fights she invariably gets into with her adversaries. Most of all, she is fiercely independent. She finds it unbearable to be vulnerable, has "a strong sense of turf," and overreacts to people, especially men, who act protectively toward her: "I have some close women friends, because I don't feel they're trying to take over my turf. But with men, it always seems, or often seems, as though I'm having to fight who I am." In her professional life, too, she asserts her independence, taking pride in the fact that "I'm the only person I take orders from, not a hierarchy of officers, aldermen and commissioners."[49] This professional

45. Paretsky, *Blood Shot* (New York: Dell, 1988), 61.
46. Paretsky, *Guardian Angel* (New York: Dell, 1992), 383.
47. Paretsky, *Bitter Medicine*, 13.
48. See note 34 above.
49. Paretsky, *Indemnity Only* (New York: Dell, 1982), 160, 186.

independence, in fact, is one of the main reasons why four years earlier she had quit her job as an attorney for the public defender in Cook County.[50] Another major reason for her starting out on her own was her feeling that as a detective she would stand a better chance of getting at the truth of a problem, at making a contribution.

> Then I got disillusioned with working for the Public Defender. The setup is pretty corrupt—you're never arguing for justice, always on points of law. I wanted to get out of it, but I still wanted to do something that would make me feel that I was still working on my concept of justice, not legal point-scoring.[51]

Much as in Scott Turow's novels, a distinction is made here between legal technicality and legal (higher) justice. By working as a private detective rather than as an attorney, Vic hopes to escape the former and pursue the latter.

Vic's independence goes hand in hand with her toughness. A karate expert, she knows how to fend for herself and does not mind getting into a fight now and again. After a long day, her favorite way of relaxing is to take a warm bath while enjoying a whiskey or two: "I headed straight for the Black Label bottle, kicking off my pumps and pulling off my panty hose while I unscrewed the cap. I drank from the bottle, a long swallow that sent a glow of warmth to my weary shoulders. Filling a glass, I took it into the bathroom with me."[52] If it were not for the pumps and the panty hose, we might think we were reading about Sam Spade! To Vic's clients as well as to her foes, her toughness signals professional competence and courage. What they do not realize is that there is another, contradictory side to Vic's personality: a vulnerable and highly sensitive one. Her bravado notwithstanding, she neither professionally nor personally ever feels secure and completely at ease. "The questioning of my professional judgment wounded me," she tells us in

---

50. Cf. also *Burn Marks,* 95: "I'd spent five years in the PD's office—I didn't want to have to start again at the beginning in a private practice. Anyway, I'd solved a case for a friend and realized it was work I could do well and get genuine satisfaction from. Plus, I can be my own boss. I should have given that as my first reason—it continues to be the most important with me. Maybe from being an only child . . ."

51. Paretsky, *Indemnity Only,* 160.

52. Paretsky, *Blood Shot,* 164.

Burn Marks, "as few other criticisms could."[53] And her relationship with Bobby Mallory, longtime friend and colleague of her father's, is marred throughout by her somewhat infantile need to show how good she is, working out there on her own. When finally, in *Blood Shot,* she gives in to her friend Lotty's insistence that she involve the police, all Vic can think of is that "I had run scared from my problems, had turned to the police, and now I was waiting like some good old-fashioned damsel in distress for rescue. It was too much . . ."[54]

In the personal domain, in matters of the heart, Vic's insecurity is even more apparent. From the very beginning, in *Indemnity Only,* and increasingly throughout the rest of the novels, she is visited by intense self-doubt and self-criticism. It all has to do with "Protection. The middle-class dream."[55] Did she, she wonders in *Indemnity Only,* make the wrong choice in preferring a life on her own in one of the most male of professions to a married life with children?[56] And does her intense dislike of protection and fear of dependence jeopardize herself and her friends? "Agnes died," Vic blurts to Lotty in *Killing Orders,* "because I involved her in my machinations. Her mother had a stroke. My aunt has gone mad. And all because I chose to be narrow-minded, pig-headed, bullying my way down a road the FBI and the SEC couldn't travel."[57] Where will it lead, this insistence on independence—"what was I going to live on when I got too old to hustle clients any longer? The thought of being sixty-six, alone, living in a little room with three plastic drawers to hold my clothes—a shudder swept through me, almost knocking me off balance."[58] Alongside the (male) story of detection a different set of (female) concerns is coming to the fore. What is emerging here as a kind of subtext is a discussion about autonomy and the relationship of self to others, and the underlying question—is autonomous selfhood an ideal worth striving for?—is immediately familiar to us from the works of the feminist writers discussed in part one of this chapter. Like that offered by these feminists, Paretsky's ultimate answer to this crucial question is a

53. Paretsky, *Burn Marks,* 212.

54. Paretsky, *Blood Shot,* 243.

55. Paretsky, *Killing Orders* (New York: Ballantine, 1985), 177.

56. Paretsky, *Indemnity Only,* 161. "There really are times when I wish I did have a couple of children and was doing the middle-class family thing. But that's a myth . . . It's just—I get scared I've made the wrong choice."

57. Paretsky, *Killing Orders,* 276.

58. Paretsky, *Burn Marks,* 33.

negative one; toward the end of the series she has Vic go through a series of remarkable reconciliations with people from her past and in general come to terms with her need to relate to and care for others.

Vic's development is not unlike the one undergone by the women participating in Carol Gilligan's abortion study. On the basis of this study, which was "designed to clarify the ways in which women construct and resolve abortion decisions," Gilligan identifies and defines three stages in female moral development toward an ethic of care. The first stage is one of selfishness. Here, the self is seen as an independent, autonomous being who is unwilling to bear any responsibility toward others. At the second stage, a shift or transition has occurred from selfishness to responsibility. This move is one toward social participation; "here the conventional feminine voice emerges with great clarity, defining the self and proclaiming its worth on the basis of the ability to care for and protect others." The third and final stage is reached when a woman realizes that she has an obligation not only toward others, but also toward herself. Though the conflict between self and other remains, "once obligation extends to include the self as well as others, the disparity between selfishness and responsibility dissolves."[59] It is only when a woman learns to claim the power to choose and to accept responsibility for that choice that she may give of herself freely without entirely losing herself in the process. Once that second transition has occurred, selfishness has become securely embedded within relationships. Evolving around the central insight that self and other are interdependent, the female ethic of care thus does not seek to leave behind but rather to incorporate male elements of autonomy and independence.

In the continued female bildungsroman of Sara Paretsky's "V. I. Warshawski Mysteries," it is hard to say exactly when and how the two transitions in Vic's moral development toward an ethic of care take place. By the time *Killing Orders* (1985) came along, however, something seems to have happened. Here, for the first time, Vic admits to herself that her close friend Lotty's critical comments on her behavior and way of thinking may have something to them: "her accusations were close to my nerve centers. Egotistical. So single-minded I would sacrifice Uncle Stefan trying to solve a problem that had the FBI and the SEC baffled."[60] Lotty has criticized Vic before, but her critical comments have

---

59. Gilligan, *In a Different Voice*, 71, 79, 94.
60. Paretsky, *Killing Orders*, 265.

mostly elicited a response of self-pity rather than serious concern. It is in *Killing Orders,* furthermore, that Vic seriously starts reflecting on matters of friendship and family. "The older I get," she says, "the less politics means to me. The only thing that seems to matter is friendship." After a quarrel, Vic and Lotty go through a period of estrangement and Vic experiences a feeling of abandonment and loneliness which brings back memories of how lost she felt after the death of first her mother and then her father. She had helped nurse them both until the very end and often has nightmares about their leaving her behind. When she finally makes up with Lotty after having admitted to being narrow-minded and pig-headed, Lotty calls her "the daughter I never had,"[61] thereby confirming Vic's assessment of their friendship: "I've known Lotty for close to twenty years. First she filled in for my mother, and then we became— friends is a weak word for it. Close, anyway."[62]

If Vic finds in Lotty a substitute for her mother, she finds in Mr. Contreras, her downstairs neighbor, a substitute father figure. We first hear of "old Mr. Contreras from the first floor" in *Bitter Medicine.*[63] From the very beginning, he insists on playing a role in Vic's life, and though she must admit that it *is* nice once in a while to have somebody—and a good meal—to come home to, it takes quite a while for her to accept his protective attitude and behavior. "You aren't going to start breathing down my neck, are you?" she says to him at some point; "repeat twenty times a day—she's a big girl, she can fall on her butt if she wants to."[64] Quietly insisting that "you are the daughter of my heart, Victoria,"[65] Mr. Contreras is not put off by Vic's protestations of independence. In *Guardian Angel,* his patience is finally rewarded when she pleads with him not to "cut me out of your life, or take yourself out of mine . . . It would bring me great pain to lose you."[66]

When, in *Blood Shot,* Vic reunites with her old childhood friend Caroline, promising her that "you will always be my sister, Caroline,"[67] her new "family" is complete. As for her real family, the only one she has ever cared about is her cousin Boom Boom, who gets killed in *Deadlock.*

61. Ibid., 88, 276.
62. Paretsky, *Bitter Medicine,* 183.
63. Ibid., 64.
64. Paretsky, *Blood Shot,* 187.
65. Ibid., 356.
66. Paretsky, *Guardian Angel,* 401.
67. Paretsky, *Blood Shot,* 356.

Like Vic herself, her mother had been an only child. On her father's side there is Uncle Peter, who has moved away from Chicago and could not care less about the rest of the family, and Aunt Elena, who, when she resurfaces in *Burn Marks* to ask for her niece's help, causes quite an upheaval in Vic's life.

With *Burn Marks* and *Guardian Angel,* numbers six and seven of the V. I. Warshawski mysteries, something again seems to have happened. Issues relating to friendship, care, and family now occupy center stage, to the point where they threaten to become more interesting than the stories of detection themselves. We are now at Gilligan's third and last stage; though still preoccupied and wrestling with problems of self and other, Vic seems well on her way toward reconciling the contradictory needs of independence and interdependence.

The appearance of Aunt Elena on Vic's doorstep at the beginning of *Burn Marks* is most unwelcome. With a long history of drinking, Elena has always been "the family problem," and her presence in Vic's life surely spells trouble. As the story unfolds, Vic finds herself reacting very strongly to her aunt. The pitiable sight of Elena's helplessness makes her wonder what her own life will be like when she reaches her aunt's age: "it was helplessness I feared. A life like Elena's, bobbing along without any channel markers to guide it." And whereas her immediate reaction is to leave Elena to her own devices, she cannot quite bring herself to do so and eventually accepts the role of helper and protector that Elena wants to force on her.

> Did I have a duty toward Elena that overrode all considerations of myself, my work, my own longing for wholeness?
>
> I'd held glasses of water for Gabriella when her arms were too weak to lift them herself, emptied wheelchair pots for Tony when he could no longer move from chair to toilet, I've done enough, I kept repeating, I've done enough. But I couldn't quite convince myself.[68]

Toward the end of *Burn Marks,* Vic is offered an apology by Bobby Mallory. Having for years taken any and every opportunity to criticize Vic, Bobby does not find it easy to admit that he has been wrong. He has thought it all over, he explains, and the conclusion he has reached is that "you're the daughter of the two people I loved best, next to Eileen, and

---

68. Paretsky, *Burn Marks,* 264, 197.

you can't do things different than you do, shouldn't do them different, not with Gabriella and Tony bringing you up."[69] The remarkable thing about Bobby's apology—other than that it is made at all—is that it is offered as a means of reconciliation by way, so to speak, of a concession to Vic's independent way of life, professional as well as personal. This mixture of acceptance and reconciliation is repeated toward the end of *Guardian Angel* during what is probably the most spectacular of Vic's reconciliations with her past: her making up with her former husband, Dick. A high-powered partner in one of Chicago's most well-known law firms, Dick moves in different legal and social circles. Yet, his and Vic's paths have often crossed in the preceding novels with disastrous results. Unable to agree on anything, they invariably quarrel and part ways loathing each other even more than before. When therefore Dick arrives at Vic's office ready to admit he has lent his support to the wrong party, the reader is taken somewhat by surprise. "I do have only myself to thank. You've always known how weak I am," he acknowledges. Upon leaving, he takes Vic's hand and exclaims, "we had some good times together, didn't we, Vic? It wasn't all fighting and contempt, was it?"[70]

Tunnel Vision *and Beyond*

"When my muscles slowed down, would I find other strengths to get me across these chasms?" Vic wonders at the very end of *Guardian Angel*. In more than one interview since the publication of *Guardian Angel*, Paretsky had made it clear that she intended her eighth novel in the V. I. Warshawski series, to be entitled *Tunnel Vision*, to terminate the series. "Since I started writing eleven years ago," she explained, "things—or perhaps rather my perception of things—have changed so much that I feel it would be wrong of me to continue. Society has become vulgarized, the violence is astonishing, solidarity has disappeared, the legal system has broken down, and people are taking the law into their own hands. I feel I can neither understand nor write about it any longer."[71] This was sad news to V. I. Warshawski fans. Yet there was a certain logic to Paretsky's decision. A continuation of the V. I. Warshawski series would be difficult as the promise of detection—and especially female

69. Ibid., 339.
70. Paretsky, *Guardian Angel*, 412–13.
71. Interview with Paretsky in the Danish newspaper *Politiken*, Nov. 14, 1993. My translation.

detection—of reaching some sort of happy end, was no longer there due to the increasing violence and vulgarization of American society and the persistent hostility toward equality between the sexes, and as Vic's moral development, outlined in the subtext of the novels, had reached at least a tentatively successful conclusion. Marrying Vic off would be unacceptable, and the thought of an aging Vic unable to fight and climb into people's offices at night was not too appealing either. All in all, therefore, it seemed, Sara Paretsky could do worse than take leave—at least for now—of her protagonist.

When *Tunnel Vision* appeared in 1993, it therefore came as something of a surprise—at least to this reader—that Paretsky leaves it completely open as to whether or not this is the last we shall see of her heroine. With her office building falling down and unpaid bills mounting up, Vic is as close to financial ruin in *Tunnel Vision* as she was fifteen years ago when she first started out as a private investigator. Her lover, Conrad, leaves her, unable to "go through another episode like this." It is not, he says, "that I resent you for being right. It's not even the bullet in my shoulder. It's watching you plunge ahead without regard for anything or anyone except your own private version of justice." She is depressed, "wrung dry" by a case that looked like a straightforward investigation but turned out to be both complex and dangerous, and cannot help wondering as that fortieth birthday is approaching whether it was all worth it: "I'm tired. I spent a month risking my life for some abstract concept of justice, and all that happened in the end was that my lover left me."[72]

There are some tough decisions to be made, concerning both the professional and the private sides of Vic's life. As the novel nears its conclusion, Vic seems on the verge of quitting as a private investigator. But then, out of the blue, she is approached by police officer Mary Louise Neely, who has a proposition for her: "I'd like to work for you." Between the two of them, Neely explains, "we could take on more work, and a wider range of it. I'm very organized. You wouldn't have to worry about the details that bore you—I'm twenty-nine, I'm very fit, and you know I'm experienced." On the very last pages of the novel, we are told that "Neely was doing freelance work for now—we were trying that for six months before considering a more formal arrangement."[73] Whether or not Paretsky has changed her mind about ending the V. I. War-

---

72. Paretsky, *Tunnel Vision* (London: Hamish Hamilton, 1993), 463, 478.
73. Ibid., 480–81, 482–83.

shawski series, we cannot know. The fact remains, however, that with the introduction of Mary Louise Neely, she very cleverly solves the problem of Vic's age, thereby opening up the possibility of continuing her popular series.[74]

Tunnel Vision opens with Vic's encounter, in the rat-infested basement of her office building, with a runaway woman and her three children, all victims of abuse by the woman's husband. What follows next is a board meeting for a battered women's shelter, on whose board Vic sits together with various women with whom she has "worked together for years, through different incarnations of women's activism." Here, as in earlier novels, the story of detection has a feminist foundation and interweaves public and private corruption and deceit. In the end, the hardest questions Vic faces are questions about herself. Conrad's criticism, familiar to us from the earlier novels, is echoed by other friends: "they didn't put compromise in your head. Look it up in the dictionary. Study it. It's a useful concept," as Conrad's sister says at some point, for example.[75]

Vic may not be able to reach a workable compromise with Conrad— indeed, if she were, as argued above, it would make a radical departure from Paretsky's portrayal of her in the previous seven novels—but she ends the novel in the company of all her best friends. "What else can I say," Paretsky has her think as she is celebrating her fortieth birthday party, "except that good friends are a balm to a bruised spirit?" The celebration is a surprise party arranged by Mr. Contreras. Vic had called him a couple of days earlier while he was recuperating at his daughter's house after having helped Vic rescue the runaway woman and her children, and she arranged to pick him up because she found her apartment building too lonely without him. "When I thought of all the times I had cursed his intrusiveness in my life," she reflected on that occasion, "I was ashamed."[76]

Able, at long last, to express and respond to love and open toward reconciliation with her past, Vic has come a long way. The V. I. Warshaw-

---

74. It is interesting to note that Vic is absent from Paretsky's most recent novel, *Ghost Country* (New York: Delacorte Press, 1998), but that Paretsky hints in her preface—to paraphrase Mark Twain—that rumors of Vic's demise may have been premature: "For those worried about V. I. Warshawski, the detective has been on strike, but we are currently in mediation and should resume work together soon" ("Thanks," ii).

75. Ibid., 8, 367.

76. Ibid., 483, 435.

ski saga has no happy end, indeed cannot have a happy end. The rest of the world has not changed along with Vic. In the later no less than in the earlier novels, Vic is met with hostility and skepticism when she introduces herself as a detective. Her authority is constantly questioned, and as she grows older she finds the struggle to be taken seriously increasingly arduous and depressing. She is taken quite by surprise, for example, when in *Burn Marks* a man wants to hire her, pleased that "someone thought I was a competent human being, not a pain in the butt who should mind her own business." It feels good for a change to have someone—especially some man—"call up and think . . . that I should be working, not that I should stay home and play with dolls."[77] There are moments—as when two of her most ardent critics, Bobby and Dick, admit to having been unjust in their treatment of her—when it seems to Vic that her struggle to establish herself as an authority is worth it. But these moments are few and far between. For the most part, she has to waste a tremendous amount of time and energy just to make men listen to her. "They could have listened to me," she exclaims in *Tunnel Vision*, bitterly summing up her complaints about the male establishment, "it's what they get for not believing women's stories."[78] The world, it seems, is not yet ready for V. I. Warshawski, private investigator.

CONCLUDING REMARKS

Much like the battle for racial equality, the fight for equality between the sexes has been a legal one. The resulting focus on a morality of rights has been much debated by feminists, especially since Carol Gilligan began in the early eighties to talk about a female "different voice" and a female morality not of rights but of care and responsibility. Gilligan's work forced feminists to look more closely at the relationship between equality and difference. Is equality a type of discourse that undermines diversity and difference, or is it somehow possible to claim that the two notions are compatible? Inspired by French postmodernist feminist attempts to deconstruct the concept of gender altogether, some American feminists have argued that the very inclusiveness so central to the pursuit of equal rights has had the unfortunate effect of undermining differences between as well as within the sexes.

77. Paretsky, *Burn Marks*, 117.
78. Paretsky, *Tunnel Vision*, 404.

The criticism against law and equal rights reasoning for relying on and catering to male norms notwithstanding, the majority of American feminists have never entirely abandoned the rhetoric of rights. Whether belonging to the sameness or difference camp of feminism, they have attempted, instead, to find a workable synthesis or reconciliation of female and male values, connecting female interests in relationships to prior male frameworks emphasizing equal rights. And in so doing, they have relied on a legal vocabulary which, in its combination of theory and practice, equity and equality, holds out a promise of incorporation and synthesis.

One arena in which the tension between the promise of individual rights and a morality of care and a possible reconciliation of the two has been in focus is feminist detective fiction. Here we have looked at the work of Sara Paretsky, who has found in the combination of realistic detective novel and female moral bildungsroman a formula for success. The choice of the hard-boiled detective novel as the medium in which to express and pursue feminist concerns has earned for her not only best-seller status, but also intellectual acclaim. Fighting to reconcile her fierce independence with an equally strong need for interdependence, and conducting that fight in a legal arena and vernacular, protagonist V. I. Warshawski embodies the modern American feminist struggle for autonomy embedded within relationships.

When we first meet V.I. or Vic in *Indemnity Only* from 1982, the first of the "V. I. Warshawski Mysteries," she has only been a detective for about four years. After law school she had worked in the Chicago Public Defender's office, but after a while she had found the sort of technical legal work with which she was involved as a public defender tedious and depressing. She had gone to law school in the first place out of a belief in the law's potential to do good. For her to be able to make a real contribution, she had increasingly felt, she would have to be out there with the needy and the downtrodden rather than inside a courtroom, and she had decided to try to make it on her own as a detective. Being a detective, moreover, she would not have her work defined for her by others— or, to put it another way, she would not have to take orders from anybody else.

In her dedication to her own "concept of justice," Vic never falters. She cannot help being frustrated and depressed at times at the lack of respect for her as a female detective with which she is constantly confronted in her dealings with men. At the end of V. I. Warshawski

Mystery number eight, *Tunnel Vision* from 1993, however, she is as seriously and genuinely concerned about protecting the rights of the have-nots as she was when we first encountered her.

Vic's will to justice serves her well as a detective. To a certain extent this is true of her urge for independence as well. Free to work at odd hours and to pursue leads that may at first look unpromising, she is able to establish herself as a tough and headstrong detective. Her unwillingness to cooperate with others, and especially with the powers that be, results in problems from time to time that might have been avoided, however. It is especially in her private life that her stubborn refusal to be dependent upon anyone else turns out to be counterproductive. The older she gets, the more important her failure to develop genuine and loving relationships with others seems.

Toward the end of the Warshawski mysteries, it is Vic's (female) concerns relating to friendship, care, and family that seem to occupy center stage. The (male) story of detection is still important, but Paretsky seems increasingly preoccupied with her heroine's effort to reconcile the contradictory needs of independence and interdependence. The eight detective novels, it would thus seem, are Paretsky's contribution to the discussion about autonomy and the relationship of self to others carried out by American feminists over the past many years. Like her feminist colleagues, Paretsky is intrigued by the question of whether autonomous selfhood is an ideal worth striving for. And by having Vic come to terms with her need to relate to and care for others, Paretsky joins the majority of American feminists, who argue that any possible solution to the feminist dilemma involves an attempt to reconcile and create a usable synthesis out of the (male) ethic of rights and the (female) ethic of care.

Her fans, intellectual or not, may not be able to identify with Vic when she throws herself into a fight and ends up in the hospital, but most of them—perhaps especially women—find the dilemmas she faces very familiar. As we leave her at the end of the eight Paretsky novels, well on her way toward establishing caring relationships yet still fighting a hostile male environment, we feel Paretsky has managed to make her protagonist a successful reflection of the feminist struggle, a successful reflection, so to speak, of the (female) *Zeitgeist*.

VII

Of Control, Absolutes, and Handmaids

The Late-Twentieth-Century Abortion Debate

When the issue is abortion, there seem to be only two things that everyone may agree upon. First of all, that this issue, within just three short decades, has come to occupy center stage in American political and cultural life; and second, that abortion itself is merely "the tip of the iceberg."[1] Books and articles about abortion are never "just" about abortion itself. For most of the participants in the abortion debate, "while the views most of us hold about abortion, whether pro-life or pro-choice or a mix of both, are not *obvious* rationalizations for policies that serve nonabortion-related interests, our views about what is the right way for American society to treat abortion may well reflect deeply held, sometimes hidden, views about the needs of society."[2]

The rapidity with which the abortion question moved from the fringes to the center of public concern may only be accounted for, then, in terms of its becoming a, if not the, major battleground in late-twentieth-century America for competing values. Back in 1962, when Sherri Finkbine, a married mother of four children now expecting her fifth, sought an abortion upon discovering that the sleeping pills she had

---

1. The phrase is Kristin Luker's, from *Abortion and the Politics of Motherhood* (Berkeley: University of California Press, 1984), 158.
2. Laurence H. Tribe, *Abortion: The Clash of Absolutes* (New York: Norton, 1992), 52.

been taking were thalidomide, nobody could predict how ferociously and emotionally the battle for abortion rights would come to be fought. Assuming that their views were representative of the public opinion, both pro-lifers and pro-choicers had begun mobilizing support before, but it was only with the Finkbine case that "what had been a trickle of public interest in the issue of abortion became a torrent."[3] Over the next decade, as the reform movement to liberalize abortion laws gathered momentum, and in turn inspired angry pro-life responses, the moral dimensions of the debate came to the fore.

The story of that reform movement—its tentative beginnings in the 1950s, the impetus provided by the suggested revision in 1959 of the Model Penal Code of the American Law Institute, as well as the Finkbine case and the rubella outbreaks of 1962–65, the increasing number of state legislatures passing cautious reforms of their strict abortion statutes after 1967, and the ultimate vindication with the 1973 Supreme Court decision in *Roe* v. *Wade*—has often been told and need not be reiterated here.[4] What is of interest in this context is first of all the nature of the messages about important matters such as sexuality and reproductive freedom, individual autonomy and dependency that are being communicated explicitly or implicitly in the contemporary abortion debate, and second the way in which an essentially moral and political problem has turned into a legal one.

At the heart of the abortion battle, I will argue, is the question of control: who can and should control whom, how, and why? At one level, there is the issue of political versus legal control, or judicial restraint versus judicial activism. The point of contention here is whether or not the activist role judges have played in umpiring, and thereby removing from state and federal legislatures, political and moral struggles of major importance to the American public, has furthered justice and equality. At another level, yet closely connected to the judicial activism question, there is the discussion about individual autonomy versus state or collective interference. Is abortion a strictly personal matter to be decided upon by the individual woman involved, in which case the woman's right to choose may be based on the legal concept of a right to privacy, or

---

3. Luker, *Abortion and the Politics of Motherhood,* 62–65.

4. See e.g., ibid., and Tribe, *Abortion: The Clash of Absolutes.* For a more recent, thorough description of the reform process, see David J. Garrow, *Liberty and Sexuality: The Right to Privacy and the Making of Roe v. Wade* (New York: Lisa Drew Books, 1994).

should the public, society as a whole, have a say in the matter? In the latter case, of course, abortion becomes a public rather than a private matter and may best be dealt with in the political arena. To these two levels of the abortion debate, the first part of this chapter will be dedicated. I shall continue my argument from the previous chapters that to most Americans, the way of the courts *is* the American way, equal justice meaning individual justice, most often formulated or defined as rights.[5]

To the pregnant woman who faces the decision of whether to get an abortion, the issue of control is a very real one. To such a woman it makes a major difference whether she herself can make that decision or whether she has to consult with and perhaps in the end relinquish control to her medical doctor, her parents (if she is underage) or her husband/boyfriend. Whatever the decision made, however, that woman— especially should she choose to carry her baby to term—will end up realizing that her decision involves others than herself. Whichever way one looks at it, there is a fetus involved too, a potential human being who, if it is allowed to live, needs to be taken care of. So does its mother. And this "double" aspect, as it were, of the abortion issue has always presented a problem to feminists. On the one hand, the right to choose for oneself ensures a high degree of autonomy for the individual woman; on the other hand, such a right isolates and defines the problem of abortions as a woman's problem. What some feminists have accordingly maintained is that "reproductive freedom is not so much a 'right' in the abstract judicial sense as it is a basic human need . . . The compression of abortion into 'privacy rights' obscures this larger issue, implying a negative or exclusionary principle and the analogy of one's body to bourgeois property."[6] The feminist level of the abortion debate will be the topic of the second part of the chapter.

The final level of the abortion battle to which I shall address myself in this chapter is what might be called the battle between religion and law.

---

5. In an interesting article, "Securing Deliberative Autonomy," James E. Fleming advances "deliberative autonomy" (or, as he also calls it, "personal self-government or self-determination") as *the* unifying theme in American (constitutional) thinking. This theme, he says, "shows the coherence and structure of certain substantive liberties on a list of familiar 'unenumerated' fundamental rights (commonly classed under privacy, autonomy, or substantive due process) . . . and is rooted, along with deliberative democracy, in the language and design of our Constitution" (*Stanford Law Review* 48 [1995]: 3).

6. Rosalind Pollack Petchesky, *Abortion and Women's Choice: The State, Sexuality and Reproductive Freedom* (Boston: Northeastern University Press, 1984), 379.

As we shall see, there is a major difference between pro-life and pro-choice views and experiences of the world. Whereas proponents of the former typically adhere to an explicit and well-articulated set of moral codes, originating in a Divine Plan, those of the latter tend to be secular pluralists who doubt whether a single, absolute moral standard can serve everyone. Once again, the issue is one of control. Pro-life people are convinced that decisions about human life are not ours to make, but that only God has sovereignty over life. The pro-choice worldview, by contrast, is centered not around faith and humility in the face of a God whose ways man may never aspire to know, but around a belief in the human capacity to reason and rationally understand and control the environment. Man, not God, is at the center of the universe; law, not religion, provides the language and general framework within which ethical decisions are made.

To pro-choicers, pro-life willingness to obey church dogma and to compromise on individual autonomy signifies a premodern, fundamentalist understanding of the world. What they tend to forget or perhaps do not quite realize, it will be argued here, is that when they set up as a modern, much more up-to-date alternative their own emphasis on the right to abortion as an individual, private choice, they make themselves "guilty" of a way of thinking and arguing that is no less absolutist than that of their pro-life opponents. Though they do not present their views with the same religious zeal that the pro-lifers often display, pro-choicers are as much informed by faith as are their opponents—only the pro-choice faith is a faith in reason, in human rationality as a faculty that enables us to assess the claims of competing beliefs and perspectives. Far from objective, such a (liberal) faith rests on implicit and often unstated moral and political assumptions about life and the world in general. The clash between pro-choice rights talk and pro-life religious fundamentalism, then, is a clash between two faiths, two very particular moral agendas.

The very fact that pro-choicers rest their case for abortion on demand on a right to privacy argumentation points to the faithlike quality of their thinking. Nothing is more intellectually "slippery" and rationally indefinable than the right to privacy. It originates in a law-review article from 1890 and has been argued over the years on the basis of substantive due process entailed in the liberty clause of the Fourteenth Amendment. There is nothing in the language or history of the Constitution that supports it, and when pro-choice activists talk about it, they use terms such as "basic," "fundamental," "deep-rooted in our society," and "as fundamental a right as a woman can possess." To Justice Hugo Black, one of the dissenters in *Griswold* v. *Connecticut* (1965), a right-to-privacy argument was "nothing but natural law and the work of the devil."[7] What is important in this context is that Warren and Brandeis, in their famous "Right to Privacy" article, saw it as a common-law right, and that the much-maligned 1973 Supreme Court decision on abortion, *Roe* v. *Wade,* to which the right to privacy argument would eventually lead, in being in line with centuries of common practice was much more consistent with the traditional common-law treatment of abortion than most people realize. In one of the most important of contemporary debates, that is, it is a common-law way of thinking and arguing that sets the parameters for discussion.

As has been the case in the preceding chapters, each of the more theoretical parts will be set off, as it were, or illuminated by a case study. The text that will be used in this chapter is Margaret Atwood's *The Handmaid's Tale* from 1985. A Canadian with American ancestors who has lived in the United States for periods of time, Atwood has the unique perspective of both in- and outsider. "The U.S.," she once declared, "is humanity's testing ground. It's like a teeming bacterial culture of everything you can imagine. It's where very different ideas are fought out."[8] The different ideas that are fought out in *The Handmaid's Tale* are, of course, ideas relating to female sexuality and reproduction. In Atwood's dystopic forecast of what is awaiting us all, open dialogue has ended: pro-choice ideas have been ousted by their pro-life counterparts. The society of Gilead, in which the action of the novel takes place, is a postmodern society that has turned premodern and especially prelegal. The inhabitants of Gilead are no longer citizens in the modern sense of the word. With the Constitution suspended, all talk of individual rights and freedom has ceased. Major decisions concerning reproduction and family life in general are made, not by the individuals involved, but by the theocratic leaders of the community.

The Handmaid's Tale, I shall conclude, is a warning to all critics of rights talk and individual autonomy: too much rights talk, too much reliance on individual rights may be bad, but no rights talk is infinitely

7. Black, quoted in Garrow, *Liberty and Sexuality,* 244.

8. Atwood, quoted in Cathy N. Davidson, "A Feminist '1984': Margaret Atwood Talks about Her Exciting New Novel," *MS.,* Feb. 1986, 25.

worse. It is likewise a warning to feminists of the Catharine MacKinnon school who would not stop at reinstating censorship to rid the world of antifeminist manifestations such as pornography.[9] Though well meant, a MacKinnon-like way of reasoning is potentially as repressive as that of the theocratic right, Atwood indicates. Somewhat ironically perhaps, given Atwood's well-known anti-American sentiments, with *The Handmaid's Tale* the traditional American regard for individualism and autonomy stands vindicated.

LEGAL CONTROL VERSUS POLITICAL CONTROL AND THE RIGHT TO PRIVACY

"How might the story of abortion have unfolded if it had been left to the legislatures to decide?" asks Laurence Tribe in *Abortion: The Clash of Absolutes*.[10] As Tribe himself reads the history of abortion law reform in the United States, there is little ground for contending that the fight for a legalization of abortion would have proceeded at a faster and smoother pace had the courts not intervened. On the contrary, up until 1973 only nineteen states had reformed their abortion laws. This cannot be said to constitute a trend, especially as the types of reforms passed by most of these states hardly increased access to abortion. As far as Mary Ann Glendon is concerned, however, *Roe* v. *Wade* "brought to a halt the process of legislative abortion reform that was already well on the way to producing in the United States, as it did all over Europe, compromise statutes that gave very substantial protection to women's interests without completely denying protection to developing life."[11] Tribe explicitly takes on Glendon and her views on abortion in *Abortion: The Clash of Absolutes,* and the "dialogue" between the two colleagues at the Harvard Law School is a good place to start our discussion about judicial activism, bringing to the fore as it does the key issues of the legal versus political control debate.[12]

9. See for example, Catharine MacKinnon, *Sexual Harassment of Working Women* (New Haven, Conn.: Yale University Press, 1979), *Feminism Unmodified: Discourses on Life and Law* (Cambridge, Mass.: Harvard University Press, 1987), and *Only Words* (Cambridge, Mass.: Harvard University Press, 1993).

10. Tribe, *Abortion: The Clash of Absolutes,* 49.

11. Mary Ann Glendon, *Rights Talk: The Impoverishment of Political Discourse* (New York: The Free Press, 1991), 58.

12. There is probably no legal issue that has been more hotly disputed than precisely

The law, says Glendon in *Abortion and Divorce in Western Law*, is the embodiment of a social dialogue, "the symbolic expression of certain cultural ideas." And family law, perhaps more than any other area of the law, carries a strong message about expected behavior and acceptable norms. By formulating abortion regulation around the right to privacy, the American legal system communicates to the female population that any American woman has a constitutional right to be let alone—and practically nothing else. Whether or not she decides to have an abortion, a woman cannot expect to receive any help from the government in the form of counseling or maternity leave, day care or child support. The United States has no explicit family policy; the problem, a woman is given to understand, is hers, and hers alone. "At present we lead the developed world in our extreme liberty of abortion, while we lag behind . . . in the benefits and services we provide to mothers and to poor families."[13] Bound up as it is with individual autonomy and isolation, the right-to-privacy foundation of the American abortion debate furthermore obscures, or relegates to a position of minor importance, Glendon argues, the fact that the taking of life is involved. In *Roe*, Justice Blackmun very deliberately avoided naming the underlying problem as one involving human life. Considering, to all extents and purposes, a fetus a nonperson very conveniently sidesteps the basic question of when it is permissible to take life. This steers the abortion debate in the wrong direction.

The American public seem to think that there is nothing unusual about the American situation, and that a compromise between the pro-life and pro-choice positions is virtually out of the question. They are wrong on both counts, says Glendon. A comparison between the cur-

---

the issue of judicial activism. "The feature of American law that remains most difficult and most important to explain," as Geoffrey C. Hazard Jr. and Michele Taruffo put it, "is why a country committed to democratic political and social principles continues to repose important law-making functions in the judicial branch of the government" (*American Civil Procedure* [New Haven and London: Yale University Press, 1993], 3). Addressing so broad a topic in only a few pages necessarily means that I will be painting with a very broad brush. Any reader interested in the more subtle details of the debate over law as a vehicle for social change should refer to the extensive literature in existence on the topic, e.g., the work of Kenneth L. Karst, Tony Lewis, David J. Garrow, Catharine MacKinnon, Robert Bork, John Hart Ely, and Richard D. Parker.

13. Mary Ann Glendon, *Abortion and Divorce in Western Law: American Failures, European Challenges* (Cambridge, Mass.: Harvard University Press, 1987), 10, 53.

rent American legal situation and that of Western European countries shows that "when the legislative process is allowed to operate, *political compromise is not only possible but typical*." The compromises reached in the various Western European countries hardly satisfy everyone, but they have been able to weigh competing interests in such a way that an all-or-nothing contest, American-style, resulting in complete frustration and even violence, has been avoided. In marked contrast to the United States, the debates in Western Europe have never focused wholeheartedly on the issue of individual *rights*. They have been on the whole less rigid and more inclined toward reaching a political consensus that would make the parties, if not entirely happy, then at least satisfied that their points of view had been listened to and considered during the process of enacting a compromise statute. The statutes presently in force in most European countries ironically parallel public opinion in the United States. The conclusion that Glendon reaches in her discussion about "American Failures, European Challenges" is accordingly that

> in the absence of a clear constitutional mandate controversial matters like regulation of abortion should not be prematurely constitutionalized. Litigation, like the legislative processes of bargaining, education, and persuasion, can contribute to the way in which a society collectively imagines reality—and revises that imagination as knowledge and experience increase. But if the courts unnecessarily decide such controversies on constitutional grounds, these potentially creative and collaborative processes are brought to a halt. The main avenue left open for *political* activity with respect to the abortion issue is then the cumbersome process of constitutional amendment.[14]

Glendon's wish to import European-style compromises as a possible solution to the abortion question in the United States is unrealizable for several reasons, argues Laurence Tribe in *Abortion: The Clash of Absolutes*. Most important, the compromise offered by Western European countries would not work in the United States, as it represents a more collectively oriented and less individualistic view of society than that held by most Americans. We should not forget, says Tribe, that "the fact that *individual rights* provide the primary focus of constitutional law in the United States is no accident." Glendon may well applaud the focus

14. Ibid., 40, 45.

in European countries on human life as a collective value, but by so doing she "underestimates the strength and value of the uniquely American ideology of individual worth that has led us to a largely rights-based legal system." To have anybody else but the woman involved make such a life-affecting decision as abortion would simply be incompatible with American legal norms of equality and would be felt as disrespect, if not disempowerment. Not only is the United States more diverse than most European countries in terms of demography and geography, education and social standing, but most Americans also harbor suspicions about a system of centralized power that allows government officials—in the context of abortion, a social worker or a physician—to interfere in their lives. If one looks at the history of the exercise of unfettered government discretion, what one sees is

> largely a history of unequal treatment based on class, race and sex . . . The contravention of law with an official wink, in our collective vision, is part of what distinguishes other countries from the United States. An approach that relies upon a strict normative judgment embodied in legislation but dramatically softened in its application by pragmatic concerns is bound, in the long run, to offend American conceptions of equal justice.[15]

Had therefore the abortion question been left to the legislative arena, the American abortion debate might have been carried out in a calmer and more dignified fashion. But a middle-of-the-road political compromise along European lines would have come—and would still come were *Roe* to be repealed by Chief Justice Rehnquist and those of his brethren who believe, like Glendon, that the kind of judicial legislation performed by the Court since the days of Earl Warren ought to stop—at a high cost to American democracy. Individual autonomy, the substantive protection of individual rights from intrusion by the state and federal governments, guaranteed to the American people by the Constitution, and more specifically by the due process or liberty clause of the Fourteenth Amendment, would be jeopardized. Though arguably anti-democratic, judicial activism is "a cornerstone of the American system of government." Without it, legislation that trod upon interests "so rooted in the tradition and conscience of our people as to be ranked as fundamental" would not be struck down. Americans would find all their most

15. Tribe, *Abortion: The Clash of Absolutes,* 74, 75.

cherished rights submitted to public vote, with the result that "any state or local government would be free to control our lives in innumerable ways, ranging from a federal abolition of birth control to a local imposition of detailed rules . . ."[16]

For both Glendon and Tribe, what is at stake in the abortion debate beyond abortion rights alone is thus the issue of individual autonomy and dependency. It is the traditional liberal regard for individualism and autonomy that is at the core of the American legal system, or, to put it in a different way, the centrality in American culture of rights talk that Tribe feels compelled to defend from Glendon's attack. Not surprisingly, therefore, the disagreement between the two legal scholars is never more intense than when the right to privacy, that "quintessential right of individual autonomy and isolation," as Glendon once called it, is at issue. To Glendon, as we saw, the right-to-privacy foundation upon which American women have built their fight for a legalization of the abortion laws merely serves to isolate abortion as a woman's problem: "no aspect of American rights discourse more tellingly illustrates the isolated character of the rights-bearer than our protean right of privacy."[17] As Tribe sees it, however, the extension of the right of privacy to abortion has helped define women's fight as a fight for female sexual autonomy. Imposing upon a woman a particular solution to her "problem" of pregnancy amounts to imposing upon her what to do or not to do with her own body, and this deprives her of the very core of liberty and privacy. "If our constitutional protection of our individual rights and human dignity means much of anything, then the freedom to decide whether or not to endure pregnancy must be deemed a fundamental aspect of personal privacy."[18]

By now "one of the most absolute rights known to the American legal system,"[19] the right to privacy has its roots in the famous Warren and Brandeis article of 1890, entitled simply "The Right to Privacy." "That the individual shall have full protection in person and in property is a principle as old as the common law," wrote Warren and Brandeis, "but it has been found necessary from time to time to define anew the exact nature and extent of such protection." Reviewing a number of both

16. Ibid., 91, 90.
17. Glendon, *Rights Talk*, 59, 48.
18. Tribe, *Abortion: The Clash of Absolutes*, 104.
19. Glendon, *Abortion and Divorce in Western Law*, 38.

English and American cases concerning intellectual and artistic property, the two authors pleaded that a distinct right was involved in all of them: the plaintiff's "right to be let alone."[20] With the Warren-Brandeis article, the legal community began to develop an argument based on the right of the individual not to have his or her thoughts or statements made public without consent. The concept was first considered a part of American tort law, but eventually made its way into Supreme Court opinions. Most lawyers refer to *Griswold* v. *Connecticut,* a 1965 case involving the use of contraception, as the decisive moment when privacy became a matter of constitutional law. In *Griswold,* Justice William O. Douglas delivered the opinion of the Court. A whole range of cases, he said, "suggest that specific guarantees in the Bill of Rights have penumbras, formed by emanations from those guarantees that help give them life and substance . . . Various guarantees create zones of privacy . . . We deal with a right of privacy older than the Bill of Rights."[21]

Justice Douglas did not say in his opinion whether the privacy right accepted in *Griswold* was an individual right or whether it included only protection for marriage and family life. The legal community and the American public had to wait seven years for a clarification of the precise scope of the new constitutional right. In the 1972 case of *Eisenstadt* v. *Baird,* the Court finally made it clear that the privacy right was not a family right so much as an individual right:

> It is true that in *Griswold* the right to privacy in question inhered in the marital relationship. Yet the marital couple is not an independent entity with a mind and heart of its own, but an association of two individuals each with a separate intellectual and emotional makeup. If the right of privacy means anything, it is the right of the individual, married or single, to be free from unwarranted governmental intrusion into matters so fundamentally affecting a person as to whether to bear or beget a child.[22]

With *Eisenstadt,* Warren and Brandeis's right to be let alone had been elevated to constitutional status. When *Roe* v. *Wade* had to be decided the following year, enough right-to-privacy ground had been covered for Justice Blackmun to declare that the decision made by a pregnant

20. Samuel D. Warren and Louis D. Brandeis, "The Right to Privacy," *Harvard Law Review* 4 (1890): 193.

21. *Griswold* v. *Connecticut,* 381 U.S. 479 (1965).

22. *Eisenstadt* v. *Baird,* 405 U.S. 438 (1972).

woman whether or not to get an abortion was protected by the concept of personal privacy.[23]

"It could be argued," says Richard F. Hixson in *Privacy in a Public Society*, "that the 'right' to privacy is more a sociological notion, even a theological construct, than it is a viable legal concept. It has as much utility . . . as the 'pursuit of happiness' or 'natural justice' or a myriad of other democratic ideals."[24] The major problem is that this construct tends to be so general that it is difficult to accommodate as a *legal* right except in specific circumstances or situations. Robert Bork was not as wide of the mark as his critics have contended when during the hearings on his nomination to the Supreme Court he saw Justice Douglas's "emanations and penumbras" analysis in *Griswold* as "less an analysis than a metaphor."[25] What Bork and other critics of the Court's various right-to-privacy analyses failed to acknowledge, however, is that the language used in both *Griswold* and *Roe* is in perfect keeping with centuries of common-law formulations. Talk of emanations and penumbras may not be good positive law, but it is good common law. Nobody put it better than Chief Justice Shaw:

> It is one of the great merits and advantages of the common law, that, instead of a series of detailed practical rules, established by positive provisions, and adapted to the precise circumstances of particular cases . . . the common law consists of a few broad and comprehensive principles, founded on reason, natural justice, and enlightened public policy, modified and adapted to the circumstances of all the particular cases which fall within it.[26]

Over the centuries, the judicial rhetoric of the best common lawyers has lent to the English language a whole variety of natural law and human rights formulations. These formulations have shaped and dominated

23. For a more detailed account of the history of the right of privacy concept, see e.g., Richard F. Hixson, *Privacy in a Public Society: Human Rights in Conflict* (New York: Oxford University Press, 1987), Mary Ann Glendon, *Rights Talk*, or David J. Garrow, *Liberty and Sexuality*.

24. Hixson, *Privacy in a Public Society*, 44–45.

25. Bork, quoted in Garrow, *Liberty and Sexuality*, 266.

26. *Norway Plains Co.* v. *Boston and Maine Railroads*, 67 Mass. (1 Gray) 263 (1854). I thank Professor Lewis Sargentich for reminding me of Chief Justice Shaw's wonderful judicial rhetoric.

important public debates. The wish for a positive, even "scientific" law expressed again and again over the last 150 years by American lawyers notwithstanding, one hears distinct common-law echoes in contemporary American rights talk. "The natural rights mentality," as Kenneth L. Karst once said, ". . . has stayed rooted in the popular folklore."[27]

It is not only the judicial rhetoric that marks *Roe* v. *Wade* as belonging within a common-law tradition. In dividing the legal regulation of abortion by trimesters, the 1973 Supreme Court decision "was much more in line with the traditional treatment of abortion than most Americans appreciate."[28] Until the first antiabortion statutes were enacted in the mid to late nineteenth century, what minimal legal regulation was in existence in the United States was inherited from the English common-law tradition. In this tradition, abortion performed before "quickening," that is, before a woman felt fetal movement, was at worst a misdemeanor. Early abortions were rarely prosecuted. So, contrary to what many Americans think today, up until about 150 years ago, abortion, at least early in pregnancy, was neither legally prohibited nor looked upon as the moral equivalent of murder.

The society of Gilead, in which the action of Margaret Atwood's *The Handmaid's Tale* (1985) takes place, is Laurence Tribe's and his fellow liberals' worst nightmare come true. It is a medieval-style theocracy that came into existence "when they shot the president and machine-gunned the Congress and the army declared a state of emergency." The first thing that the new regime did was to suspend the Constitution. After that, "newspapers were censored . . . The roadblocks began to appear, and Identipasses."[29] Individual initiative and autonomy were increasingly curbed until a point was reached where everything was forbidden that had not explicitly been allowed. By the time the novel opens, speaking freely in Gilead is a capital offense. Indeed, most things are.

What makes *The Handmaid's Tale* so gripping and terrifying is that the Republic of Gilead, projected as it is only into the end of the twentieth century, both is and is not the world we know. The political, demographic, and environmental causes leading to the Gilead takeover, for example, are all too familiar: the widespread availability of birth

27. Kenneth L. Karst, *Belonging to America: Equal Citizenship and the Constitution* (New Haven, Conn.: Yale University Press, 1989), 222.

28. Luker, *Abortion and the Politics of Motherhood*, 14.

29. Margaret Atwood, *The Handmaid's Tale* (New York: Fawcett Crest, 1985), 225.

control, including abortion, has contributed to a significant decline in birthrates, especially among Caucasians; government failure to monitor chemical pollution and to prevent large-scale plunder of natural resources has produced an unsafe environment; and the AIDS epidemic along with other sexually transmitted diseases has spread throughout the population at large. Military mobilization has made a coup possible in the first place. And right-wing, pro-life, pro-home attempts to control sexuality—to which feminist campaigns against pornography, rape, and child abuse have unintentionally lent their support—have found their logical conclusion in a patriarchal demand for female subordination. In an interview, Margaret Atwood carefully distinguished her novel set in the near future from futuristic fantasy: "It's not science fiction. There are no spaceships, no Martians, nothing like that." In fact, "there is nothing in *The Handmaid's Tale*, with the exception maybe of one scene, that has not happened at some point in history. I was quite careful about that. I didn't invent a lot. I transposed to a different time and place, but the motifs are all historical motifs."[30]

The society of Gilead, then, is a logical extension of what is already happening in contemporary America. Atwood envisions in her first attempt at dystopic or speculative fiction only the present tendencies that made a Gilead possible.[31] Her choice of genre, to which we shall return in more detail toward the end of the chapter, is a happy one; it gives her some distance from the contemporary scene, a better vantage point from which to take it all in and present it in a comprehensive way. "I think this particular genre is a walking along of a potential road, and the reader as well as the writer can then decide if that is the road they wish to go on. Whether we go that way or not is going to be up to us."[32] As a Canadian with at least one American ancestor—the Mary Webster to whom the novel is in part dedicated—who did her M.A. at Radcliffe, moreover, Atwood speaks from an elsewhere that knows its enemies to be close by and, what is more, internalized. America is where it is going to happen first, it is "what's in store for us, what we are turning into," as she put it in her other famous novel about abortion, *Surfacing*, from

30. Davidson, "A Feminist '1984,' " 24.

31. In "Control and Creativity: The Politics of Risk in Margaret Atwood's *The Handmaid's Tale*," in *Critical Essays on Margaret Atwood*, ed. Judith McCombs (Boston: G. K. Hall, 1988), Lucy M. Freibert quotes Atwood as referring to her novel as a piece of "dystopia, a negative utopia" or "speculative fiction" (290, notes 2, 9).

32. Davidson, "A Feminist '1984,' " 26.

1972. Americans "spread themselves like a virus, they get into the brain and take over the cells and the cells change from inside and the ones that have the disease can't tell the difference."[33] In more than one way, "Gilead is within you."[34]

The message of *The Handmaid's Tale* is openly political: unless we take seriously the rise of the New Right and other fundamentalist manifestations, we may easily slide into a monolithic theocracy like the Republic of Gilead, which is more oppressive even than early Puritan rule. The focus of the novel is the violation of individual autonomy, especially female autonomy. The system that Fred—to whom the protagonist Offred has been assigned for a period of two years—and the other high-ranked officials in the Gilead regime called Commanders have devised for themselves tolerates no resistance or dissent. Heretics are hunted down, their bodies eventually hung from hooks embedded in the barbed-wire brick walls of what used to be Harvard Yard. These heretics, mostly doctors and other professionals who have assisted women in getting abortions, the people are told, "are like war criminals. It's no excuse that what they did was legal at the time: their crimes are retroactive."[35] A veritable military hierarchy of Commanders, Eyes, Guardians, Angels, and Aunts is in place, monitoring every single step the inhabitants of Gilead take through the use of advanced electronic devices and a detailed network of checkpoints. Everybody is dependent upon everybody else—you never know who is an Eye—and everything from loitering to looking into each others' eyes when talking, as already noted, constitutes a major offense in the heavily regulated political structure of Gilead.

Since the primary goal in Gilead is to return the birthrate to positive, women, or rather procreation, occupy a special position. Getting pregnant is what it is all about for Gilead's women. Handmaids are given three chances to become pregnant; if, after their third "posting" with a Commander and his wife they have not succeeded in conceiving, they are declared Unwomen and "discards" and are shipped off to the Colonies, where they have to clean up city ghettoes, toxic dumps, and radiation spills. "Be fruitful, and multiply, and replenish the earth"[36]—is the biblical justification repeated *ad nauseam* to the Handmaids for the sex-

---

33. Atwood, *Surfacing* (New York: Fawcett Crest, 1972), 153.
34. Atwood, *The Handmaid's Tale*, 31.
35. Ibid., 44.
36. Ibid., 323, 114.

ual subjugation they suffer at the hands of the theocracy. The Bible is invoked on every occasion, whether during the Ceremony, on Birth Days, or at the Prayvaganzas or Salvagings, in order that every woman may come to recognize the Divine Plan behind the Gileadean society and the religious nature of the role she plays. "The religious trappings that pervade the political structure foster the idea that the primary purpose of the system is to protect women, while the actual purpose is to control them and reinforce the notion that their biology is their destiny."[37]

Regardless of the caste to which she belongs—whether she is a Wife wearing a blue habit, a Handmaid dressed in red, a green-clad Martha, or an Econowife wearing striped blue/red/green dresses—the Gilead female inhabitant is never recognized as an individual with personal qualifications. "We are," records Offred, "for breeding purposes . . . We are two-legged wombs, that's all: sacred vessels, ambulatory chalices." The official message to the women is precisely to forget about their own egos, to renounce their pasts, to make sacrifices and to subsume their own needs under those of society at large: "what we prayed for was emptiness, so we would be worthy to be filled: with grace, with love, with self-denial, semen and babies . . . Oh God, obliterate me." And one of the most scary aspects of *The Handmaid's Tale,* to which we shall come back later, is precisely how easily and how fast a woman like Offred can be brainwashed into self-denial. "We were," Offred is told during her "reeducation" at the Rachel and Leah Center, "a society dying . . . of too much choice." Back then, there was "freedom to. Now you have freedom from. Don't underrate it."[38]

If the similarities of Gilead to contemporary American society are easy to spot, Gilead's ties to early Puritan rule are no less so. Indeed, the very fact that Atwood dedicated the novel to Mary Webster and Perry Miller is a clear indication of her wish to immediately alert her reader to those ties. Of the former, Atwood once said: "New England . . . is the land of my ancestors, and one of my ancestors was a witch. Her name was Mary Webster, she lived in Connecticut, and she was hanged for 'causing an old man to become extremely valitudinarious'."[39] Perry Mil-

---

37. Freibert, "Control and Creativity," 283–84.

38. Atwood, *The Handmaid's Tale,* 176, 251, 33–34.

39. Atwood, quoted in Mark Evans, "Versions of History: *The Handmaid's Tale* and Its Dedicatees," in *Margaret Atwood: Writing and Subjectivity,* ed. Colin Nicholson (London: St. Martin's, 1994), 177.

ler needs no introduction; any student of American history has encountered his by now classic works on Puritan America. Atwood was a student of Miller's during her period of study and residence at Radcliffe in the early 1960s,[40] and it is not hard to divine his influence behind a comment such as the following, made much later by Atwood: "The founding fathers had wanted their society to be a theocratic utopia, a city upon a hill, to be a model and a shining example to all nations. The split between the dream and the reality is an old one and it has not gone away."[41] Mary Webster died in 1683, almost exactly three hundred years before the time of Atwood's writing of *The Handmaid's Tale*. This makes it tempting to see the novel as a kind of tercentennial document in the best of the American jeremiad tradition,[42] lamenting what the American experiment has come to.

The seeds for the Gileadean theocracy, the numerous hints and references to Puritan America throughout the novel remind us, can be found in the early American utopia. What is especially interesting in this context is the way in which Gilead, like the Puritan theocracy of old, is a prelegal society. There is no shortage of rules and regulations in Gilead, but "there are no lawyers anymore." Indeed, with the Constitution suspended, there is no need for lawyers, because there is nothing and nobody to defend. At a Particicution toward the end of the novel, for example, a supposed rapist is exposed to the wrath of a group of women. He is eventually killed, but only after the women have tortured and maimed him. "This man," the women are told, "has been convicted of rape . . . The penalty of rape, as you know, is death. Deuteronomy 22:23–29."[43] It is as clear-cut as that—the man has committed a crime for which the Bible prescribes a specific penalty. In Gilead, the words "due process of law" are no longer part of the official vocabulary.

In Puritan New England, according to Jerold S. Auerbach, "legal dispute settlement was explicitly discouraged." When a conflict devel-

---

40. Evans quotes Atwood as saying during a lecture on "Canadian-American Relations" that "Canadian critics felt [*Survival*] owed much to the noxious influence of Northrop Frye, under whom I'd studied up there, but they overlooked the noxious influence of Perry Miller, under whom I'd studied down here" (Evans, "Versions of History," 180–81).

41. Atwood, quoted in ibid., 181.

42. See Sacvan Bercovitch, *The American Jeremiad* (Madison: University of Wisconsin Press, 1978).

43. Atwood, *The Handmaid's Tale,* 31, 358.

oped, it was solved without recourse to the legal process as "litigation was perceived as a form of self-aggrandizement contrary to the best interests of the community." Attempts to restore communal harmony initiated, not with lawyers and the courts, but with the church. "Nothing resembling legal due process existed in church proceedings, which varied among congregations."[44] As Auerbach sees it, nonlegal dispute settlement in colonial society expressed a strong communitarian impulse toward reasserting harmony and consensus—an impulse that is sadly missing in today's litigious America. To Atwood, however, the price to be paid for such community consensus, a loss of autonomy as guaranteed by due process of law, is too high. For all her often voiced anti-American feelings, *The Handmaid's Tale* makes a surprisingly strong statement in favor of liberal ideas and concerns, American-style.

ABORTION AS AN "INTRA-FEMINIST POLEMIC"

New technologies and the changing nature of work . . . give women—for the first time in history—the option of deciding exactly how and when their family roles will fit into the larger context of their lives . . . While on the surface it is the embryo's fate that seems to be at stake, the abortion debate is actually about the meaning of women's lives.[45]

By 1974, Kristin Luker writes, more than 80 percent of both pro-life and pro-choice activists were women—a fact that clearly speaks of the importance to women of the abortion issue. The data collected by Luker in her survey of pro-life and pro-choice movements suggest, moreover, that whereas the social background of male activists—their place of birth, educational and income levels, number of children, and present occupation—tended to be similar whether they belonged to one camp or the other, the women who made up the ranks of the movements were clearly divided into "two different social worlds and the hopes and beliefs those worlds support."[46] To a considerable extent, it would thus seem, the abortion debate is "an intra-feminist polemic."[47]

44. Jerold S. Auerbach, *Justice without Law? Resolving Disputes without Lawyers* (New York: Oxford University Press, 1983), 23, 22, 24.

45. Luker, *Abortion and the Politics of Motherhood*, 193–94.

46. Ibid., 194. For this and the following two paragraphs, I rely on Luker, 194–97 and 159–86.

47. The phrase is that of Barbara Ehrenreich, who used it in "Feminism's Phantoms," *The New Republic,* Mar. 17, 1986, 35.

As for the pro-choice activists in Luker's survey, they almost all worked in the paid labor force. Their educational background was considerable—about a third had undertaken some graduate work beyond their B.A. degree—and this had allowed them to be employed in the major professions where they made good salaries. They had typically married comparatively late and had only one or two children. The pro-life activists, by comparison, tended to be housewives, to have scarcely any educational training beyond high school, to have married early, and to have at least three children. Last but not least, the pro-choice women differed dramatically from their pro-life counterparts in terms of the place and importance in their lives of religion. By far the majority of pro-lifers were religious, mostly Catholic, and they considered their religion and their church one of the most important aspects of their lives. To about two-thirds of the pro-choicers, on the other hand, religious affiliation and religious issues were not considered of vital importance.

These differences in social background not surprisingly led to differences in the way in which pro-lifers and pro-choicers perceived the world. First of all, pro-life activists saw men and women as intrinsically different and as consequently belonging to different spheres. The male sphere is the workplace, the public world, whereas the female sphere is the home and the family. This means that for women, the most fulfilling and "natural" role is to raise and care for children and families. Sex between men and women was viewed as sacred as long as it served a procreative purpose. Contraception, premarital sex, and infidelity were unacceptable not just because they may have dire social consequences, but also because they take away from the sexual experience an important element, the bringing into existence of human life. The moral codes on which pro-lifers based their views on what constitutes moral and responsible behavior were well defined, absolute, and God-given; they would not change over time, and they were not open to discussion.

The views of the pro-choice activists were diametrically opposed to all of the above. Pro-choicers believed in equality between the sexes; if men and women are different, it is nurture and not nature that has made them so. Rather than divide the world up into two different spheres, public and private, therefore, men and women ought to share and take part in both spheres. There is no natural law that says only women may raise families; if given the time and opportunity, men may develop caretaking abilities that are just as impressive as those most often seen in women. Having sex, according to the pro-choice activists, is a fundamental part of a relationship, and it carries a value in and of itself in that it strengthens the emotional ties between the partners. Moral codes are not eternally valid, but depend on time, cultural setting, and individual beliefs. Moral judgments consequently rely upon a subjective application of personal ethical guidelines. "All of these factors, combined with a staunch belief in the rights of the individual, lead [pro-choice activists] to believe that only individuals, not governments or churches, can ultimately make ethical decisions"—about abortion, for example. Luker concludes on the basis of her survey that

> Pro-choice and pro-life activists live in different worlds, and the scope of their lives, as both adults and children, fortifies them in their belief that their own views on abortion are the more correct, more moral, and more reasonable. When added to this is the fact that should "the other side" win, one group of women will see the very real devaluation of their lives and life resources, it is not surprising that the abortion debate has generated so much heat and so little light.[48]

The deeply religious nature of their commitment notwithstanding, the pro-lifers have opted, like their opponents, for a rights talk–based formulation of their position. Embryos may be in a state of utter dependency and helplessness, but they are human, the pro-life argument goes, and as such they are entitled to all the rights of personhood. Not everyone within the pro-life movement is entirely happy with the legalistic turn of "official" antiabortion rhetoric, however. To build a pro-life case against abortion on the assertion of personhood as a natural or inborn right, professor of theological ethics Stanley Hauerwas has maintained, for example, amounts to surrender to secular, liberal premises of argumentation. Rather than participate in a liberal debate about facts and principles, pro-lifers ought to concentrate on the *Christian* basis of their views. "The Christian prohibition against taking life rests not on the assumption that human life has overriding value, but on the conviction that it is not ours to take—that as God's creatures we have no basis to claim sovereignty over life."[49]

Within pro-choice ranks, too, there is widespread disagreement about

---

48. Luker, *Abortion and the Politics of Motherhood,* 184, 215.
49. Stanley Hauerwas, "Why Abortion Is a Religious Issue," in *The Ethics of Abortion: Pro-Life v. Pro-Choice,* ed. Robert M. Baird and Stuart E. Rosenbaum (Buffalo: Prometheus Books, 1993), 162.

the desirability and usefulness of conducting the battle for free abortion in terms of rights talk. "The claim for 'abortion rights' seeks access to a necessary service," maintains Rosalind Petchesky, for example, "but by itself it fails to address the social relations and sexual divisions around which responsibility for pregnancy and children is assigned." When women are politically and sexually powerless, a right to choose means very little. Many feminists, moreover, as we saw in the preceding chapter, perceive an overriding right to autonomy and privacy to be a characteristically male ideal which ignores female beliefs in nurturing and responsibility for others. What is needed, therefore, is a feminist argument that, rather than mirror the abstract moral language of a right to autonomy derived from a male tradition of liberal individualism and property rights, instead rests first of all on an awareness of women's oppression and a commitment to ending it, and second on an emphasis on abortion as a *female*, that is a nonneutral, right. Issues of class and especially gender are very much to the point here; indeed, some feminists argue, they are what the whole debate is all about. Abortion, concludes Petchesky, in the best of American feminist "embedding rights within relationships" tradition (see chapter six), "is a positive benefit that society has an obligation to provide to all who seek it, just as it provides education and health benefits. Put another way, abortion is not simply an 'individual right' (civil liberty) or even a 'welfare right' (for those 'in need') but a 'social right.' "[50]

The extent to which the abortion debate, in raising issues of female self-definition and family policy, has tended to polarize especially the female American population is reflected in Margaret Atwood's *The Handmaid's Tale*. "This tale is an absorbing novel, as well as an intrafeminist polemic," as Barbara Ehrenreich wrote in a review of the novel.[51] Offred's recording of her life before and during the Gilead Regime is a highly ambivalent document in the sense that it exposes not only the victimization of women, but also women's complicity in their own undoing. We never quite know what to make of Offred. Being raised by a feminist of the old, radical school, who participated in proabortion marches and pornographic book burnings, she has become wary of the feminist fight and has sunk into a political passivity from which she never really recovers. "You're just a backlash," her mother

---

50. Petchesky, *Abortion and Women's Choice*, 7, 387.
51. See note 47.

would say to her. "You don't know what we had to go through, just to get you where you are."[52] It is only after Offred has been through her reeducation at the Rachel and Leah Center and has lost her husband and daughter that she starts to appreciate her mother and everything that she stood for. This appreciation does not turn her into an activist, though. What she does do, of course, is record her story. The very act of telling her Handmaid's Tale, of reporting for the benefit of later generations what actually happened, is the only indication of a political commitment on Offred's part.[53] With the exception of this arguably political act, throughout the novel she remains a passive observer: "what is to be done, I thought. There is nothing to be done . . . After the first shock, after you'd come to terms, it was better to be lethargic. You could tell yourself you were saving up your strength."[54]

After the takeover of the Gilead Regime, Offred tells us, "there were marches, of course, a lot of women and some men. But they were smaller than you might have thought. I guess the people were scared. . . . I didn't go on any of the marches." Later, after she has been posted to the Commander Fred and has become Of-fred, the only name by which we ever know her, she again passes up the possibility of getting involved. Fred is "at the top, and I mean the very top," Ofglen tells her. The two Handmaids are doing their shopping, and Ofglen reveals to Offred that she is a member of a resistance movement that would like to recruit Offred to its ranks. The movement has found out that Offred is having an illicit affair with Fred and wants her to use her unique access to "the very top" of the regime to "find out and tell us . . . Anything you can." Offred—admittedly—makes an attempt one evening to pry out of the Commander "what's going on," but it is a feeble and halfhearted at

---

52. Atwood, *The Handmaid's Tale,* 156.

53. According to Barbara Hill Rigney, it is Offred's willingness to pass on her version of what really happened in Gilead that validates her experience. "For Atwood, writing itself becomes a political act; the writer is always a reporter of truth, even when her subject is fiction" (*Margaret Atwood* [London: Macmillan, 1987], 110). This argument makes one wonder whether what is at stake for Atwood in her portrayal of Offred, in addition to or perhaps beyond her political message, is a version of the Henry Jamesian problem of "seeing" versus "being": does the very act of writing constitute enough activity for a writer to claim to be not merely a passive observer of, but indeed an active participant in, what is going on in society?

54. Atwood, *The Handmaid's Tale,* 68, 91.

tempt and is treated as such by Fred. She never uses her influence with him to gain really useful information; what she gains instead is some hand lotion and access to old magazines. "Maybe I don't really want to know what's going on," she says. "Maybe I'd rather not know. Maybe I can't bear to know. The Fall was a fall from innocence to knowledge." And toward the very end of the novel, when she has fallen head over heals in love with the chauffeur, Nick, she finally loses what interest she might have had in the Commander and the Regime altogether: "the fact is that I no longer want to leave, escape, cross the border to freedom. I want to be here, with Nick, where I can get at him."[55]

"You were always such a wimp," Offred's oldest and closest friend, Moira, says to her at some point—Moira, who is living proof that it *is* possible to fight the system, and of whom Offred has come over the years to expect "swashbuckling, heroism, single-minded combat. Something I lack." Offred is never more scared than when she is presented with a choice. Thus when the doctor at one of her mandatory monthly checks, in an ironic reversal on Atwood's part of the role formerly played by doctors in providing women with abortions, offers his "services" to help get her pregnant, she panics. "I put on my clothes again, behind the screen. My hands are shaking. Why am I frightened? I've crossed no boundaries, I've given no trusts, taken no risks, all is safe. It's the choice that terrifies me. A way out, a salvation."[56]

Offred's apathetic noninvolvement reflects two basic concerns of her author: first of all that victimization, in a real sense, is at least partly a matter of choice. Passivity is as much a choice as is activity. "In the long sorry story of human cruelty and pillage," as Ehrenreich puts it, "women are actors as well as victims, even when, like Offred, we choose to turn our backs and burrow into the narrow world of daily life."[57] Second, and equally important, the kind of moral cowardice displayed by Offred reflects Atwood's fear that should the New Right and other fundamentalist movements presently on the rise in the United States ultimately succeed in their endeavors to return the country to a premodern theocracy, it would not take them too long to brainwash nonbelievers into becoming believers. *The Handmaid's Tale* is never more scary than when

55. Ibid., 232, 289, 243, 252, 348.
56. Ibid., 324, 80.
57. Ehrenreich, "Feminism's Phantoms," 35.

it shows Offred being deeply influenced by official Gileadean teachings, or when it shows the female community of Gilead, in the beginning unwillingly, yet increasingly willingly, participating in the Particicution ceremony involving an alleged rapist. When, early on, Gilead is visited by a group of Japanese tourists, the women in the group seem curiously "undressed" to Offred. "It has taken so little time to change our minds, about things like this," she reflects. And when later the ludicrous Impregnation Ceremony is about to begin, she thinks to herself when she sees the Commander's wife all dressed up, "no use for you . . . you can't use them anymore, you're withered. They're the genital organs of plants." Already, she is dividing up her fellow sisters according to Gileadean philosophy: "There are only women who are fruitful and women who are barren."[58]

"For the generations that come after," Aunt Lydia had told the Handmaids at the Rachel and Leah Center, "it will be so much better. The women will live in harmony together, all in one family . . . Women united for a common end!" Back in the old days, women were raped and made the victims of pornography and sexual harassment. None of this will happen in the society of Gilead, where men and women live in totally separate spheres and rape has become a capital offense. Men, being "sex machines, said Aunt Lydia, and not much more," are reduced, for all practical purposes, to stud services, while women are put on a domestic pedestal, their procreative ability and the sanctity of the home highly praised from on high. "Mother," Offred cannot help thinking after a Birth Day to which the only male contribution has been the chauffeuring of the women to and from the house where it took place, "you wanted a women's culture. Well, now there is one. It isn't what you meant, but it exists."[59]

With its separation into male and female spheres, its emphasis on the sanctity of the home and of procreation, its punishment for sexual intercourse engaged in for pure pleasure, and its finding in the Bible the justification for it all, the "women's culture" forced into existence in Gilead constitutes pro-life ideas of the world writ large, or rather magnified to distortion. But it also constitutes a warning that there is a repressive tendency within feminism itself. On issues such as rape, child abuse, and pornography, radical feminists have voiced opinions that

58. Atwood, *The Handmaid's Tale*, 38, 104–5, 79.
59. Ibid., 209, 186, 164.

coincide with those of the antifeminist Right. Of this we ought to beware, warns Atwood.

ABORTION AS A CLASH OF ABSOLUTES: RELIGION VERSUS LAW

At the most basic level, as we saw, the clash between pro-life and pro-choice people is one between a religious and a secular understanding of the world. "In contrast to the peace, environmental, and antinuclear movements, which also contain many religious activists and groups, the antiabortion movement, which encompasses not only Catholics and fundamentalist Protestants, but also Orthodox Jews, Mormons, and Black Muslims, is narrowly religious and anti-secular."[60] When it comes to moral decision making, and especially decision making about childbirth and sex, pro-lifers, in denying the role of human will and judgment so central to pro-choicers, oppose every intellectual and philosophical tradition that has grown out of the Enlightenment and secularism. They find it presumptuous, even downright blasphemous, of their opponents to want to exert control over something as sacred as human life. The question for pro-lifers, as Stanley Hauerwas so aptly puts it, is "not 'when does life begin?,' but 'who is the true Sovereign[?]' . . . the Christian respect for life is first of all a statement, not about life, but about God."[61]

Pro-life professions of faith and trust in a Divine Plan and strict adherence to an absolute moral code are seen by pro-choicers as manifestations of a longing for a world order that no longer exists. That the latter, despite their avowed orientation toward cultural relativism and pluralism, at times speak up for the protection of human values that are no less absolutist and diffuse as those to which their opponents adhere, they rarely want to admit, however. Laurence Tribe is a case in point. "The story of abortion in America," he writes, "may . . . help us to see that while the clash over abortion is one of absolutes, absolutes themselves may be contingent . . . Far from being inevitable outgrowths of the natural order of things, these competing values are socially constructed." Yet, when it comes to the protection of individual autonomy from interference by state or federal governments as guaranteed by the liberty clause of the Fourteenth Amendment, there is nothing "contingent"

60. Petchesky, *Abortion and Women's Choice,* 252.
61. Hauerwas, "Why Abortion Is a Religious Issue," 163.

about Tribe's line of reasoning. "To impose virtue on *any* person de-means that person's individual worth," he declares. "Respect for in-dividual autonomy and reverence for the privacy of intimate human relations . . . [are] traditionally central among the values for whose protection the U.S. and its Constitution stands." In fact, the decisions judges make as to whether a right is so "fundamental" as to be specially protected by the liberty clause of the Fourteenth Amendment concern nothing less than "the meaning of America."[62] Such rhetoric is every bit as absolutist and morally and intellectually "slippery" as that em-ployed by right-to-lifers. We do not have to listen hard for echoes of Justice Douglas's emanations and penumbras, and other common-law "metaphors."

The abortion debate, I will conclude by arguing, is in a very real sense a clash of absolutes: a clash between a pro-life religious funda-mentalism and a pro-choice liberal absolutism, formulated as rights talk. It is no coincidence that the pope and the Catholic church, in what is perhaps their last desperate fight for ideological supremacy—their fight against abortion, against allowing women into the priest-hood, and against breaking the celibacy of Catholic priests—have found it necessary to fortify their ranks by aligning themselves with Islamic and other fundamentalists, thereby breaking centuries-old traditions. What the Catholic church has correctly perceived is that modern, es-sentially secular man and woman no longer need or are ready to receive "the truth" from above. They have found for themselves a new truth, a secular, liberal truth, which is centered around individual auton-omy and independence as defined by the law, and with which they find it much more comfortable to live. This new truth is informed by a belief in reason as a faculty that operates independently of any par-ticular worldview. Indeed, as Stanley Fish has argued, "liberalism de-pends on not inquiring into the status of reason, depends, that is, on the assumption that reason's status is obvious: it is that which enables us to assess the claims of competing perspectives and beliefs." Lib-eral arguments to the contrary notwithstanding, reason or rationality itself rests on belief, on a very particular, often unstated but implicit, moral agenda "that has managed, by the very partisan means it claims to transcend, to grab the moral high ground, and to grab it from a discourse—the discourse of religion—that had held it for centuries."

---

62. Tribe, *Abortion: The Clash of Absolutes,* 27, 103, 91.

To the faithlike quality of liberal thinking as well as to its foundation in legal, especially common-legal, ways of arguing I shall return in my last chapter on the law and literature movement. Suffice it to say, here, again with Fish, that "the clash between liberals and fundamentalists is a clash between two faiths . . . between two ways of thinking undergirded by incompatible first principles, empirical verification and biblical inerrancy."[63]

For her attempt with *The Handmaid's Tale* to vindicate American liberal democracy, Atwood, as noted above, could not have chosen a better genre. As is the case with the detective fiction of Sara Paretsky (see chapter six), the form, the literary conventions operating within the genre of science fiction, to which Atwood's dystopic novel is closely connected even though it does not have a specifically scientific theme, underscores the contents or message of the novel. Science fiction is a modern, secular, and didactic literary mode which relies on human reason to explain events and phenomena. Everything shown must in principle be interpretable empirically and rationally. In contrast to fantasies that offer a supernatural explanation of phenomena, that is, science fiction is about a "this-worldly other world," to borrow a phrase from Darko Suvin.[64] Joanna Russ sums it up this way:

> Science Fiction is . . . the only modern literary form (with the possible exception of the detective puzzle) which embodies in its basic assumptions the conviction that finding out, or knowing about something— however impractical the knowledge—is itself a crucial good. Science fiction is a positive response to the post-industrial world, not always in its content (there is plenty of nostalgia for the past and dislike of change in science fiction) but in its very assumptions, its very form.[65]

More than one critic has tried over the years to think of a workable definition of science fiction. One of the broadest and most useful is the one Kingsley Amis came up with many years ago. In *New Maps of*

63. Stanley Fish, *There Is No Such Thing as Free Speech: And It's a Good Thing Too* (New York: Oxford University Press, 1994), 135, 138, 136.

64. Darko Suvin, *Metamorphoses of Science Fiction: On the Poetics and History of a Literary Genre* (New Haven, Conn.: Yale University Press, 1979), 42.

65. Joanna Russ, "Towards an Aesthetic of Science Fiction," in *Science Fiction Studies: Selected Articles on Science Fiction 1973–75,* ed. R. D. Mullen and Darko Suvin (Boston: Gregg Press, 1976), 13.

Hell (1961), he saw science fiction as a form of narrative that derived from "some innovation in science or technology, or pseudo-science or pseudo-technology."[66] As Mark R. Hillegas points out, "science fiction according to [Amis's] definition is not possible until the world-view shifts from a supernatural explanation of phenomena to a rational explanation based on known or hypothesized laws of the universe."[67] As the name implies, that is, science fiction coincides with the rise of science and the scientist.

In "Utopias and Science Fiction," Raymond Williams distinguishes between four types of *dys*topia, each of which is the negative of four types of *u*topia: the hell, the externally altered world, the willed transformation, and the technological transformation. In the first two types, it is the element of otherness that steals the attention, whereas in the willed and the technological transformations the element of transformation is in focus. *The Handmaid's Tale* is a dystopia of the third type, the willed transformation, "in which a new but less happy kind of life has been brought about by social degeneration, by the emergence or re-emergence of harmful kinds of social order, or by the unforeseen yet disastrous consequences of an effort at social improvement." It is, suggests Williams, this third type which, in the strict sense, is "the characteristic . . . dystopian mode." The kind of transformation we meet in the willed transformation has come about as a result of "some social agency, explicit or implicit." This is not the case in the other type of dystopian writing in which transformation also plays a vital role, the technological transformation (type four). Here, it is technological development, more than social agency, which has worsened the conditions under which people live. If only in its broadest sense, as secularity and rationality, all the four types of dystopia are inspired by the "spirit of science" and may consequently be viewed as belonging to the genre of science fiction. "We must note also," Williams goes on, "that there are important examples of type (3) in which the scientific spirit and applied science are subordinate to or simply associated with a dominant emphasis on social and political (including revolutionary) transformation; or in which they are neutral with respect to the social and political transformation, which

66. Kingsley Amis, quoted in Mark R. Hillegas, "The Literary Background to Science Fiction," in *Science Fiction: A Critical Guide,* ed. Patrick Parrinder (London: Longman, 1979), 2.

67. Ibid. This paragraph is based on Hillegas's article.

proceeds on its own terms."[68] *The Handmaid's Tale* is precisely such an "important example of type (3)." Even if, therefore, its author has never herself considered it a work of science fiction, it may—at least in Williams's terminology—be claimed as one.

Finally—and paradoxically—it is in Atwood's choice of a Puritan, premodern setting for her novel that *The Handmaid's Tale* reveals its ties to science fiction. "Science fiction," as Joanna Russ, referring back to Darko Suvin, points out, "is quasi-medieval"; it "presents an eerie echo of the attitudes and interests of a pre-industrial, pre-Renaissance, pre-secular, pre-individualistic culture." Like much medieval literature, science fiction is an educational literature; it is, in fact, not only openly didactic, it is also often worshipful, even religious in tone—"science is to science fiction (by analogy) what medieval Christianity was to deliberately didactic medieval fiction." The tendency Russ finds in science fiction toward awe and a religious or quasi-religious attitude toward the world she traces back to the way in which science fiction paints ideas, that is, addresses itself to our minds, our capacity to rationalize and extrapolate from known to unknown, rather than to our senses. Its "ultra-American, individualistic, muscle-flexing" qualities notwithstanding, concludes Russ, "science fiction (largely American in origins and influence) is nonetheless collective in outlook, didactic, materialist, and paradoxically often intensely religious or mystical. Such a cluster of traits reminds one not only of medieval culture, but, possibly, of tendencies in our own, post-industrial culture."[69]

Modern, secular, empirically and rationally interpretable, yet often quasi-medieval, worshipful, even religious in tone—that is the picture that emerges of science fiction. What genre could more successfully convey a support for pro-choice rights talk based on the traditional American regard for individual autonomy—a rights talk that claims to be modern, secular, empirically and rationally interpretable, yet reveals a tendency toward absolutism?

CONCLUDING REMARKS

Few debates have more thoroughly fragmented contemporary society than the debate about abortion. Beyond abortion itself, it has been

68. Raymond Williams, "Utopia and Science Fiction," in Parrinder, ed., *Science Fiction*, 52, 54, 53.

69. Russ, "Towards an Aesthetic of Science Fiction," 9, 10, 9, 13.

argued in this chapter, it is the issue of control that is at stake in this debate. At various levels what is being discussed is *who* ought to make those life-affecting decisions involved in abortion. At one level, lawyers and politicians fight over the tendency throughout American society for important matters concerning abortion to find their way into the courts rather than into the legislatures. At a different level, abortion has become a forum for intrafeminist debates about the role of motherhood in women's lives and issues of family policy in general. And at yet a third level, the abortion debate has highlighted the attempt on the part of pro-life activists to turn the tide of modernity, as it were, and return the American population to the religiously motivated lifestyles of yesteryear.

In the tale told by Offred, the protagonist of Margaret Atwood's *The Handmaid's Tale,* we find the various levels of the abortion debate reflected. It is precisely to the issue of control, and by implication individual autonomy and dependency, that Atwood's novel addresses itself. Offred is a Handmaid in the Republic of Gilead, a medieval-style theocracy that has come about as a result of a violent coup d'état in the late 1980s or early 1990s. For Offred and the other women in Gilead, the crucial question in the contemporary discussion as to who will control women's bodies is no longer up for debate. Reproduction and family policy is held in tight control by the leaders of the community. There are hardly any choices to be made any longer. Offred may leave the home of the Commander to whom she is currently posted only once a day to do some shopping at the local food markets. Every step she takes is heavily surveyed. Once a month she must "offer" herself to the Commander and pray that he makes her pregnant—if not, she will be shipped off to the Colonies as an Unwoman.

Offred's story of events before and during the Gilead Regime constitutes a warning on her author's part that unless we beware of tendencies in contemporary America toward repression and fundamentalism—tendencies that may be found not only at the right but also at the left end of the political spectrum—a future along Gileadean lines may not be so very far away.

VIII

American Law and the Search for Cultural Redemption

A Discussion of William Gaddis's
A Frolic of His Own

I t was quite an event when William Gaddis published a new novel. It did not happen very often. *A Frolic of His Own* from 1994 was Gaddis's fourth novel in an almost forty-year career. His first novel, *The Recognitions,* came in 1955. It was followed by *JR* (1975) and *Carpenter's Gothic* (1985). Unlike many of his fellow writers, Gaddis had "never been in a rush to get into print," as he put it in a recent interview.[1] In preparation for each of his novels he did careful research into the area of American society or culture that would form the background for the plot. In his first novel, the plot is shaped around the American art world. *JR* takes place within the world of business, and *A Frolic of His Own* takes us through the complexities of American law. "The law is an immense attempt to establish order or to rescue it—I'm not sure which," Gaddis said when the book was published. "And yet, it's led to a carnival of disorderly conduct on all sides. This kind of paradox fascinates me."[2]

The opening sentence of the novel announces its theme: "Justice?— You get justice in the next world, in this world you have the law."[3] The law is everywhere in *A Frolic of His Own.* To begin with, the novel's title

1. William Gaddis, telephone interview with Laurel Graeber, *The New York Times Book Review,* Jan. 9, 1994, 22. Gaddis died in December 1998.
2. Ibid.
3. William Gaddis, *A Frolic of His Own* (New York: Simon & Schuster, 1994), 13.

is a legal phrase used in cases of imputed negligence. It describes the activities of an employee that, though resulting in job-related injuries, do not entitle the employee to compensation. The main character of the novel, Oscar Crease, is the failed offspring of a famous legal family. His grandfather sat on the U.S. Supreme Court together with Oliver Wendell Holmes, and his ninety-seven-year-old father is a distinguished judge in Virginia. A middle-aged community-college history teacher and would-be playwright, Oscar has managed to write a play based on his grandfather's Civil War experiences. The play, entitled *Once at Antietam,* has never been published, nor has it ever been produced on stage.[4] It is not a particularly good play, but it constitutes Oscar's last hope for fame, respect, and recognition—especially from his father, who has always paid more attention to his legal career than to his son. When a Civil War movie is released whose plot is suspiciously close to that of his play, Oscar does not hesitate to bring a copyright infringement suit against the movie's producer.[5]

The plagiarism suit is not the only legal matter in which Oscar is involved. When we first meet him, he is in the hospital, recuperating from injuries inflicted by his own car, which ran over him while he was trying to jump-start it. His injuries are by no means severe—within days he is perfectly able to walk again—but that does not prevent him from embarking on a million-dollar suit for pain and disfigurement. As both owner of the car and victim of the accident, Oscar is suing himself, thus becoming the ultimately litigious American. This suit is neither more nor less absurd or pathetic—or hilariously funny, for that matter—than

4. In his review of *A Frolic of His Own* ("Jarndyce U.S.A.," *Times Literary Supplement,* no. 4757, June 3, 1994), Zachary Leader mentions that like Oscar, Gaddis himself wrote an unpublished play in the 1950s entitled *Once at Antietam.* This may indicate that Gaddis saw himself in Oscar—at least to a certain extent. There is not much to like about Oscar. He is so pretentious and so pathetic that the reader cannot help wondering whether he constitutes an exercise of autobiographical self-criticism on Gaddis's part. "Projections of this type," writes David Cowart, "constitute the examined life of the artist, at once an exorcism of unworthy versions of the self and a rhetorically effective shielding of the vulnerable ego, whose pretensions might otherwise be dismissed by captious readers" ("Heritage and Deracination in Walker's 'Everyday Use,'" *Studies in Short Fiction* 33: 3 [Summer 1996], graciously supplied to me by David Cowart).

5. The ten-million-dollar lawsuit brought in October 1997 against Steven Spielberg's company, Dream Works SKG, by Barbara Chase-Riboud, the author of the 1989 novel *Echo of Lions,* claiming that Spielberg has ripped off her book for his film *Amistad,* makes one wonder whether Chase-Riboud has read *A Frolic of His Own!*

the various suits in which the other characters of *A Frolic of His Own* are engaged. Take for example the $700 million trademark infringement suit brought by the Episcopal Church against Pepsi-Cola on the grounds that the anagrammatic relationship of their names is no accident. Or the two suits involving the socialite Trish, who gets herself pregnant by a young man and proceeds to have an abortion without consulting him. Trish hires one set of lawyers to bring damages for "fetal endangerment" and another to defend her abortion.

There are suits everywhere. And for every suit there is a countersuit or an appeal, all of which run up enormous costs. Scattered throughout the novel are legal opinions, complaints, answers to complaints, and depositions, many of which at first seem ludicrous but eventually turn out to serve some purpose. Gaddis's characters all seem convinced that the place to turn in search of answers, definitions of right and wrong, is the country's justice system. *A Frolic of His Own* reflects how "the civil complaint [has become] . . . the sonnet of our times," as Robert Weisberg puts it. Oscar and his fellow characters are "not so much aberrant in [their] mental condition as representative of us all in [their] belief that the civil justice system is the best medium for all desperate hopes for recognition, respect, and solace."[6]

Gaddis ridicules law-permeated America; he exposes the obsession with law and lawyers that he sees all around him. But his satirical attacks never obscure his affection for the law and for the people for whom it has developed into an ideology. In this, as well as in the levels of complexity and subtlety that he succeeds in creating as the plot unfolds, *A Frolic of His Own* differs from other "lawyerly" novels on the contemporary American cultural scene. But there is one other thing that makes *A Frolic of His Own* stand out, and that is the sincerity with which Gaddis attempts to reopen discussions that have been declared dead or at least obsolete by deconstructionist and postmodernist critics. The novel is about old-fashioned themes such as divided selves, the originality of art (or lack thereof), the corruption of the ideal and the aspirational by the vulgar; at the same time it concerns more contemporary themes such as the impact of multiculturalism on national and personal identity. It will not do to dismiss Gaddis curtly as an elitist snob. Old and new, the questions he raises truly matter, and readers find refreshing the honesty

6. Robert Weisberg, "Taking Law Seriously," *Yale Journal of Law and the Humanities* 7.2 (1995): 446.

with which, leaving them acutely, painfully aware of the contradictions and absurdities of the legal system, the author tacitly admits that he, too, can only guess at possible answers.

A Frolic of His Own touches upon a myriad of themes and aspects within American history and culture. One chapter cannot do justice to them all. In what follows, the focus will be on Gaddis's discussion of law as an engine for cultural redemption. When Gaddis describes how his fellow Americans grasp at the machinery of law to lend their lives some dignified order, it will be argued, he puts his finger on an important contemporary phenomenon. While the country's legal system may once have been able to supply redemptive justice, it has become too wordy and bureaucratic to do so today, he implies, thereby wisely advising his readers not to ask too much of the country's judges and other legal servants. I shall take as my point of departure the copyright infringement suit in which Oscar Crease is involved, and around which most of the plot revolves. My discussion of this lawsuit will be preceded by an analysis of law as a powerful form of expressing and defining meanings in American public life.

LAW AND THE EXPRESSION OF PUBLIC VALUES

In an important discussion of Gaddis's first novel, *The Recognitions,* Tony Tanner relates "the notion that the ordinary individual and the artist alike may be living their lives within an intricate system or pattern of fictions" to the "search for some recognition of non-fictional reality." Together, he says, these "form a recurrent American theme which no one has explored at greater length than William Gaddis in his novel *The Recognitions.*" The relationship between recognition and invention is worth examining, Tanner continues, since a true act of recognition for Gaddis "is more profound than any act of invention, and . . . the greatest achievement of any invention or art work is when it frees you into a recognition of reality."[7] Tanner's insight is as pertinent to *A Frolic of His Own* as it was to Gaddis's first novel. Gaddis remained preoccupied with the recognition of reality and possible ways in which to facilitate it. It will be argued here that Gaddis sought a contemporary American reality—transcendental or material—in the law.

---

7. Tony Tanner, *City of Words: A Study of American Fiction in the Mid-Twentieth Century* (London: Jonathan Cape, 1971), 395–96.

He did not make it easy for his readers. As in his other novels, in *A Frolic of His Own* he used the technique of nearly continuous, minimally punctuated speech. Dashes indicate dialogue, and it takes a real effort on the reader's part to sort out the various voices—to figure out who says what. Language is obviously important; it is through language that we get to know the characters and their feelings and problems. In Gaddis's work, as Jonathan Raban points out in his review of *A Frolic of His Own,* "language is where we live and what we are. It's all we have."[8]

At first sight, the world of words that Gaddis elaborates merely seems pointless and chaotic. The characters ramble on in a manic and self-centered way. They constantly interrupt each other, making it impossible for anyone to express a coherent line of thought. In addition, their author keeps interrupting the narrative, such as it is, by inserting a variety of texts, chiefly legal documents, but also Oscar's play *Once at Antietam,* of which we get close to seventy pages. In the first of these legal documents, Oscar's father's opinion in *Szyrk* v. *Village of Tatamount et al.,* old Judge Crease addresses the problem of language. The Szyrk case, which is one of the most ridiculously funny in the novel, involves a dog belonging to a small black boy in Tatamount, Virginia, which runs into a massive free-standing sculpture, Cyclone Seven, and cannot get out. When the creator of Cyclone Seven, Mr. Szyrk, "a sculptor of some wide reputation in artistic circles," learns that the fire brigade is all set to help the dog get out with the aid of acetylene torches, he seeks an injunction to prevent the village and its fire brigade from tampering with his masterpiece. It is Mr. Szyrk's claim "to act as an instrument of higher authority, namely 'art'" that gives rise to the following observations on Judge Crease's part:

> . . . we may first cite [the] dictionary definition [of "art"] as "(1) Human effort to imitate, supplement, alter or counteract the work of nature." Notwithstanding that Cyclone Seven clearly answers this description especially in its last emphasis, there remain certain fine distinctions posing some little difficulty for the average lay observer persuaded from habit and even education to regard sculptural art as beauty synonymous with truth in expressing harmony . . . obliging us for the purpose of this proceeding to confront *the theory that in having become self-referential art is in itself theory* without which it has no more substance than Sir Arthur

---

8. Jonathan Raban, "At Home in Babel," *New York Review of Books,* Feb. 17, 1994, 4.

Eddington's famous step "on a swarm of flies," here present in further exhibits by plaintiff drawn from prestigious art publications . . . *serving only a corresponding self-referential confrontation of language with language and thereby, in reducing itself to theory, rendering it a mere plaything,* which exhibits the court finds frivolous.[9] (my emphases)

Judge Crease is basically making fun here of contemporary postmodern attempts to textualize everything. Yet his mandarin discourse is itself in danger of slipping into wholesale reflexivity, so that Harry, Oscar's stepsister Christina's lawyer-husband, presently understands him to be saying precisely the opposite of what he is in fact saying. When Christina complains to Harry that it is only lawyers who can understand legal language, and that it is all a conspiracy anyway, Harry defiantly shoots back, echoing Judge Crease,

> But, but damn it Christina that's what we're talking about! What do you think the law is, that's all it is, language . . . it all evaporates into language confronted by language turning language itself into theory till it's not about what it's about it's only about itself turning into a mere plaything the Judge says it right there in this new opinion. . . .[10]

Precisely because of the tendency of Gaddis's characters to ramble on at the most frantic pace without seemingly getting anywhere, we are tempted to take such outbursts as an invitation to see the fictional world Gaddis creates for us as a postmodern one full of plurality and indeterminacy. As we move further into the novel, however, we realize that "the confrontation of language with language" exposed by Gaddis does not so much reduce language to theory as it simply constitutes an attempt on the part of his characters to make the most of it, to do the best they can in their daily late-twentieth-century struggle to communicate. "Gaddis' nasty exposés of legal language do not really purport to show," as Robert Weisberg explains, "that law is ultimately about language, but that law is, unpostmodernistly speaking, about injustice or at least the visceral human feel of injustice."[11]

The various documents interleaved throughout Gaddis's massive tome may strike the reader as annoying and unnecessarily tedious inter-

9. Gaddis, *A Frolic of His Own,* 29, 33.
10. Ibid., 251.
11. Weisberg, "Taking Law Seriously," 452.

ruptions of the narrative, but they are full of shrewd observations and common sense. They have a peculiar power of their own and "provide the novel's only moments of stability, illusory flickers of presence, agency, closure, respite, justice even."[12]

When Christina wonders why it is that her stepfather "spends his precious time on this piece of junk sculpture and some dead dog," her husband Harry answers: "Trying to rescue the language, Christina. Wait and see."[13] The implication is that judges such as Judge Crease may help rescue language from postmodern attempts to textualize everything—the kind of textualization that the old judge pokes fun at in his opinion quoted above. It is not that lawyers and judges are better or more lovable persons than anybody else. There are in fact a number of highly unflattering portraits of jurists in the novel, Judge Crease himself being one of them. It is just that in the 1990s it is to the law that people look for order and discipline. "The point is," says Robert Weisberg,

> that even though the legal system is a "jerrybuilt evasion" of reality, there is a reality to evade. Though the characters are fools to believe that the legal system they have made or inherited will bring them justice—or even that they deserve justice—they are not fools to believe that something like justice could exist and perhaps has existed. For Gaddis, justice is not quite so distant as Utopia . . . It is a "real ideal" and one which this species should be capable of achieving, but which, in Gaddis' almost vindictively angry view, this species has idiotically botched.[14]

In addition to being the area of contemporary American culture that may further what Tony Tanner calls "the pilgrimage" toward reality,[15] the law has increasingly come to be seen over the past few years as a form of expression that is extremely powerful "in defining meanings in our public life."[16] In his most recent book, *Law's Promise, Law's Expression,* Kenneth L. Karst argues that the United States is presently witnessing a "cultural counterrevolution," a "profound disquiet" felt by a number of Americans who have felt left out, even threatened by the successes of the

12. Leader, "Jarndyce U.S.A.," 22.
13. Gaddis, *A Frolic of His Own,* 251.
14. Weisberg, "Taking Law Seriously," 452.
15. Tanner, *City of Words,* 397.
16. Kenneth L. Karst, *Law's Promise, Law's Expression: Visions of Power in the Politics of Race, Gender, and Religion* (New Haven, Conn.: Yale University Press, 1993), 3.

civil rights movement, the women's movement, and the gay rights movement. This cultural counterrevolution evokes visions of an earlier social order, a traditional rank-ordering of groups, and it is inextricably bound up in law.

> Because the political aspect of a clash of cultures is a contest over public meanings, the law is a natural focus of contention, as the community's definitive expression of those meanings. It is this function that makes law, in Thurman Arnold's words, "a great reservoir of emotionally important social symbols."[17]

To the counterrevolutionaries, according to their hostile critics, the promise of law is first of all to impose order on a chaotic society and to have that order "embodied in a formal public acknowledgment of the dominance of their values." Second, and not unrelated, law's promise is to uphold an ideology of masculinity that treats power as its own justification and equates the proof of manhood with the expression of dominance.

> The heart of the ideology of masculinity is the belief that power rightfully belongs to the masculine—that is, to those who display the traits traditionally called masculine. This belief has two corollaries. The first is that the gender line must be clearly drawn, and the second is that power is rightfully distributed among the masculine in proportion to their masculinity—as determined not merely by their physical stature or aggressiveness, but more generally by their ability to dominate and to avoid being dominated.

What the counterrevolutionaries are asking for, in other words, is "the political and cultural equivalent of a copyright or a trademark."[18] They want the country at large not only to acknowledge that their cultural and political points of view are the "correct" ones, but also to elevate these views into official public policy and law.

With *A Frolic of His Own*, William Gaddis enlisted in the ranks of the counterrevolutionaries. His is an unusually sophisticated contribu-

17. Ibid., 2, 8.
18. Ibid., 43, 33–34, 59.

tion to the cultural debates presently ravaging the United States, to be sure. Unlike the mainly southern, lower income, evangelical or fundamentalist Protestants and practicing Catholics with limited formal education that make up the largest number of the constituency for cultural counterrevolution,[19] Gaddis did not act out of status anxiety, out of fear that he is losing out politically and economically. What he did share with the average counterrevolutionary, however, was a profound confusion as to what the effects have been on traditional American values of the inclusion of a number of new groups of Americans as full participants. Are the nation's subcultures correct when they claim that legal and cultural universalism threaten to undermine them? And if so, does this mean that the kinds of things Americans used to believe in, such as American exceptionalism and civic culture, solidly anchored within Western philosophy and culture and aspiring to embrace everyone, have now become obsolete and ought to be discarded altogether? These are some of the questions that preoccupy Oscar Crease—and his author—as he embarks on a quixotic defense of originality that may or may not become a crusade for that "cultural copyright" Karst speaks of.

INTELLECTUAL PROPERTY AND ANXIETIES OF MANHOOD: OSCAR CREASE'S COPYRIGHT INFRINGEMENT SUIT

Copyright Law: History and Current Definitions

The Congress shall have power . . . to promote the progress of science and useful arts by securing for limited times to authors and inventors the exclusive right to their respective writings and discoveries.

Article 1, Section 8, Clause 8 of the United States Constitution does not use the terms *copyrights* and *patents,* but it has been understood from its very beginning to cover both.[20] The clause is simple and direct, but not entirely clear. Is copyright, for example, a form of property, a personal right of the author, or a combination of personal and property rights? Was it conceived by the framers for the benefit of the author or the

19. Ibid., 7.

20. The following pages are based upon Robert A. Gorman and Jane C. Ginsburg, *Copyright for the Nineties,* 4th ed. (Charlottesville, Va.: The Michie Company, 1993), 1–83. The Shaler, Holmes, and Harlan quotes may be found on 29, 37, and 37, respectively.

public? And what does "useful arts" mean—is a soap opera as useful as a novel by William Faulkner? These are just some of the questions upon which scholars have been unable to agree over the years.

The Copyright Act of 1909 states:

> The enactment of copyright legislation by Congress under the terms of the Constitution is not based upon any natural right that the author has in his writings . . . but upon the ground that the welfare of the public will be served and progress of science and useful arts will be promoted by securing to authors for limited periods the exclusive rights to their writings . . . Not primarily for the benefit of the author, but primarily for the benefit of the public, such rights are given.

As some legal scholars have since seen it, however, copyright ought not so much to foster the creation and dissemination of intellectual works for the public welfare as to benefit the individual author. Here is Harvard law professor Nathaniel Shaler commenting, in 1936, on the special kind of rights an author has to his work.

> When we come to weigh the rights of the several sorts of property which can be held by man . . . it will be clearly seen that intellectual property is, after all, the only absolute possession in the world . . . The man who brings out of the nothingness some child of his thought has rights therein which cannot belong to any other sort of property.

The interpretation of the words "useful arts" has been linked over the years to the issue of whose benefit is more important, that of the general public or that of the author. Those who have been chiefly concerned with the public good have attempted to answer questions that look very familiar to students of American studies. Do the words "promote" and "useful" indicate an assessment of a work of art in terms of its educational value, and if this is indeed the case what is and is not educational? Is there a qualitative difference between a highbrow and a lowbrow piece of art, and if so who is qualified to say so? In a famous case from 1903, *Bleistein* v. *Donaldson Lithographing Co.,* Justices Holmes and Harlan discussed precisely these issues. The case concerned the copying in reduced form of three chromolithographs prepared as advertisements for a circus. Holmes delivered the opinion of the court:

It would be a dangerous undertaking for persons trained only to the law to constitute themselves final judges of the worth of pictorial illustrations, outside of the narrowest and most obvious limits. At the one extreme some works of genius would be sure to miss appreciation. Their very novelty would make them repulsive until the public had learned the new language in which their author spoke . . . At the other end, copyright would be denied to pictures which appealed to a public less educated than the judge. Yet if they command the interest of any public, they have a commercial value—it would be bold to say that they have not an aesthetic and educational value—and the taste of any public is not to be treated with contempt.

To this, Holmes's colleague on the Court, Justice Harlan, countered in his dissent that "if a chromo, lithograph, or other print, engraving, or picture has no other use than that of a mere advertisement, and no value aside from this function, it would not be promotive of the useful arts, within the meaning of the constitutional provision, to protect the 'author' in the exclusive use thereof. . . ."

More recently, the issue of copyright has also been connected to First Amendment debates involving freedom of speech. Thus, in *Harper & Row Publishers, Inc.* v. *Nation Enters* (1985), Justice O'Connor invoked the potentially beneficial interdependence of copyright and the First Amendment by emphasizing that "it should not be forgotten that the Framers intended copyright itself to be the engine of free expression. By establishing a marketable right to the use of one's expression, copyright supplies the economic incentive to create and disseminate ideas."[21] Intellectual property and patent rights have furthermore become hot issues in relation to current genome and other genetic engineering research as well as to computer technology. Gaddis's choice of copyright law as the framework for his critical analysis of the current state of American culture is therefore an excellent one. Before we turn to Oscar's copyright infringement suit, however, we need to take a quick look at the nature and the subject matter of copyright as currently defined.

A copyright is a set of exclusive rights in literary, musical, choreographic, dramatic, and artistic works. The rights under copyright per-

---

21. Sandra Day O'Connor, quoted in Gorman and Ginsburg, *Copyright for the Nineties,* 30.

tain to the reproduction, adaptation, public distribution, and public display or performance of the work. For copyright to be available, the work of authorship in question must be original and fixed in a tangible medium. As to what the first of the two fundamental criteria of copyright protection, originality, means, the Supreme Court recently explained that

> The *sine qua non* of copyright is originality. To qualify for copyright protection, a work must be original to the author . . . Original, as the term is used in copyright, means only that the work was independently created by the author (as opposed to copied from other works), and that it possesses at least some minimal degree of creativity . . . To be sure, the requisite level of creativity is extremely low; even a slight amount will suffice . . . Originality does not signify novelty; a work may be original even though it closely resembles other works so long as the similarity is fortuitous, not the result of copying.[22]

The copyright owner's exclusive rights are limited in two important ways. First of all, because a copyright protects only against copying (or paraphrasing) the copyrighted work, a copyright does not prohibit another author from *independently* producing the same or a similar work. Second, neither *ideas* nor discrete *facts* from a copyrighted work are protected; copyright protects only the particular *expression* of ideas and facts. The latter limitation has been the subject of much discussion, the distinction between an idea and its expression not always being immediately apparent. As we shall see, this very elusiveness of the idea/expression dichotomy gives rise to some interesting points of contention during Oscar's plagiarism suit.

Crease v. *Erebus Entertainment, Inc.*

Discussing with Christina how Oscar will react if he loses the copyright infringement suit he has brought against the producers of the Civil War movie *The Blood in the Red White and Blue,* Harry suggests that Oscar has been "going on a frolic of his own." Christina wants to know where on earth he has dug up that phrase. Going on a frolic of one's own, Harry explains, is

---

22. *Feist Publications, Inc.* v. *Rural Telephone Service,* 499 U.S. 340 (1991), as quoted in Gorman and Ginsburg, *Copyright for the Nineties,* 86.

Just a phrase, comes up sometimes in cases of imputed negligence, the servant gets injured or injures somebody else on the job when he's not doing what he's hired for, not performing any duty owing to the master, voluntarily undertakes some activity outside the scope of his employment . . . like an office worker puts out an eye shooting paper clips with a rubberband . . .

"Isn't that really what the law is all about?" Christina then asks Harry, "where it's all laws, and laws, and everything's laws and [Oscar's] done something nobody's told him to, nobody hired him to and gone off on a frolic of his own I mean think about it Harry. Isn't that really what the artist is finally all about?"[23]

The next time somebody refers to this legal technicality, it is old Judge Crease in his instructions to the jury in the case of *Fickert* v. *Ude*. The Reverend Elton Ude of Mississippi is accused of negligence in the baptismal drowning of a small boy called Wayne Fickert in the Pee Dee River. "In bringing a new soul into the fold through the baptismal ceremony," writes Judge Crease, the Reverend Ude was "engaged on his master's business . . . and not, in the words of a later English jurist, 'going on a frolic of his own.' " The Reverend Ude's master is, of course, God, and what Judge Crease is suggesting in his instruction to the jury is that the drowning is God's fault rather than the Reverend Ude's, especially since in this particular case, "the instrument of imminent catastrophe is the master's control, as must the crest and current of the Pee Dee River have been."[24]

The connection made throughout the novel between the artist and God in relation to the legal phrase "a frolic of his own" is an interesting one. In the Fickert case, God is literally "indicted for negligence—is absent, elusive, unstable."[25] Like a number of Gaddis's other fictional creations, Oscar is engaged in a search for his father, human and divine. His real reason for embarking on the plagiarism suit is to win his father's approval by showing him that he has been capable of producing a valuable and important play about the Crease family. As already mentioned, the old judge does not show too much interest in his offspring; he is always too busy thinking and writing about legal matters to get in

23. Gaddis, *A Frolic of His Own*, 348, 349. Here, it would seem, Gaddis, qua artist, somehow sees himself in his pathetic protagonist.

24. Ibid., 376.

25. Leader, "Jarndyce U.S.A.," 22.

touch with Oscar. The ultimate irony of the novel is that when his father finally exerts himself on Oscar's behalf by writing the appeal in his plagiarism case, he merely does it for "love of the law," as his old law clerk informs Oscar and Christina upon the judge's death.[26] This is devastating news to Oscar, who thought that his father really wanted to help him out.

Though most of his family came from the South, Oscar has lived all his life as "a wealthy recluse" (or, as his somewhat silly girlfriend Lily thinks the papers have called him, "a wealthy excuse") on Long Island.[27] The silent pond beyond the window of his by now somewhat rundown mansion, to which the characters turn their attention when everything gets to be too much in and around the house, recalls Walden Pond, and scattered throughout the book are passages from *Walden* itself as well as from Longfellow's *Song of Hiawatha*. Oscar Crease, that is, is an American historian and playwright with a New England background and frame of mind. Traditionally, as Tony Tanner reminds us, in New England human creativity was somewhat problematic. Creating something out of nothing was perceived to be God's prerogative, and if a human being engaged in creative activity he or she risked being accused of blasphemy. Oscar does not seem to suffer from precisely this kind of guilt. Instead, "his reverence is now directed to the creative acts of the Old Masters."[28] Again, Tony Tanner is speaking here about Wyatt from *The Recognitions,* but his observation is just as relevant in regard to Oscar Crease.

In *A Frolic of His Own,* Gaddis is as much preoccupied with the theme of the American artist as copyist as he was in his earlier work. For Oscar as well as for his author, remembering is more important than inventing—"notions of originality give way to copying," as Tanner puts it. The general feeling in *The Recognitions*—and, we may add, also in the later novel—Tanner goes on,

> seems to be that in their quest for originality, contemporary artists merely synthesize products to vaunt their own egos. Such art works obscure reality. Great art forgets self altogether and contains a recognition of reality. Copying such works to re-experience that recognition may thus become

26. Gaddis, *A Frolic of His Own,* 487.
27. Ibid., 266, 267.
28. Tanner, *City of Words,* 396–97.

an authentic, selfless mode of access to reality. Gaddis's book keeps returning to the difference between the fictions or fabrications which hinder, and those which facilitate, that recognition of reality which, truly understood, is the most original act of which man is capable.[29]

American copyright law, as we saw above, specifically concerns itself with notions of originality, novelty, ideas and their expressions or, to put it in a different way, with the American artist as copyist. By focusing the plot of *A Frolic of His Own* on a copyright infringement suit, Gaddis has thus succeeded in creating a piece of work that speaks both to his own key concerns as a writer and to the key cultural concerns of this country.

It is when Oscar is recuperating in the hospital from the injuries inflicted by his own car that he first reads about the production—and enormous success—of *The Blood in the Red White and Blue.* He is greatly upset and exclaims to his brother-in-law, "no, but [that man Kiester who made it] stole my idea, the same story all of it, it's even the same battle it's not a, just a nuisance it really happened, it was my own grandfather wasn't it?" Always the lawyer, Harry immediately tries to warn Oscar about taking this any further: "Oscar you can't just, you can't own the Civil War. You can't copyright history, you can't copyright an idea. . . ."[30] Oscar does not heed Harry's advice, of course. He proceeds to hire a lawyer, Harold Basie. Basie, who is black and later turns out to be a complete fraud, encourages Oscar to go ahead with his plagiarism suit. When the producers of the Civil War epic offer to settle for $200,000, it is Basie who persuades Oscar to turn the offer down and instead try his luck in court. Because of his injuries Oscar is unable to attend the regular court meetings. Kiester's lawyers therefore have to pay a visit to his Long Island home to take his deposition.

Enter the attorney for the defendants, Mr. Jawaharlal Madhar Pai, Esq., of the firm of Swyne & Dour. Madhar Pai, we learn through Harry, is "real red brick university product all English tailoring really full of himself, Swyne & Dour's token ethnic they came up with when they got a look at Mister Basie." Before long this "token ethnic," who, as it soon turns out, is every bit as clever and knowledgeable about cultural issues as Oscar, engages his opponent in a fascinating discussion about art and culture. Pai starts out by asking Oscar about the title of his

29. Ibid.
30. Gaddis, *A Frolic of His Own,* 18.

play—where it comes from and what Oscar intended it to convey. The title "Once at Antietam," Oscar answers, echoes a line in Shakespeare's *Othello* and is intended to evoke the dramatic death scene in which Othello stabs himself. Would this kind of sophisticated reference make sense to a mass audience, Pai wants to know next.

> A. To anyone who's read Shakespeare.
> Q. Would you characterize that as a general audience? Or a rather narrow one?
> A. As a theater going audience.
> Q. As a relatively narrow audience, then, a traditionally elite audience? In other words you wouldn't have expected a mass audience to make this Shakespeare connection?[31]

Having successfully exposed Oscar's highbrow leanings, Pai pursues the topic of possible sources of inspiration for *Once at Antietam.* Certain passages of the play remind him of Eugene O'Neill's Civil War trilogy *Mourning Becomes Electra,* for example. Are these similarities accidental, he asks. Appalled that Pai may think he has taken his material and his characters from O'Neill's play, Oscar hastens to say that this is most "certainly not" the case. He would never dream of taking anything from "that sham thing" of O'Neill's—"I mean you wouldn't see me writing 'Does it pain dreadfully? You poor darling, how you must have suffered!' "[32] In addition to emphasizing the fact that Oscar prefers his play to be associated in people's mind with Shakespeare rather than with O'Neill, the O'Neill comparison allows Pai to drive home the point that similarities may indeed occur without copying—a point of which he intends later to remind Oscar in relation to the movie *The Blood in the Red White and Blue.*

When Pai next directs Oscar's attention to Book One of Plato's *Republic* and to the striking similarities between this classic and his own work, Oscar's reaction is entirely different. Plato, Oscar readily acknowledges, is a chief source of inspiration for his play. He would certainly expect people not only to recognize this, but also to recognize the fact that his play is meant as a kind of homage to Plato, one of the greatest Western thinkers of all times.

31. Ibid., 171.
32. Ibid., 189.

A. . . . I obviously expected people to recognize these passages, these pieces of Socratic dialogue, any civilized person would recognize them from the Republic. It's all simply, it was all simply meant as a kind of homage, that's obvious isn't it?

Q. Please let me ask the questions. When you say any civilized person, are we back to that somewhat narrow, rather exclusive audience envisioned in connection with your play's title's slightly remote echo of Shakespeare?

A. I answered that didn't I? That he played to both the stalls and the pits?

Q. We are speaking now of Plato. Are you saying, then, that this very broad audience, which you have characterized as the pits, would be expected to recognize these random passages from his Republic?

A. It doesn't matter, no. No not the specific passages but it doesn't matter, that's the . . .

Q. Not the specific passages, then, but the approach, the Socratic method as it's known. What Dale Carnegie called the 'Yes yes' response?

A. Who?

Q. Dale Carnegie, the author of How to Win Friends and Influence People.

A. God! Yes, speaking of the pits but that's the point, it doesn't matter. They don't have to know it's the Republic, they may never have heard of Plato but they're carried away by it, by the dialogue, by the wit and the timeliness of it, and the timelessness of it. That's the greatness of Plato, finding a wider audience, that's the point. That's what I mean by homage.[33]

It is this "timeless" quality of Plato's work, according to Oscar, as well as the fact that "any civilized person" would recognize the similarities between his own work and that of Plato, which makes it acceptable for him to lift whole passages from Plato. It is this timeless quality, moreover, that he aspires to in his own writing. What he has attempted to capture in his play are "the voices of men a hundred years ago swept by the tide of events toward the end of innocence? to bring them to life caught up in the toils of history, struggling vainly with the great riddles of human existence, justice and slavery, war, destiny." When a work of art succeeds in touching upon the great timeless themes of Western civilization, idea and expression become one, and copying such a work

33. Ibid., 195–96.

becomes a means of gaining access to an authentic recognition of reality. The legal distinction between idea and expression no longer applies— except in cases where a timeless idea is copied in a vulgar and demeaning way. This is for example the case, Oscar claims, with the blockbuster movie *The Blood in the Red White and Blue,* which is full of sex scenes and gory special effects. What he seeks to have redressed in this lawsuit, he explains to Pai, is "on the one hand . . . the theft of my play without giving me credit and on the other what offends me is when my work is, when vulgarity and grossness and stupidity debase my work."[34] The difference between his copying from Plato and Kiester's copying from him lies not in the act of copying itself, but in the end product. Whereas his play has preserved the timeless quality and essence of the *Republic, The Blood in the Red White and Blue* is a piece of popular junk that caters to all the worst in human beings. Or, as Tanner would have defended Oscar had he been his attorney, whereas *Once at Antietam* facilitates, Kiester's movie hinders "that recognition of reality which, truly understood, is the most original act of which man is capable."[35]

As intriguing as he may find his views on copyright, Pai subsequently informs Oscar, he feels obliged to point out that they will not hold up in a court of law. Copyright law makes a clear distinction between an idea and its expression, and anybody involved in a copyright infringement suit must do likewise. But Oscar is not only wrong in a legal sense, Pai says; culturally speaking his theories about copyright and art are erroneous too. His elitist preferences blind him to the real issues in contemporary America. The so-called timeless problems of the so-called civilized person with which Oscar deals in his play are luxury problems. To the large majority of Oscar's fellow Americans, "the portrayal of man the microcosm of his nation's history, of man against himself, of self delusion and self betrayal" is by and large irrelevant. What chiefly interests the average American are the poverty, the drug problems, the ethnic fights going on in the streets of multicultural America, and of these there is precious little in Oscar's play. The important division is not that within a person, but that between ethnic groups. When Oscar tries to defend himself by saying that his Civil War play is really "not about these quarrels between black people and Jews that burst out on the front page is it?" Pai, warming to his subject, indignantly retorts:

34. Ibid., 300, 207.
35. See note 29.

Drugs, gunfire, let them fight it out, turn off the news and go in to dinner, not our fight is it? like your wounded pheasant burrowing for refuge in the stone wall, trying to flee from what was happening? the hollow essence of this Christian hypocrisy? . . . John Israel and Kane out there, both sides of your equation manipulating your hero's profoundly hypocritical capacity for guilt, the black and the Jew parading their real grievances they're not appealing to his conscience, they're not even fighting each other to seize hold of his conscience Oscar they're fighting for which one will fill this yawning sentimental churchgoing flag waving vacant remnant of the founding fathers, which one will finally be the conscience of this exhausted morally bankrupt corpse of the white Protestant establishment and that! . . . that's the heart of it, the heart of the American dilemma.[36]

Pai does not stop here. Having dealt Oscar's already shaky self-esteem a heavy blow by showing him how obsolete the concerns of his play are and how his preoccupation with those elitist concerns prevents him from noticing—and taking responsibility for—what is happening around him, Pai proceeds to attack the very foundation on which Oscar builds his notions of great and timeless art. "I don't really trust your Plato," he tells Oscar.

Look at his record on slavery, subjugation of women and the welcome mat out on Queer Street you get the feeling in this Cratylus that it's all really just a game he's playing, cardboard characters and their arguments so full of holes the whole thing ends in confusion and the flaws in his method show right through, your plea in your deposition back there as homage? as timely and timeless? In the end he's pretty much a dictator isn't he, a censor, can't trust him . . .[37]

Oscar is shocked and genuinely confused by these devastating attacks on everything he has always believed in. He never really recovers. Toward the end of the novel, he regresses back into childhood. In the last glimpse we get of him, he bursts out from behind a door and starts tickling Christina until she can hardly breathe—an act oddly enough presaged by Christina herself at the beginning of the novel. She and Oscar, she tells her husband,

36. Gaddis, *A Frolic of His Own*, 50, 325–26.
37. Ibid., 330.

used to talk about one of us buying the other one out when we grew up, but if something happened to him and the whole place would come to me he'd get violent because it had belonged to his mother when Father married her and he'd say he'd come back and haunt me, he'd jump out from behind doors to show me what he'd do, grabbing me and tickling me till I screamed, till I couldn't breathe.[38]

Oscar's, or rather his author's, "revenge" is to "feminize" Madhar Pai in ways that recall Kenneth Karst's theories about current counter-revolutionary attempts to uphold an ideology of masculinity. Pai is portrayed not only as an effeminate product of the British private school system, who throws in an "old sport" or "old fellow" at regular intervals, but also as an opportunistic intruder, who only has an affair with social-ite Trish in order to gain access to the America of the rich and famous. "He's quick all right," Harry says to Christina after Pai has helped Trish defraud a devoted family servant by breaking Trish's mother's will, "sometimes he's a little too quick . . . one of these men who has to show that he's smarter than you are even when nothing's at stake . . . He'd rather win than be right."[39] Politically correct or not, it is not to Madhar Pai or "Mudpye," as Harry and Christina nickname him, that our sympathy flows. In the end, all his obvious flaws and snobbishness notwithstanding, Oscar is the one whose plight mostly touches us.

Oscar's confrontation with Pai mainly concerns the concept of cul-ture. Throughout *A Frolic of His Own*, however, the discussion of high culture versus low culture is closely paralleled by a no less interesting and significant discussion about justice versus law. In both his lawsuits, Oscar wants more than just victory from the law. He wants vindication, or justice—"that's why I'm suing and it's not just the money, loss of earning capacity, career in jeopardy no, it's the principle of the thing," as he informs us from the very beginning.[40] For Pai, on the other hand, the issue of justice—or rather, the dream of justice—is just as obsolete and ridiculous as the issue of timeless values and great themes within West-ern civilization. Winning is what counts, not being right—just as the fight in the street is more important than old-fashioned WASP philo-sophical inquiries into the depth of the soul.

38. Ibid., 15.
39. Ibid., 339.
40. Ibid., 85.

In being more interested in winning than in being right, Pai recalls Anthony Kronman's lawyer-technician. He is precisely the sort of lawyer, described by Kronman in *The Lost Lawyer,* for whom the law is nothing more than a technical means to an end, and for whom the ideals of the common-law lawyer-statesman—practical wisdom, excellence of judgment, and a devotion to the public good—have become obsolete, even embarrassing.[41] It is interesting to note in this connection, also, that Gaddis has Oscar—and later on also Harry—reflect on the justice-versus-law issue by comparing Oscar's grandfather (the hero of Oscar's play) to his colleague on the Court, Justice Oliver Wendell Holmes. Trying to explain to Harold Basie "what it was between them," Oscar notes at some point that

> for Holmes everything was the law and when somebody held forth about justice like my grandfather did Holmes argued that he was refusing to think in terms of the evidence, to think in legal terms that's what it was all about between them right to the end, these clashes and passionate opinions he was as obsessed with justice as Holmes was with the law.[42]

Later on, during a conversation between Harry and Christina about old Judge Crease's opinion in the Tatamount case, the contrast between Justice Thomas Crease and Justice Holmes is again brought up.

> A story you hear in first year law school, same argument Oscar's grandfather got into with Holmes . . . Justice Learned Hand exhorting Holmes 'Do justice, sir, do justice!' and Holmes stops their carriage. 'That is not my job,' he says. 'It's my job to apply the law.'[43]

Applying the law is precisely what Pai and most of his fellow lawyers and judges do in today's legal system. Justice Holmes and his followers have prevailed.[44] This does not prevent Oscar and his fellow Americans from

41. Please see chap. 3 for a discussion of Anthony Kronman's theories.

42. Gaddis, *A Frolic of His Own,* 98.

43. Ibid., 251.

44. It is interesting to note in this connection that what Duncan Kennedy calls the "critical strategy," or "the left/mpm (modern/postmodern) project," started with Oliver Wendell Holmes: "My view is that there is an actual, dramatic historical moment when this critical strategy was first formulated. It occurred in 1894, when Oliver Wendell Holmes published his article, 'Privilige, Malice, and Intent.' In discussing recent English

dreaming about justice, however. And though they are foolish to expect to be rescued by the legal system they have made or inherited, Gaddis implies, "they are not fools to believe that something like justice could exist and perhaps has existed."[45]

CONCLUDING REMARKS

Oscar Crease, the protagonist of William Gaddis's *A Frolic of His Own,* sees himself as "the gentleman poet, the last civilized man." The themes that he deals with in his play *Once at Antietam* are the great themes of Western civilization. The play is based on the experiences during the Civil War of Oscar's grandfather, Thomas Crease, who hired substitutes to take his place in the army. For various reasons, one substitute ended up serving on the Confederate side whereas the other joined the Union army, and as fate would have it they met at the bloody battle of Antietam. As he grew older, Thomas Crease became "increasingly haunted by the conviction that the two had killed each other and that he was thus in some fanciful way a walking suicide."[46]

When Oscar brings suit against the producer Constantine Kiester and his film company for having created with the Civil War epic *The Blood in the Red White and Blue* a vulgar travesty of his own play, he is ostensibly doing so out of a wish to vindicate his family. What he is really after, though, claims his stepsister Christina, is recognition and attention. Christina is right in more than one way. Oscar wants to be taken seriously by his father, who has never had any time for him. But he also wants the world at large to recognize that the great themes of Western civilization around which his play revolves are still valid—even in today's multicultural America where the various subcultures are claiming that all talk of absolute, timeless values merely serves to under-

---

and American labor and common law anti-trust cases, he wrote this sentence: 'The ground of decision really comes down to a proposition of policy of rather a delicate nature concerning the merit of the particular benefit to themselves intended by the defendant, and suggests a doubt whether judges with different economic sympathies might not decide such a case differently when brought face to face with the issue.' The rest is history" (Duncan Kennedy, *A Critique of Adjudication (fin de siècle)* [Cambridge, Mass.: Harvard University Press, 1997], 85). See chap. 9 for a longer discussion of Duncan Kennedy and his legal theories.

45. Weisberg, "Taking Law Seriously," 452.
46. Gaddis, *A Frolic of His Own,* 348, 350.

mine them. In this endeavor, Oscar ultimately fails. He wins his suit only to discover that all he gets out of it is one-fifth of the movie's net profits. He gets his father enlisted in his cause only to find out that his father's interest stems from love of the law rather than love of his son. He learns upon his father's death that he had been lied to by his father about what really happened to his grandfather during the Civil War—what he believed to be historical facts are not facts at all. And on top of it all he has to suffer the embarrassment of being told by Kiester's attorney, a "token ethnic" at the prestigious law firm of Swyne & Dour, that the philosophical concerns of his play not only are old-fashioned and irrelevant to a contemporary American audience, but also make a convenient excuse for not dealing with the real problems. Utterly confused and disillusioned, Oscar tells his brother-in-law Harry that "it doesn't really matter does it, just a lot of, it's all those ideas I had that got in the way it's all sort of stiff and old fashioned, characters making speeches and those ideas that just got in the way that's what happened, it doesn't matter."[47]

If Oscar's play is full of "characters making speeches," so is *A Frolic of His Own* itself. The novel is crowded with voices and dialogue. There is a constant need for words as if putting words on certain key problems will help keep those problems at bay. The one theme that preoccupies everyone is the law. That is no wonder—one way or the other, every character in the novel is involved in at least one lawsuit. Oscar himself is involved in two. In addition to the copyright infringement suit concerning his play, around which most of the plot revolves, there is the personal injury suit that derives from his getting run over by his own car while trying to jump-start it. This latter suit becomes more and more complex—chiefly due to the fact that Oscar is basically suing himself—and Oscar never really seems to know what is going on. "You're suing the hit and run driver who ran over you aren't you?" asks Christina at some point. "No," Oscar answers, "I'm suing his, I mean my, I'm suing the insurance company for the owner of the car who are suing the, I think they're suing the dealer, the original dealer who's suing the car's maker it's all in the letter I got . . ."[48]

It may be exaggerated to call Oscar a walking legal suicide, but his legal predicament clearly echoes the moral problem of divided selves that haunted his grandfather. "To put it in plain language you might

47. Ibid., 110, 427.
48. Ibid., 385.

almost say that this is a suit between who you are and who you think you are, the question being which one is the plaintiff and which one is the defendant," as one of his lawyers explains the situation.[49] In the latter part of the nineteenth century, it was "the great riddles of human existence" with which human beings struggled. A hundred years later, it is the law. The legal arena is where the action is in late-twentieth-century America, Gaddis indicates. He is right. In contemporary law-permeated America, every major problem—be it of a political, moral, or social nature—eventually turns into a legal one.

"Questions that do have answers," Harry says to Oscar at one point, "that's what the whole of law's all about."[50] In the world of words created by Gaddis, the legal vernacular serves to make things concrete and thereby manageable. When problems are framed as legal problems, the law *does* have the answer. But there is more to it than that. The longing for lost values and cultural unity that is so pronounced throughout *A Frolic of His Own* is similar to the visions of an earlier social and cultural order evoked by what Kenneth Karst has called the cultural counterrevolution. As the cultural counterrevolutionaries see it, law is the most powerful form of expressing and defining meanings in public life. They have consequently waged their war for cultural copyright in the legal arena. For the right side of the American political spectrum no less than for the left, that is, the social issues agenda has been an agenda that is heavily focused on law and its promise.[51]

49. Ibid., 474.

50. Ibid., 398.

51. The special investigation into President Bill Clinton's credibility—personal as well as professional—led by Independent Council Kenneth Starr, which led to the second impeachment trial in the history of the United States, is one recent example of a rightwing attempt to use the law for a particular political purpose.

To Have or
Not to Have "a Project"
The Law and Literature Movement

I f the law has become central in the life of the nation at large, it has become no less so in academic circles. Thus, since the mid-seventies a new intellectual field or movement has emerged at American universities: law and literature. The highbrow or intellectual version, as it were, of Tom Wolfe's *The Bonfire of the Vanities,* Scott Turow's *Presumed Innocent,* or *The People's Court,* this interdisciplinary invention has expanded at a remarkable pace. Within the past two decades, a whole range of scholarly books have been published that deal with the combination of law and literature. Robert A. Ferguson, Richard H. Weisberg, Robert Weisberg, James Boyd White, Brook Thomas, Sanford Levinson, Ronald Dworkin, Richard A. Posner, Owen M. Fiss, and Stanley Fish are some of the scholars whose names have come to be associated with the new field. Of particular interest to these scholars are matters relating to the interpretation of American law. Like any other kind of text, a legal text must be interpreted, and since literary critics have a long and thorough experience in interpreting texts, legal scholars may benefit from the use of literary theories and methods in their

---

The chapter's title is a phrase of Stanley Fish's. Fish writes about his disagreement with Ronald Dworkin in *There's No Such Thing as Free Speech: And It's a Good Thing Too* (New York: Oxford University Press, 1994), 230: "That finally is what is at stake between us, whether or not Dworkin has a project."

interpretation of the law. In every polemic concerning such interpretation, however, what is ultimately at stake, it will be argued in this last chapter, is the question of American identity and nationhood.

There is nothing new or surprising about this preoccupation with the issue of identity. Ever since the first English immigrants arrived on the North American continent to form "a City upon a Hill," every generation of Americans has tried to identify what it means to be an American. What *is* new about this academic attempt to come to terms with the question of Americanness, however, is the realization of the importance for the American experiment of the law. The discourse of the modern, and by implication of America, scholars have come to see, is a legal discourse. Having no common religion and no common ethnic and ancestral origins on which to found their nation, Americans have formed their identity around what Kenneth L. Karst has described as "the ideology of the American civic culture." The central components of this ideology, as we saw in chapter one, are individualism, egalitarianism, democracy, nationalism, and tolerance of diversity, and within the civic culture the law has acted as a kind of "cultural glue," serving "communitarian purposes by standing as a totem, a symbol that community exists."

> A minimum requirement of nationhood is a set of universal norms . . . The American civic culture, as I use the term here, embraces not only citizen alliances and participation but also a widely shared ideology, a creed that is both manifested in our constitutional doctrine and shaped by it . . . When we look closely at what is supposed to be special, it turns out to be an ideology . . . The ideological component of the American civic culture performs its unifying function in the way that myth and religion unify, providing the focus for individual self-identification in a system of belief that is founded more on feeling than on logic.[1]

From the time of America's founding, Karst has furthermore maintained, "American courts have performed a dual constitutional role: not just delimiting the boundaries of individual autonomy and governmental power, but maintaining the institutional base for our nationhood. In our society as in any other, law—including constitutional law—mainly

---

1. Kenneth L. Karst, *Belonging to America: Equal Citizenship and the Constitution* (New Haven, Conn.: Yale University Press, 1989), 29, 193, 31–32.

serves to reinforce the existing distribution of power. But the role of our constitutional law in maintaining the American nation is more complex."[2] It is with the unifying function of American law that the law and literature movement is concerned, and to a discussion of which this chapter is consequently dedicated. Underlying the law and literature discussion of interpretation and rhetoric is a more general concern as to whether or not it still makes sense in this pluralistic and relativistic day and age to talk about a multicultural nation of more than 250 million people as a community. Will the incorporation into the disciplines of law, and perhaps first of all constitutional law, of the tools and methods of postmodern critical literary theory jeopardize, to the point of destroying, the modernist foundation for American self-identification? What will happen to the concept of nationhood once the possibility of unity of the law and of reconciliation of differences which has always been at the core of modernist jurisprudence is removed by the condition of postmodernity? These are the questions that form the subtext of the law and literature movement.

The law and literature polemic, that is, is a polemic about modern versus postmodern ways of thinking. Before I move on, let me briefly clarify what I mean by the terms "modern" and "postmodern." First and foremost, what chiefly interests me here is the aesthetic or theoretical part of the projects of modernity and postmodernity, respectively. The distinction between the two projects is an arbitrary one. Some critics have chosen to conflate them altogether or simply to see the postmodern as a continuation of the modern. In *A Critique of Adjudication,* for example, Duncan Kennedy pursues his own version of what he calls "a left/mpm [modernist/postmodernist] project."[3] As I see it, however, the difference between modernism and postmodernism is fairly substantial and has to do primarily with the belief (or lack thereof) in the power of the individual to know and control his or her world. "To be modern," T. S. Eliot quotes Irving Babbitt as once saying, "has meant practically to be increasingly positive and critical, to refuse anything on an authority 'anterior, exterior, and superior' to the individual."[4] It is this modern

---

2. Ibid., 215.

3. Duncan Kennedy, *A Critique of Adjudication (fin de siècle)* (Cambridge, Mass.: Harvard University Press, 1997), 8.

4. Irving Babbitt, as quoted by T. S. Eliot in "The Humanism of Irving Babbitt" (1928), in *Selected Essays* (London: Faber & Faber, 1951), 477–78.

glorification of the individual as the *creator* of culture—and of art—that the postmodern critiques. As far as postmodern theorists are concerned, the individual is no more than the *product* of his or her culture, and the modern belief that all can still be totalized or theorized as an aesthetics and an ethic, even a heroic ethic, is a total myth—the result being, to paraphrase Karl Marx slightly, that all that was/is believed to be solid melts into air.

In the polemic of modern versus postmodern, it will be argued in the following, it is mostly the former, the modern ways of thinking, that come out victorious. On the part of "antifoundationalists" no less than on the part of "foundationalists," to use Stanley Fish's terminology, we find a surprisingly strong willingness to defend a modernist view in the face of postmodern attacks. In chapter five on race and the law, for example, we saw Patricia Williams and other radical minority scholars express apprehension at the attack launched by Critical Legal Studies scholars on the procedural formality of (modernist) law. And in chapter six on gender and the law, we traced in the various feminist attempts to "embed rights within relationships" a deep-seated reluctance to let go of liberal (male) rights talk altogether. This defense of liberal rights talk on the part of the alleged victims of legal and other subordination is especially noteworthy in view of their explicitly stated sympathies for critical legal views. What seems to be going on here is something that for want of a better term, I will call *a leap of legal faith:* their awareness of the "deficiencies" and pretenses of modern American law notwithstanding, these scholars express *a will to believe* in the ability of the law by setting up impartial procedures to keep alive the professed American ideals of liberty and equality for all.

What is being said and done in American academic circles does not always correspond to what is going on in the population at large. In their willingness to defend some version of modern law's authority— some version of that liberal reign of justice—from metaphysical attacks of a postmodern deconstructive kind, however, scholars of both founda-tionalist and antifoundationalist leanings are *on a par* with their fellow Americans. In one cultural text after another, we find an acting out, so to speak, of what Karst calls the civic culture's ideals. Even as American cultural life has become saturated with talk of pluralism and cultural diversity, the longing for wholeness remains. From Tom Wolfe's *The Bonfire of the Vanities* and Scott Turow's novels, through the television show *The People's Court,* to the detective fiction of Sara Paretsky, Margaret Atwood's *The Handmaid's Tale,* and William Gaddis's *A Frolic of His Own*—and many other examples can be found—the message is the same: the American legal system may have degenerated into a power-game between greedy lawyers, and the American public may have become too sue-happy, but the law is still one of the defining characteristics of American community. It offers at least one common ground on which all subcultures can meet and demand that America live up to its professed ideals.

What the protagonists of the works I have dealt with in this book seem, more or less consciously, to be aware of, moreover, is that the affirmation of their belief in law's possibilities—at which they arrive only after a long castigation of the way in which the legal system presently works—is "itself founding, and constitutes a kind of contract between the legal institution and the public, each believing in the other's belief about itself and thus creating a world in which expectations and a sense of mutual responsibility confirm one another without any external support."[5] In popular as in high culture, that is, there seems to be a fundamental agreement as to the importance for the American experiment of the law—an importance which, in times of crisis, merits a leap of faith.

Americans have always had high expectations from the courts, especially the Supreme Court. Much like oracles with direct access to heavenly justice, the nine justices have been supposed to fill the void created by other segments of society. With particular pride, as we have seen in the preceding chapters, lawyers and scholars point to the common law with its combination of theory and practice, universal justice and contextual, individualized remedy as the source of these high expectations. Chief Justice Rehnquist and his Brethren make front-page news frequently enough for many Americans to have familiarized themselves with their names and at least some of their major decisions. Yet, to the average citizen, it is more likely to be somebody like Judge Wapner of *The People's Court* who embodies the best of the common-law tradition. Wapner was never more beloved than when he addressed himself eloquently to the topic of life, liberty, and the pursuit of happiness in general, in order then—equally eloquently—to direct his attention to the case at hand. In the following, we shall see how this kind of authori-

5. Fish, *There's No Such Thing as Free Speech,* 214.

tative decision-making, and the appeal such decision-making holds for Americans high and low, has always both intrigued and baffled scholars of American law and/or literature.

OF FOUNDATIONALIST AND ANTIFOUNDATIONALIST VIEWS IN GENERAL

Poststructuralism, as Costas Douzinas and Ronnie Warrington have put it, "has pronounced the end of all grand narratives and references, whether of God, truth, or form, and has insisted on the death of man as creative author and the centered subject of history and representation." The task for postmodern jurisprudence is "to open a clearing for reason(s), ethics and law(s) once all strategic moves of modern philosophy and jurisprudence to ground them on some single principle, form or meaning lie shattered." The principle of systematic unity and the possibility of value-free interpretation, on which Western metaphysical thought has always based itself, have become untenable, even "slightly comical," during the current cultural, intellectual, and political moment of postmodernity:

> The western rule of law or *rechtsstaat* was conceived as an answer to the degeneracy of moral consensus. The conditions that led to its genesis, however, further exacerbated by the onslaught of full-fledged modernity, prevent it from ever being able to deliver what it claims, a neutral, non-subjectivist resolution of value disagreement and social conflict . . . A theory of legislation is by definition a theory of choice and conflicting values and versions of the good in an epoch of nihilism.[6]

The two major "grand narratives" whose foundational belief in "the *topoi* of order, identity and unity" postmodern or contextual theories of law seek to deconstruct are the ones advanced by the schools of positive and natural law. As for the former, legal positivism, it is "both the dominant and the typically modernist school of jurisprudence," according to Douzinas and Warrington. The law is looked upon as a system, a set of formal, coherent rules that may be mastered and subsequently used. Learning the law therefore means learning to think within formal

6. Costas Douzinas and Ronnie Warrington, with Shaun McVeigh, *Postmodern Jurisprudence: The Law of the Text in the Texts of Law* (London: Routledge, 1991), 28, 18, 27, 14, 13.

categories, general frames of concepts, and working within them once a certain amount of classification has been grasped. A conclusion may always be reached on any given legal issue; all it takes is arguing long enough. "The formalism of the enterprise is evident in the assertion that all correct legal statements—both legislation and adjudication—are the outcome of a process of subsumption of inferior to superior norms."[7]

The second grand narrative and target of postmodern criticism, the school of natural law, shares with legal positivism a faith in law's possibilities. Douzinas and Warrington talk about two subschools or versions of natural law: a classical natural law, which finds its principle in divine truth and the cosmic order, and a more modern rational natural law, whose claim to naturalness rests on "the 'universal faculty of reason' to extract these norms from the facts of psychic and social life." About this modern version of natural law—and especially about its most recent mutation in the theory of fundamental human rights—there is something suspicious, or at least "strange." Historically situated as it is within the modern period, it can no longer take for granted the religious orientation of classical natural law, yet nostalgically longs for the cohesion and overall meaning this very orientation gave to its predecessor. "In its self-presentation as natural, modern law mimics the law of the lost *polis*. Its appeal to nature is the sign and desire for order."[8] Unlike legal positivism, natural law, in both of its versions, perceives the law as having a moral argument, as inviting a moral discourse. The law is not a system in and of its own right that works independently of what is going on in society at large.

Compared to what the two schools have in common, the presentation of the law as a united and coherent system, however, the question of whether or not legal argument is discontinuous with moral argument is of only minor importance. To all practical extents and purposes, both schools are within "the Enlightenment habit of thought."[9] A different way of putting it would be to say, with Stanley Fish, that the schools of positive and natural law are both "foundationalist":

By foundationalism I mean any attempt to ground inquiry and communication in something more firm and stable than mere belief or unex-

---

7. Ibid., 25, 21.
8. Ibid., 19.
9. Sabina Lovibond, "Feminism and Postmodernism," *New Left Review,* 178 (1989): 11.

amined practice. The foundationalist strategy is first to identify that ground and then so to order our activities that they become anchored to it and thereby rendered objective and principled. The ground so identified must have certain (related) characteristics; it must be invariant across contexts and even cultures; it must stand apart from political, partisan, and "subjective" concerns in relation to which it must act as a constraint; and it must provide a reference point or checkpoint against which claims to knowledge and success can be measured and adjudicated.[10]

When therefore, in the current law and literature debate, scholars of a positivist inclination take on proponents of natural law, "there is less debate here than the debaters believe."[11] The real and important argument is not the one among foundationalists, but the one between foundationalists and proponents of postmodern critical legal views, or "antifoundationalist" views.[12]

To participants in the law and literature enterprise of both foundationalist and antifoundationalist leanings, the transfer to the field of law of the tools and methods of literary criticism raises provocative questions of far-reaching importance. Chief among these is the question of interpretive constraints. It is the fear on the part of those adhering to foundationalist beliefs that, once the antifoundationalist beliefs that occupy a prominent position in current literary discourses gain ground within the ranks of legal scholars and practitioners, chaos will ensue. If there is no meaning prior to interpretation, the foundationalists ask, how are subjectivity and mere arbitrariness to be curbed? And more important, if the modernist liberal belief in universal, enduring values, such as the ones outlined in the Constitution upon which the American experiment was founded, collapses altogether, will not that experiment itself prove to have been but a failure, a hopelessly utopian dream?

10. Stanley Fish, *Doing What Comes Naturally: Change, Rhetoric, and the Practice and Theory in Literary and Legal Studies* (Durham, N.C.: Duke University Press, 1989), 342–43.

11. Robert Weisberg, "The Law-Literature Enterprise," *Yale Journal of Law and the Humanities* 1: 1 (Dec. 1988): 45.

12. In Fish's terminology, "Antifoundationalism teaches that questions of fact, truth, correctness, validity, and clarity can neither be posed nor answered in reference to some extracontextual, ahistorical, nonsituational reality, or rule, or law, or value; rather, antifoundationalism asserts, all of these matters are intelligible and debatable only within the precincts of the contexts or situations or paradigms or communities that give them their local and changeable shape" (*Doing What Comes Naturally,* 344).

What is ultimately at stake here is the feasibility of modernity, and consequently of the American experiment of liberty and equality for all. It is no wonder, therefore, that even arch-antifoundationalists show misgivings about the implications for American unity and nationhood of the dismantling of modernist jurisprudence. As we shall see, the position most often reached, even by antifoundationalists, is one of compromise, of leaving the door at least somewhat ajar to modernist views. What follows is first a brief look at two foundationalists, Richard Posner and Ronald Dworkin, whose contributions to the law and literature debate will be seen as modern versions of the positivist and natural law schools of thought, respectively.[13] Before we then turn to the antifoundationalist or postmodern side of the debate, as exemplified by the work of members of the Critical Legal Studies movement and of feminist and minority legal scholars, we shall consider the views of Stanley Fish. A transitional figure with a leg in each camp, as it were, Fish offers a piercing and insightful criticism of both foundationalist and antifoundationalist views.

FOUNDATIONALIST VIEWS: RICHARD POSNER AND RONALD DWORKIN

In *Law and Literature: A Misunderstood Relation,* Richard Posner distinguishes between two modes of reading or interpreting texts. The first mode is "intentionalist," the second "New Critical." Whereas an intentionalist reader will attempt to figure out from the words, the structure, and the background of a text what meaning or message the author of that text intended to communicate to the reader, a New Critic will consider a text an artifact and assign to it "a coherent and satisfying meaning" regardless of its author's original intention.[14] Taken out of context, the activity of legal actors—judges in particular—may seem similar to that of artists and writers, but the difference is that when judges interpret a statute, they take people's property, liberty, or lives. Pragmatically speaking, that is, the law is an instrument of considerable

13. I am aware that this is a controversial classification. Douzinas and Warrington, for example, see the school of law and economics, of which Posner is a founding member, as a modern version of natural rather than positivist law (see *Postmodern Jurisprudence,* 20). Perhaps this only goes to show the affinity between the two schools of thought.

14. Richard A. Posner, *Law and Literature: A Misunderstood Relation* (Cambridge, Mass.: Harvard University Press, 1988), 219.

political power and sanction. Legal judgments thus have much more far-reaching consequences than do literary ones. Were a reader to use the intentionalist approach in interpreting a literary text, it might perhaps impair the richness of that text. But conversely, were that same reader to use a New Critical approach in a reading of the Constitution, he or she would take the words of that document out of their historical context, thereby cutting him or herself loose from any constraints inherent in the text.

It is precisely this loss of constraint, which he sees as the inevitable result of a New Critical approach to the interpretation of legal documents, that concerns Posner throughout *Law and Literature*. By treating a legal document as a piece of literature, New Critics and poststructuralist critics (such as Robin West and the legal feminists and Roberto Unger and the Critical Legal Studies movement) come dangerously close to opening Pandora's box. For, in transferring to the legal field the tools of the literary trade, New Critics and poststructuralist critics will also transfer the self-referentiality and exaggerated freedom of interpretation that has characterized the postmodern literary arena. And if a judge achieves this kind of "freedom," what will stop him or her from bending the law according to his or her own subjective taste or whim?

Rather than go along with "the Dionysian impulse" or "Romantic" temperament of so much present-day literary theory, lawyers should be the first to realize that the law is "a bastion of Apollonian values." The emphasis ought to be on "professionalism, logic, strict rules, sharp distinctions, positive law" in order that "the human factor" and "the specific circumstances of a case" may be minimized.[15] Precisely because the law is a generalizing and abstracting mechanism, it may at times be necessary to supplement its professionally detached and rational voice with a more human and passionate one. This is where literature comes in. Literary works, dealing with "the perennial concerns of humankind," transcending "boundaries of period and culture," can teach lawyers empathy and give them insight into the concerns and problems of other people. What lawyers can furthermore learn from literature and literary theory is what Posner calls its "craft values": "Impartiality (detachment, empathy, balance, perspective, a complex awareness of the possibility of other perspectives than the writer's own), scrupulousness,

15. Ibid., 140, 155, 107.

and concreteness. These values . . . can be summarized in the term 'aesthetic integrity.' "[16]

Expressing in *Law and Literature* "a warm though qualified enthusiasm for the field of law and literature,"[17] Posner points to a number of important connections between the two fields: the issue of interpretation is central to both; legal texts resemble literary texts in being highly rhetorical; literature is subject to legal regulation under such rubrics as defamation, obscenity, and copyright; judicial opinions often employ literary devices. Finally, the legal process has a significant theatrical dimension to it that is attractive to writers of literature.[18] To a certain extent, therefore, the field of law and literature deserves to be taken seriously in legal teaching and research. Present law school curricula would benefit from a certain integration of courses in law and literature. Such courses would provide a healthy outside perspective on the law, just as they would introduce students to interdisciplinary studies in general.

When it comes to some of the larger and more ambitious claims made on behalf of the field by poststructuralist critics, however, Posner's attitude is less positive. Though claims may be made for the potential of the law and literature enterprise, they are not as substantial as those that can be made for the law and economics enterprise. Unlike the study of economics, the study of literature is not an exact science, and the development the latter has undergone in recent years toward subjectivity and skepticism, even nihilism, is a frightening one. Skepticism may be interesting and perhaps even irrefutable as a philosophical stance, Posner concedes, but when it is pushed as far as a critic such as Stanley Fish pushes it, it becomes "incapable of guiding action and interpretation."[19]

In *The Problems of Jurisprudence* (1990), Posner continues his discussion about whether or not literary theories of interpretation may be of use to the legal establishment. Though referring, in a footnote, to the several "fruitful analogies" suggested in *Law and Literature*,[20] he has by now come to the conclusion that "the differences between legal and

16. Ibid., 74, 241, 303.
17. Ibid., 353.
18. Ibid., 8–9.
19. Ibid., 263–64.
20. Richard A. Posner, *The Problems of Jurisprudence* (Cambridge, Mass.: Harvard University Press, 1990), 264 n. 4.

literary texts are so great that the lawyer . . . cannot expect much help from the methods of literary interpretation." When talking about interpretation and law, Posner argues, it is important to distinguish between common law and statute law. The former is a conceptual system in which the concept, not the text, controls.

> Because of its conceptual character, common law is unwritten law in a profound sense. Indeed, a common law doctrine is no more textual than Newton's universal law of gravitation is. The doctrine is inferred from a judicial opinion, or more commonly from a series of judicial opinions, but the doctrine is not those opinions or the particular verbal formulas in them just as Newton's law, although first learned from the words in which Newton published it, is not those words.[21]

The conceptual nature of the common law means that interpretation plays a marginal role in common-law decision-making. In fact, says Posner, "we do not need, and I can think make little sense of, the concept of interpretation in order to understand and evaluate the common law." As for statute law, it differs from common law in that

> the statutory text—the starting point for decision and in that respect (but only that respect) corresponding to judicial opinions in common law decision making—is in some important sense not to be revised by the judges, not to be put into their own words. They cannot treat the statute as a stab at formulating a concept. They have first to extract the concept from the statute—that is, interpret the statute.[22]

This difference would appear to make interpretation central to statutory decision-making. Repeating his assertion from *Law and Literature* about the lack of any kind of consensus within literary circles as to the meanings of great literary texts, however, Posner does not want his colleagues in American law to pursue the analogy between a legal and a literary text any further. The law and literature path does not lead anywhere. Epistemic questions concerning textuality are of only limited help to the practicing jurist, and tend to carry him or her away from "the important question concerning statutory interpretation, which is political rather than epistemic: how free *should* judges feel themselves to be

21. Ibid., 264, 248.
22. Ibid., 261, 248.

from the fetters of text and legislative intent in applying statutes and the Constitution?" It makes far more sense to see a statute not as a literary work but as a command issued by the legislature to the judiciary, and to speak "in pragmatist fashion" of the consequences of competing approaches to the role of the judge in statutory as well as constitutional cases.[23]

As an alternative to present tendencies within the academy and the judiciary to focus on the rhetoric and textuality of law and a corresponding lack of focus on consequences, Posner sets up a pragmatic—and very common-law inspired—view of law "as a deep-rooted custom fulfilling powerful social needs." The sense of pragmatism that appeals to him

> means looking at problems concretely, experimentally, without illusions, with full awareness of the imitations of human reason, with a sense of the "localness" of human knowledge, the difficulty of translations between cultures, the unattainability of "truth," the consequent importance of keeping diverse paths of inquiry open, the dependence of inquiry on culture and social institutions, and above all the insistence that social thought and action be evaluated as instruments to valued human goals rather than as ends in themselves.[24]

The economic approach allows the law "to be reconceived in simple, coherent terms and to be applied more objectively than traditional lawyers would think possible." The project of reducing the law to a

23. Ibid., 271. It should be noted, however, that in a later work, *Overcoming Law* (Cambridge, Mass.: Harvard University Press, 1995), Posner does mention one particular way in which the study of literature may be of professional use to lawyers. Inspired by Thomas C. Grey's *The Wallace Stevens Case: Law and the Practice of Poetry* (1991), he comments, "I now see with the aid of my own interpretive struggles with the poems of Wallace Stevens discussed by Grey that there is another and more favorable light in which to regard [the principle that the reader of a statute or contract or other legal rule or instrument should assume that every meaning was placed there for a purpose]. It is an antidote to hasty, careless, lazy reading. If we assume that every word is there for a purpose, we are made to read and ponder—every word, as we would surely be led to do by a good teacher of poetry. It is only when that principle of interpretation is transformed from a discipline to an algorithm that it is aptly criticized as unrealistic and misleading. At some level, then, law and literature . . . do converge" (480–81).

24. Posner, *Problem of Jurisprudence*, 398, 465. See also *Overcoming Law,* in which Posner continues his discussion about the pragmatic approach to law. In the later work, he characterizes the "pragmatic outlook" as "practical, instrumental, forward-looking, activist, empirical, skeptical, antidogmatic, experimental" (11).

handful of mathematical formulas may seem odd, Posner admits, but once the essentially economic nature of the law (and especially the common law) is understood, it will become obvious that "a few principles" such as for example cost-benefit analysis and the prevention of free riding "can explain most doctrines and decisions."[25]

The declared wish on Posner's part via a reduction of the law to a handful of formulas to "point the way to a clearer understanding of the law" shows that Posner never really leaves behind his positivist belief in law's possibilities.[26] He may declare himself a pragmatist and reject the idea of a grand narrative of the law, but, as Stanley Fish puts it, he still believes "in some benefit to be derived for practice from the pursuit of theory or antitheory."[27]

Ronald Dworkin sees more potential in the law and literature enterprise than does Posner. "Legal practice," he declares in his essay "Law as Interpretation," "is an exercise in interpretation, not only when lawyers interpret particular documents or statutes, but generally." Lawyers may therefore improve their understanding of the law "by comparing legal interpretation with interpretation in other fields of knowledge, particularly literature." Seeing law as interpretation necessarily means seeing legal practice as a political activity. This does not make of the law "a matter of personal or partisan politics," however. It is only, Dworkin hastens to add, "in the broad sense of political theory" that lawyers and judges cannot avoid making political decisions.[28] Though willing, unlike Posner, to make certain concessions to the postmodern insistence on the law as open-ended and politically manipulable, Dworkin is no less intent on addressing the problem of indeterminacy than is Posner. He does so, as we shall see, by means of invoking an aesthetic model, the chain novel, which holds out a promise of textual constraint.[29]

---

25. Posner, *Problem of Jurisprudence*, 361.

26. Ibid., 465.

27. Stanley Fish, *There's No Such Thing as Free Speech*, 230.

28. Ronald Dworkin, "Law as Interpretation," *Texas Law Review* 60 (1982), 527.

29. Since *Law's Empire* (Cambridge, Mass.: Belknap Press, 1986), in which he affirmed his commitment to the chain novel model as discussed in "Law as Interpretation," Dworkin has added little to this model of adjudication. In *Life's Dominion: An Argument about Abortion, Euthanasia, and Individual Freedom* (New York: Knopf, 1993), for example, he focuses on the constitutional question of legalized abortion and euthanasia. "Throughout it," as legal philosopher Douglas Lind puts it, "he provides only a thin sketch of a theory of legal interpretation. What sketching he does comes straight out of

It is in his wish for and anticipation of textual completeness that Dworkin reveals himself as a foundationalist. There is a certain irony in the fact, therefore, that he sets out in his writing to overcome the jurisprudential tradition of legal positivism. Postmodern critical views on the law would have made a much more obvious target, one would have thought. In the context of law and literature, his criticism of the positivist position takes the form of a polemic against "doctrinaire author's intention theories," or original intention à la Posner. The author's intention school is far too simplistic, Dworkin contends, in that it "makes the value of a work of art turn on a narrow and constrained view of the intentions of the author." First of all, in neither literature nor law is it necessarily always the heart of the matter to discover what the author had in mind while writing his or her text. Why, for example, must we know "whether Shakespeare thought Hamlet was mad or sane pretending to be mad in order to decide how good a play he wrote?" When we demand to know the relevance of original intent, all we get in the way of an answer is a circular argument: "value or significance . . . attaches primarily to what the author intended, just because it is what the author intended." Second, a novelist's or legislator's intention "is complex and structured in ways that embarrass any simple author's intention theory." Often, especially in a legal context, it is not even possible to say who the author is or was. Which one or how many of the delegates to the Constitutional Convention are we thinking about when we attempt to divine the original intent behind the Constitution, for example? And who may possibly discover "what was 'in the mind' of all the judges who decided cases about accidents at one time or another in our legal history?"[30] Furthermore, an author may not always be aware of his or her intentions as he or she writes. What he or she succeeds in putting down on paper may not correspond to what he or she set out to write, or may be the result of a simple change of mind in mid-writing.

Behind the intentionalist attempt to trace the value of a text back to the author's meaning or intent is the belief that "propositions of law"— that is, the pronouncements lawyers make as to what the law is on some question or other—"are indeed wholly descriptive: they are in fact pieces of history." It is with this underlying positivist view of propositions of

---

Law's Empire" (Douglas Lind, "A Matter of Utility: Dworkin on Morality, Integrity, and Making Law the Best It Can Be," Constitutional Law Journal 6.2 [Spring 1996]).

30. Dworkin, "Law as Interpretation," 536, 540, 537, 547, 548.

law as mere descriptions of decisions made by legislators and legal institutions in the past that Dworkin's main quarrel lies. What the intentionalist fails to see is that propositions of law are neither uncompli-
catedly descriptive of legal history nor purely evaluative. They are,
rather, "interpretive of legal history, which combines elements of both
description and evaluation but is different from both." Dworkin's idea
of interpretation as a technique of legal analysis is much more inclusive,
that is, than the one we encountered in Posner's account of the law and
literature enterprise. What to Posner is an activity sui generis, beyond
the neatly defined borders of which lawyers may find little of genuine
use, in Dworkin becomes "a general activity" or "mode of knowledge."[31]
Dworkin consequently invites every lawyer to immerse him or herself in
the debates currently taking place within the discipline of literature. The
picture that emerges of interpretation in these debates is a highly complex one and is bound to baffle. But that is indeed the point. The more
familiar a lawyer gets with the thoughts and arguments of the various
schools of literary thought, the more obvious it becomes to him or her
that propositions of law—or literature—are not just out there waiting to
be found, but are the result of active interpretation on the part of the
individual advancing them.

With "Law as Interpretation" Dworkin intends to show, in fact, that
literary interpretation may be used as a model for the central method of
legal analysis. An interpretation of a literary text, he suggests, "attempts
to show which way of reading (or speaking or directing or acting) the
text reveals it as the best work of art." In a parallel way, acknowledging
that law, unlike literature, is not an artistic but a *political* enterprise, a
plausible interpretation of any body or division of law "must show the
value of that body of law in political terms by demonstrating the best
principle or policy it can be taken to serve." Deciding difficult or hard
cases at law, Dworkin expands his argument about the usefulness for
lawyers of literary interpretation, "is rather like [the] strange literary
exercise" of writing a chain novel. One novelist writes the opening
chapter, which is then sent on to the next novelist who adds a chapter
and then sends the by now two chapters on to the next novelist, and so
on. The similarity is most obvious when judges consider and decide
cases at common law.

31. Ibid., 528, 529.

Each judge is then like a novelist in the chain. He or she must read through what other judges in the past have written not simply to discover what these judges have said, or their state of mind when they said it, but to reach an opinion about what these judges have collectively *done,* in the way that each of our novelists formed an opinion about the collective novel so far written.[32]

To make the chain of law work, each judge must make sure that his or her interpretation of all that went before—the decisions and conventions that make up the history of the case at hand—stays within the path carved out by these earlier decisions. In a Hercules-like fashion,[33] he or she "has a responsibility to advance the enterprise in hand rather than strike out in some new direction." Critics, who may have been uneasy about what might at first glance have looked like a confusion on Dworkin's part of interpretation with criticism or even a relativization or reduction of the whole enterprise of interpretation to a question of choice, pure and simple, may therefore now rest assured. Neither of his two "banal suggestions" concerning interpretation—his "aesthetic hypothesis" about literary interpretation and his "political hypothesis" about legal interpretation—celebrates unlimited interpretive choice. In the dual assumption that it is possible with a chain novel or a chain of legal decisions to create a unified text, and that a reader/novelist/judge approaches this text as purposeful, wishing "to show *it* as the best work . . . *it* can be," lies a recognition of textual and interpretive constraint.[34] As Douzinas and Warrington put it, Dworkin's "theory of interpretation is the hermeneutical circle in disguise":

> The chain novel "genre" asserts the possibility of a harmonious interplay between the constraints of the past and the principled freedom of the present. As a *chain* novel it recognizes the claims of the canon and the

32. Ibid., 531, 544, 542.

33. Hercules, that "lawyer of superhuman skill, learning, patience, and acumen," was assumed to accept "the main uncontroversial constitutive and regulative rules of law in his jurisdiction. He accepts, that is, that statutes have the general power to create and extinguish legal rights, and that judges have the general duty to follow earlier decisions of their court or higher courts, whose rationale, as lawyers say, extends to the case at bar" (Ronald Dworkin, "Hard Cases," *Harvard Law Review* 88 [1975]: 1083).

34. Dworkin, "Law as Interpretation," 543, 531, 546, 531.

constraints of formal identity. As a chain *novel* it promises authorial freedom but announces its future totalisation which, although infinitely delayed, demands of its authors to write as if theirs is the last chapter that would bring the book to a close. But furthermore and crucially, the image of writing-as-interpretation claims that the text is a sub-species of the hermeneutical act, a recovery and a transmission of meaning.[35]

BETWEEN FOUNDATIONALIST AND ANTIFOUNDATIONALIST VIEWS: STANLEY FISH

Even though the foundationalist position is remarkably resistant and resourceful in the face of attacks, it has, states Stanley Fish in *Doing What Comes Naturally,* over the past few decades become "increasingly untenable and problematical." Ultimately a conservative, static vision that is afraid of wandering beyond certain well-defined limits, it is defensive rather than self-assertive, "a secular version of a familiar theological paradigm in which the passionate and the carnal must be submitted to the corrective teaching of an already revealed Word." In various ways and in various disciplines from philosophy to the social and natural sciences, it has been driven into a corner by the antifoundationalist argument to which Fish himself subscribes. It is not, he emphasizes, that important concepts cannot be made within an antifoundationalist framework. It is just that these concepts and judgments, rather than being independent of the social and historical context in which they occur, are the products of that context. The counterattack made by foundationalists, that the antifoundationalist argument will result in the loss of all that is sacred and necessary to rational reasoning and successful communication, thus will not hold. For,

> Even if one is convinced (as I am) that the world he sees and the values he espouses are constructions, or, as some say, "effects of discourse," that conviction will in no way render that world any less perspicuous or those

35. Douzinas and Warrington, *Postmodern Jurisprudence,* 62, 63. As far as Douzinas and Warrington are concerned, the promise for the law of wholeness held out by Dworkin's suggestion of the chain of law is immediately deconstructed by his theory of rhetoric and aesthetics—"the law of aesthetics undermines the hermeneutics of reason" (73). This may indeed be the case. But if it is, I would like to suggest that Dworkin's will to hermeneutic reason, the attempt he makes at a leap of legal faith, is so much more, not less, the significant for his awareness—as witnessed by the rhetorical moves he makes—of legal contingency.

values any less compelling. It is thus a condition of human life to be operating as an extension of beliefs and assumptions with an absoluteness that is a necessary consequence of the absoluteness with which they hold—inform, shape, constitute—us.[36]

If the foundationalist opposition to the local, the historical, or the contingent is misplaced, so is the foundationalist fear of individual or subjective, unconstrained preference. The foundationalist assumption of an interpreter—whether in the field of law or the field of literature— who is at least in theory free to determine meaning in any way he or she desires, and who consequently needs to be constrained by something external like rules or laws, is false. Such an interpreter does not and cannot exist according to Fish, as each interpreter will necessarily "always and already" be part of a particular context, "thinking (and perceiving) with and within the norms, standards, definitions, routines, and understood goals that both define and are defined by that context." The dangers of excessive interpretive freedom not only have been "neutralized"; they are also *"unrealizable,"* as the self is not free but constrained by what Fish terms "interpretive communities," contexts of practice that shape and direct it.[37]

Every person is a member of several "interpretive communities," each one of which gives him or her an internalized sense of what is relevant. No fancy theoretical apparatus is needed to provide the rules that any settled practice will provide. Posner, Dworkin, and other foundationalists or semifoundationalists therefore need not worry about the possibly dangerous consequences an incorporation of the methods and practices of literary theory into the field of law may have. Any lawyer who has successfully passed through professional training will have learned how to consult laws and rules. No additional constraints are needed to give such a lawyer the direction or way of thinking his or her initiation into the professional community of jurists has already given him or her— "the brakes . . . are always and already on."[38]

With his positing of "interpretive communities" of practice, Fish hopes to have accomplished at least two things: first, to have allayed foundationalist fears of subjectivity in legal (and literary) interpretation,

36. Fish, *Doing What Comes Naturally,* 441, 245–46.
37. Ibid., 126–27, 138.
38. Ibid., 12.

and second, to have assured foundationalists that although one believes in historical contingency and cultural relativism, one does not have to give up the claim to foundations and values. Declaring himself "a card-carrying antifoundationalist" and "strong interpretivist," Fish nonetheless shares the desire of Posner, Dworkin, and other foundationalists "to defend adjudication in the face of 'nihilist' and 'subjectivist' arguments."[39] His sympathy—and scorn—are, that is, extended to both sides in the controversy concerning law and literature.

In the world of dialectic and postmodern critique, "we find a philosophy of suspicion, of systematic *dis*trust," and this relentlessly negative tradition on the Left ultimately leads to a protective—and therefore unproductive—stance that is just as rigid as the one assumed by the foundationalists. "Acknowledging as inescapable the condition of historicity, but claiming nonetheless to have escaped it," Left critical theory often ends up being trapped in what Fish calls "antifoundationalist hope." This "critical self-consciousness fallacy" is similar in kind to the mistaken assertion made by the Right that biases and prejudices may be overcome once they are exposed and dealt with "rationally." Such critical or "heightened" consciousness is simply not attainable, for "being situated not only means that one cannot achieve a distance on one's beliefs, but that one's beliefs do not relax their hold because one 'knows' that they are local and not universal." The intellectual Left ought to beware of the trap of pure objectivity and pure subjectivity into which conservative thinkers fall in their attempt to guard against interest-laden behavior and partiality, and to stick to the main tenet of antifoundationalist or interpretivist theory: "when we act impartially (and again I agree that we can) we do so 'by our lights,' which means that we act within and as an extension of an interpretive and therefore partial notion of what being impartial means."[40]

What the intellectual Left tends to forget when it subjects the law to a philosophical or metaphysical analysis, moreover, Fish continues in his argument in *There's No Such Thing as Free Speech,* is that there is a second, more pragmatic side of the law, "the activity of simply (or not so simply) doing law." At this day-to-day practical level of the law, the law is not a failure, but "an amazing kind of success." Under enormous social, political, and economic pressures, braving attempt upon attempt

39. Ibid., 347, 245, 138.
40. Ibid., 442–43, 456, 466, 467, 43.

at dismantling its integrity, it has *kept going*. Adherents of postmodern critical thought have done their best over the past couple of decades to raise our consciousness to the fact that the law has fabricated its own identity and authority, that the law is rhetorical and has managed to cover up how it works and manipulates. They are perfectly right, says Fish, in pointing to how the law produces its own authority, but the conclusion they draw from this—that the whole thing will and ought to collapse like a set of cards—is not the correct one. Most of us have realized by now that the law is what we make of it. What we have also realized, however, is how dependent we and society in general have grown on the belief that the decisions judges make are indeed constrained by law and by reasoned argument. The intellectual Left underestimates this public will to believe in the law and its servants and fails to acknowledge how "law emerges because people desire predictability, stability, equal protection, the reign of justice, etc., and because they want to believe that it is possible to secure these things by instituting a set of impartial procedures." The law will only work, and we want and need it to work, if the metaphysical entities critical thinkers would remove "are retained." And "if the history of our life with law tells us anything, it is that they will be retained no matter what analysis of either an economic or deconstructive kind is able to show." The law's job, in fact, which it has performed remarkably well, is precisely "to stand between us and the contingency out of which its own structures are fashioned."

> In a world without foundational essences . . . there are always institutions (the family, the university, local and national governments) that are assigned the task of providing the spaces (or are they theaters) in which we negotiate the differences that would, if they were given full sway, prevent us from living together in what we are all pleased to call civilization. And what, after all, are the alternatives? Either the impossible alternative of grounding the law in perspicuous and immutable abstractions, or the unworkable alternative of intruding that impossibility into every phase of the law's operations, unworkable because the effect of such intrusions would be so to attenuate those operations that they would finally disappear. That leaves us with the law as it is, something we believe in because it answers to, even as it is the creation of, our desires.[41]

41. Fish, *There's No Such Thing as Free Speech*, 22, 156, 213, 179.

In positing the belief in the law as it is as "itself founding," as con-
stituting "a kind of contract between the legal institution and the public," Stanley Fish comes close to describing what I have called a leap of
legal faith. What interests him about the willingness to let the law go on
performing its job in spite of our awareness that it may all be a sham is
its inherently pragmatic quality of "truth is what works." Of the foundationalist aspirations, likewise inherent in such a leap of legal faith, to
make of the law a chief provider, in this nihilistic and multicultural day
and age, of holistic meaning and truth, of course, Fish remains deeply
skeptical. As far as Fish is concerned, as we saw in the preceding chapter,
there is not much to choose between a religious and a foundationalist
liberal rights talk–oriented view of the world. Though claiming to have
moved beyond and to have replaced the discourse of religion, liberalism
rests every bit as much on faith as does religion. Fish sums it up by
saying that it is the belief in having "a project" that marks his disagreement with foundationalists of the legal positivist school such as Richard
Posner and foundationalists of the modern rational natural law school
such as Ronald Dworkin. Whatever differences separate these two
thinkers, "they are alike in thinking that they have something to recommend that will make the game better." By contrast, all Fish has to
recommend "is the game, which, since it doesn't need my recommenda-
tions, will proceed on its way undeterred and unimproved by anything I
have to say."[42]

Fish positions himself, as we have seen, somewhere in the middle
between foundationalists and antifoundationalists. His self-pronounced
antifoundationalist views notwithstanding, he is as—if in fact not
more—critical of antifoundationalism as he is of foundationalism. Ultimately, he is closer to the latter than to the former. And it is, oddly
enough, his pragmatic insistence on practice that makes him so. Precisely *because* truth is what works for Fish, he ends up defending the
same thing for which the foundationalists fight so hard: a belief in the
law as it is—that is, in a modernist reign of justice. The means by which
he gets there are different. For Fish, what legitimates such a reign of
justice is that it works, and that the people want it to go on working—
not the theoretical underpinnings of modernist jurisprudence. Foundationalist theory and antifoundationalist practice work toward the same

42. Ibid., 179, 230.

end here: a reaffirmation of the modernist legal foundation on which the American experiment rests.

ANTIFOUNDATIONALIST VIEWS: CRITICAL LEGAL STUDIES AND FEMINIST JURISPRUDENCE

The foundationalist search for an overarching principle for resolving legal disputes, members of the Critical Legal Studies movement and feminist and minority legal scholars claim, has merely served in the past to belie and divert attention from those relations of power and conflicts of interest so central to an understanding of modern liberal American society.[43] Such conflicts must be brought out in the open, for everyone to see and discuss. Foundationalist claims about legal reasoning—that it is capable of taking us from legal premises (for example, precedents, notions of rights or of social policy) to determinate answers, determinate solutions to particular problems—must be exposed as the blatant falsehoods that they are. And the voices of all those who have been "textually excluded—those robbed of subjectivity and speech" during the emergence and present reality of the Rule of Law—must be heard.[44]

The Critical Legal Studies movement, explains one of its founding members, Roberto M. Unger, "arose from the leftist tradition in modern legal thought and practice"—a tradition that has been marked by two overriding concerns: the critique of formalism and objectivism, and "the purely instrumental use of legal practice and legal doctrine to advance leftist aims." Formalism sees impersonal, objective purposes, policies, and principles as indispensable components of legal analysis, and objectivism believes that authoritative legal texts embody and sustain an intelligible moral order. Formalism and objectivism come together, according to Unger, in the two most influential schools of legal thought in America today: the law and economics school, which invokes "practical

43. Strictly speaking, neither all the members of the Critical Legal Studies movement nor all the Critical Race Theory scholars with whom this last part of the chapter is concerned may be considered participants in the law and literature debate. As their arguments are constantly referred to and commented on by both the foundationalist and the antifoundationalist camp, however, a survey of the field of law and literature would be incomplete without them.

44. Robin West, "Communities, Texts and Law: Reflections on the Law and Literature Movement," *Yale Journal of Law and the Humanities* 1.1 (1988): 143.

requirements (with normative implications) that supposedly underlie the legal system and its history"; and the rights and principles school, which locates "an underlying moral order that can then serve as the basis for a system of more or less natural rights" within the legal order itself. Taken together, these two sets of ideas express the dictum that "the laws are not merely the outcome of contingent power struggles or of practical pressures lacking in rightful authority." The law and economics and the rights and principles schools are but feeble reminders of the project of nineteenth-century legal science, "the search for a built-in legal structure of democracy and the market."[45] Nothing ever came of this search; finding a universal legal language of democracy and the market has proven to be but a utopian dream. And whereas contemporary law and legal doctrine have done their very best to minimize the subversive implications of this "discovery," Unger and the Critical Legal Studies movement intend to pursue these implications to the bitter end.

What starts as a negative project in Unger's work of debunking or deconstructing the fictions of the two major contemporary schools of legal thought, however, soon turns into a project of "construction." Out of the critique of formalism and objectivism, Unger develops what he calls "the deviationist doctrine." This doctrine aims at enlarging the class of legitimate doctrinal activities so as to incorporate the "fight over the right and possible forms of social life."[46] Such a fight, legal scholars have hitherto maintained, belongs in the political rather than the legal arena. As relations of power and conflicts of interest in regard to class, race, and gender increasingly claim the attention of modern American society and its legal system, however, Unger counters, the genre of legal analysis, as it is presently understood, is far too confined to be of any but superficial use. What does or does not come under the auspices of the law needs to be radically revised.

As the name implies, Unger's deviationist doctrine is first of all a deviation from or redefinition of existing legal theory, and second a doctrine. What Unger offers us, that is, is an "internal argument" rather than a radical departure from the formalism and objectivism he criticizes—"legal doctrine, rightly understood and practiced, is the conduct of internal argument through legal materials." As to why a self-

<hr>

45. Roberto M. Unger, *The Critical Legal Studies Movement* (Cambridge, Mass.: Harvard University Press, 1986), 1, 4, 12, 13, 2, 5.

46. Ibid., 18.

proclaimed radical such as himself should be interested in preserving doctrine in the first place, he defends his position by claiming that "the ideas supply the visionary thought . . . as a complement and a corrective." Working from within a well-established tradition of doctrines of course means that he cannot entirely break free of but must respect the ground rules already laid out, but this drawback is made up for by "the richness of reference to a concrete collective history of ideas and institutions." The concrete history of ideas and institutions to which Unger's internal argument applies, it eventually becomes clear, is the tradition of American liberalism.

> The program I have described . . . represents a superliberalism. It pushes the liberal premises about state and society, about freedom from dependence and governance of social relations by the will, to the point at which they merge into a large ambition: the building of a social world less alien to a self that can always violate the generative rules of its own mental or social constructs and put other rules and other constructs in their place.

For all his subversive critical legal views, it would thus seem, Roberto Unger too has a project: to reform or reconstruct entrenched forms of human connection and communal experience. His point of departure, the concrete collective history of ideas and institutions, as well as the antifoundationalist means with which he aims at reconstructing forms of solidarity and subjectivity, are not unlike Stanley Fish's. But his social ideal itself, thought out as it is "in legal categories and protected by legal rights," displays foundationalist overtones that recall the work of a scholar such as Ronald Dworkin.[47]

In later works, Unger continues his attempt to redirect the attention of contemporary legal theorists to the original promise of liberal democracy. "No component of public interest," he says in *What Should Legal Analysis Become?* from 1996, for example, "seems more important than the commitment to assure people of the practical conditions effectively to enjoy the rights of free citizens, free economic agents, and free individuals." Lawyers and judges have done their very best over the years to uphold the part of the original liberal framework that concerns individual rights—to such an extent, in fact, that rights talk has turned into an obsession. But they have neglected the political side of the liberal demo-

47. Ibid., 18, 117, 91, 18, 41, 37.

cratic project, the attempt to create an institutional structure within which such rights and resources can be justly and fairly redistributed. The reigning belief among jurists that social evils can and should effectively be redressed by legal means alone is not only erroneous, it is also superficial and patronizing in that it deepens the division between elites and the rank-and-file of the benefited groups. "We must be sure that our judicial practice leaves open and available, practically and imaginatively," Unger concludes, "the space on which the real work of social reform can occur."[48]

Unger's criticism of rights talk but general wish to remain within a broad, liberal framework of law is shared by most critical legal scholars. As far as Duncan Kennedy is concerned, for example, rights discourse is "internally inconsistent, vacuous or circular." Within the framework of rights reasoning, a plausible rights justification may be found for virtually any result. This does not so much present a problem in "the occasional case on the periphery where everyone recognizes value judgments have to be made." But in cases where fundamental questions concerning justice between social classes, races, or sexes are at stake, rights reasoning offers no guidance: "because it is logically incoherent and manipulable, traditionally individualist, and willfully blind to the realities of *substantive* inequality, rights discourse is a trap." From the other available Left theoretical approach, that of instrumental Marxism, the radical law student or legal scholar bent on exposing the ideological message behind most legal education—namely, that the legal rules in force not only follow their own inner logic, but also "are a good thing, and . . . are there because they are a good thing"—will not receive much help either.[49] Unlike Left-liberal rights analysis, Marxism is not inherently vacuous. But in the criticism traditional Marxists have always launched against law, they have gone too far; they have failed to see the potential for social change presented by legal activism. Legal rules and rhetoric are far more than "mere window dressing," and what is needed, Kennedy suggests, "is to think about law in a way that will allow one *to enter into it, to criticize without utterly rejecting it.*" "Existentialist-Marxist" and "anarcho-syndicalist" as Kennedy may be, and much as he

48. Roberto M. Unger, *What Should Legal Analysis Become?* (London: Verso, 1996), 47, 113.

49. Duncan Kennedy, *Legal Education and the Reproduction of Hierarchy: A Polemic against the System* (Cambridge, Mass.: AFAR, 1983), 23, 47.

dislikes rights discourse, that is, his mode of resistance is ultimately just as informed by a *"modernist point of view"* as is Unger's.[50]

In a later work, *Sexy Dressing, Etc.: Essays on the Power and Politics of Cultural Identity* (1993), Kennedy's criticism of Marxism and of liberal rights talk is incorporated into a larger theory about the distribution of wealth, income, power, and knowledge in capitalist society. The law plays a much larger "causal" role in distribution than is acknowledged in either conventional Marxist or conventional liberal accounts, he argues. In the former, the relationships of the capitalist class and the proletariat to capital and land do have a legal form, but "that form is merely reflective of an underlying set of material conditions." And in the liberal model, "the distributive issue is present, but understood as a matter of legislative intervention (for example, progressive taxation, labor legislation) to achieve distributive objectives by superimposition on an essentially apolitical private law background."[51] The role assigned in both accounts to the combatants in the economic struggle is too passive. Each of the two parties in a struggle over the distribution of wealth or power does have a certain bargaining power, and it is legal ground rules that determine who gets what kind of bargaining powers.

The basic point that Kennedy makes, following Robert Hale and the legal realists, concerning the centrality of law to distribution may be applied "to distributive issues wherever they arise." Whether we are talking distributive conflicts between classes, races, or genders, we are talking conflicts of interest, and the best way to deal with such conflicts of interest (especially where one is oneself one of the parties involved) is to use the language of cost/benefit or law and economics. Cost/benefit analysis, says Kennedy—bowing in the direction of Richard Posner, yet using the language of law and economics in a way that may not be entirely to Posner's liking—"provides a clearly gendered, male-developed, male-identified language, of which I am a more-or-less native speaker. . . . It is more 'authentic,' for me, than the voice of role-reversed male sensitivity—the voice of total empathy with women as victims."[52]

The decision on Kennedy's part to use the language of cost/benefit or law and economics may be due to what he terms, in *A Critique of*

---

50. Ibid., 25, 26, 84. My emphasis.

51. Duncan Kennedy, *Sexy Dressing, Etc.: Essays on the Power and Politics of Cultural Identity* (Cambridge, Mass.: Harvard University Press, 1993), 90.

52. Ibid., 100, 130.

Adjudication, "the iron law of methodology": "*The more 'hard'* (capable of being counted, highly verifiable and replicable, intersubjectively 'valid'), *the more 'narrow'* (partial, fragmentary, meaningless)." Since the issues that chiefly interest him happen to be "broad" ones like "justice and liveliness," his response is to use "the hard/narrow methods of representation strategically, in the interest of making the soft/broad methods plausible. . . ." Among the broader issues that he deals with in his latest book is the loss of faith in rights discourse and by implication also in the idea of the objectivity of adjudication that resulted in the pursuit of a left/mpm project. His own personal loss of faith in legal reasoning occurred when he was still in law school, Kennedy writes, but as a general process within legal thought, it has gone on at least since Jeremy Bentham criticized the legal arguments of William Blackstone. What is interesting to note in this connection is that Kennedy is careful to point out how "the critique of rights recognizes the reality of rule-making, rule-following, and rule-enforcing behavior . . . Having lost one's faith in rights discourse is perfectly consistent with, indeed often associated with, a passionate belief in radical expansion of citizen rights against the state." In the end, therefore, he and others who have embarked on a left/mpm project "make the leap into commitment or action. That we don't believe we can demonstrate the correctness of our choices doesn't make us nihilists, at least not in our own eyes."[53]

Implicit in the wish on the part of members of CLS to criticize without utterly rejecting liberal legal theory, a number of Critical Race Theory and legal feminist scholars have maintained, is a tendency toward an objectivist epistemology—an epistemology that is based on the norms of the white male. Members of the CLS movement have done a fine job in bringing to light conflicts of interest in American society based on class, but when it comes to conflicts involving race and gender, their record is less impressive. In much the same way that the liberal ideal of equality belies relations of power and hierarchical structures, so the members of CLS have failed to understand and incorporate the reality of gender and race discrimination in contemporary America. With their concern for the worth of the "principles" expressed or unexpressed in a legal text, they have tended to misrepresent, even to exclude, the actual experience, history, culture, and intellectual tradition of

53. Kennedy, *A Critique of Adjudication,* 17, 333–34, 362.

women and people of color. The time has therefore now come to make audible the voices of what Robin West calls "the textually excluded." One way of doing so is to listen carefully to the personal and subjective experiences of those textually excluded Americans. Like Posner, West and other feminist legal scholars see the main potential of the law and literature movement in the possibility of literature to give lawyers an insight into the perspectives of people with whom they normally would not be in contact. The texts by means of which they want to get to know "the concrete other" are not necessarily Posner's great literary texts, transcending "boundaries of period and culture," however; any kind of text will do as long as it speaks of concrete, real-life human experiences.

> We need to listen, then, not just to the great stories and classic texts that constitute our cultural and legal tradition. We also need to listen to the lawyers, legal academics, lay people, poets, novelists, and anyone else who is able to tell the stories of those who have been textually excluded from that cultural past.[54]

Of what do they tell, these stories of the textually excluded? They tell of slavery, of oppression and violence suffered at the hands of a system founded on male notions of power. Yet, they also interestingly enough tell of the value to women and people of color of the (male) discourse of rights talk. Thus, the main feature on the progressive agenda offered by CLS, against which Patricia Williams directs her scorn in her personal story of textual exclusion, *The Alchemy of Race and Rights,* for example, is the dismissal of rights talk. When Tushnet, Kennedy, and other members of CLS argue that rights discourse is alienating and legitimates hierarchy, she points out, as we saw in chapter five, they tend to forget how historically, within the black community, the prospect of attaining important legal rights has always been a semireligious source of hope.

> "Rights" feels new in the mouths of most black people. It is still deliciously empowering to say. It is the magic wand of visibility and invisibility, of inclusion and exclusion, of power and no power. The concept of rights, both positive and negative, is the marker of our citizenship, our relation to others. . . . In discarding rights altogether, one discards a

54. West, "Communities, Texts and Law," 143, 156.

symbol too deeply enmeshed in the psyche of the oppressed to lose without trauma and much resistance.[55]

Patricia Williams's wish to "Reconstruct Ideals from Deconstructed Rights" is shared by many CRT and feminist legal scholars.[56] As we saw in chapter six, the conclusion most often reached by American feminists in their criticism of male rights talk is not to disregard it altogether and to strike out in a new direction, but to "embed rights within relationships"—to embed, that is, in a feminist or female framework of values the promise of liberty and equality for all held out by the American tradition of rights talk. What applies to the debate between legal positivists and proponents of natural law, therefore, also applies to the quarrel between CLS and legal feminists and minority scholars: "there is less debate here than the debaters believe."[57] Their differences of opinion are ultimately of minor importance compared to what these two groups of scholars on the Left have in common, a progressive agenda that exposes hierarchical structures and power relations in today's America, focuses on the concrete and local, believes in the law as a means to social change, and prefers to fight from *within* the liberal tradition of American law. We are talking reconstruction rather than deconstruction, inclusion into the discourse of rights rather than downright refusal to continue that discourse.

This willingness on the part of antifoundationalist scholars, who spend much of their time and energy exposing the contingent and relativistic nature of the law and legal theory and the power struggles at the heart of American liberal thinking, to remain dedicated to the belief in liberal legal discourse as an effective discourse to bring about social change amounts to a leap of legal faith. What we see here are the contours of an antifoundationalist project. Though based on a critically pragmatic or relativistic assessment of the law as naked power, that is, on the very antithesis of foundationalist myths about abstract, universal legal principles, this antifoundationalist project works toward much the same end as does the project undertaken by scholars of a foundationalist observation: a reaffirmation of the modernist legal tradition that pro-

---

55. Patricia J. Williams, *The Alchemy of Race and Rights: Diary of a Law Professor* (Cambridge, Mass.: Harvard University Press, 1991), 164, 165.

56. Williams, "Alchemical Notes: Reconstructing Ideals from Deconstructed Rights," *Harvard Civil Rights–Civil Liberties Review* 22 (1987).

57. Lovibond, "Feminism and Postmodernism," 11.

vides the foundation not only for American dreams of fundamental individual freedoms and rights, but also for maintaining the American nation. Were the postmodern implications of the antifoundationalist progressive agenda to be pursued to their final conclusions, antifoundationalists are no less aware than are their foundationalist opponents, not much would remain of the legal system as "the institutional base for our nationhood."[58] Liberal legal discourse, to rephrase Patricia Williams slightly, is and remains the marker of American citizenship.

To sum up: the disagreements among the participants in the law and literature debate are many and extensive. Yet, when it comes to one of the main features of liberal democracy, American style, the reliance on the law as a force for social change and social cohesion, foundationalists and antifoundationalists alike show themselves ready to defend it—even if such a defense takes a leap of legal faith. This pledge of renewed faith in law's possibilities gives to antifoundationalist arguments an overtone of foundationalist beliefs in universal, enduring values, but it also provides foundationalist emphases on principles and abstract themes with a solid foundation in *practice*. For virtually all the scholars I have dealt with here, it is with the concrete, everyday experiences and customs of the community that every legal argument must start. What we see once again, that is, is practice and theory working hand in hand. It is law as custom transformed or common law to which these scholars remain dedicated. When Dworkin, for example, invokes the aesthetic model of the chain novel as holding out a promise of textual constraint, as we saw, he sees the similarity between literary and legal interpretation as being most apparent when judges decide common-law cases. And when both Unger and Kennedy express the wish to "think about law in a way that will allow one to enter into it, to criticize without utterly rejecting it," they operate within the flexible framework of the common law.

The strength of the common law, it bears repeating, has always been twofold: its doubly dualist nature—material as well as ideological, and spreading upward from the bottom and not merely downward from the top—and its ability to respond, in time, to changes that are taking place in society so as to assimilate these changes into the existing system without bursting its bonds. For most American scholars, who are interested in issues relating to the American experiment and American democracy, therefore, the common law provides a framework and a ver-

58. Karst, *Belonging to America*, 215.

nacular that is adaptable enough to make forays into postmodern ways of thinking unattractive.

CONCLUDING REMARKS

To have or not to have a project—that is one of the major questions under discussion in the law and literature debate. The project in question concerns the feasibility of upholding, in the current cultural, intellectual, and political moment of postmodernity with its emphasis on plurality and diversity over authoritarian unity, the belief in liberal legal discourse as an effective discourse to bring about social change and to act as a kind of "cultural glue." Realizing that what is at stake here is the modernist legal foundation on which the American experiment rests and thus ultimately nothing less than American self-identification, most of the participants in the law and literature debate have shown an unwillingness to endorse current critical intellectual tendencies in their entirety. Even scholars who would otherwise lend a sympathetic ear to postmodern theories have warned that what may seem attractive as a thought experiment in the field of literary theory may turn out within the framework of legal practice to have direct and unpleasant effects.

The dividing line in the law and literature debate roughly follows the old tension between what Stanley Fish calls foundationalism and anti-foundationalism: on the one hand, the belief in universal, enduring values and literal meaning, serving as a constraint on interpretation; and, on the other, the belief in contingent and relative values subject to the accidents of history and culture, and the unavailability of literal meaning. That foundationalists are prepared to go to war to defend the old liberal belief in law's possibilities should come as no surprise. It is somewhat more surprising to encounter a similar willingness in scholars of an antifoundationalist observation. The intellectual move these latter make most of all resembles a leap of legal faith—they pledge allegiance to the law as a force for social change and social cohesion knowing full well that the law has fabricated its own authority and authenticity. This move is a common-law move in the sense that it is founded on an insight into the concrete *mores* of American society, yet has as its aim something more lofty and intangible; the affirmation of what Kenneth Karst calls the civic culture's ideals. To the extent that it has an inner logic, this logic is familiar to us from American culture, high as well as low. Countless are the cultural texts that, after setting out to expose the rottenness at the core of the American democracy by means of showing the sorry state in which the legal system currently finds itself, then move on to affirm the promise of fundamental legal rights expressed in the Constitution and the other legal texts that form the foundation for American nationhood. For once, it would thus seem, what is going on in academia mirrors what is going on in American culture at large.

Conclusion

While Americans look to the courts to pronounce the norms for many relation-ships, only in extreme cases do they resort to actual enforcement. In this light, civil justice is as much a mechanism for community debate and civic instruc-tion as for redressing legal wrongs. A society as culturally heterogeneous and morally centered as ours may have a fundamental need for such a mechanism. If providing civic instruction is an undeclared function of the judiciary, then calculation of the costs and benefits of civil justice should take that benefit into account.

Geoffrey C. Hazard and Michele Taruffo, *American Civil Procedure*

Government does teach lessons in behavior, and a time-honored method of getting its pupils' attention is the criminal law.

Kenneth L. Karst, *Law's Promise, Law's Expression*

But spectator sport though it may have been, O.J.-mania was still a dangerous game, indeed a deadly political exercise. It was that great conversation about race Lani Guinier implored us Americans to have . . . perhaps it would do us a world of good to just own up to the fact that racial passion plays, from the Scottsboro Boys to the Clarence Thomas hearings, have emerged as a uniquely American art form, like jazz—our own stylized form of Kabuki theater.

Patricia Williams, "American Kabuki"

I n the mid-1990s, most foreigners were amazed at and perhaps also slightly amused by the American obsession with the O. J. Simpson murder trial—carried live on all three national television networks and on CNN. As time has gone by, it has become clear that this obsession may not be accounted for solely in terms of the entertainment value—high as it may have been—of this "event." "Something more was going on," says Toni Morrison in her introduction to *Birth of a Nation 'hood: Gaze, Script, and Spectacle in the O. J. Simpson Case,* "something more than a hot property of mayhem loaded with the thrill that a mixture of fame, sex, death, money and race produces."[1] That something was the construction by the mass media of an official public story that refused to let alternative stories be heard. Underneath the already understood and already agreed upon interpretation of what had happened and why, broadcast by the media as public truth, there was a cultural story—a cultural story about race, gender, class, and justice in American society. In much the same way that the intense controversy surrounding the Clarence Thomas confirmation hearings in 1991 raised issues of profound social and political importance,[2] it was during and as a result of the O. J. Simpson trial that a much-needed post–Civil Rights discourse on race, gender, class, and justice was initiated.

It is precisely the way in which the law has become the forum for discussion of issues of importance to the American people that has been the concern of this book. The American legal system and American law, it has been argued throughout, occupy a unique position in American culture and society. Americans may complain about litigiousness and overcrowded court dockets, about greedy lawyers and an adversarial system run wild, but if and when they have problems it is to their lawyers and their courts that they turn for help. This is reflected in the cultural life of the nation. Countless are the cultural texts—books, films, and television series—that, after setting out to expose the sorry state of American law, then move on to affirm its promise. Within the context of this book, whether we talk about the nonfiction works of legal and

---

1. Toni Morrison, "Introduction," in Toni Morrison and Claudia Brodsky Lacour, *Birth of a Nation 'hood: Gaze, Script, and Spectacle in the O. J. Simpson Case* (New York: Pantheon Books, 1997), xv.

2. The subtitle of *Race-ing, Justice, En-gendering, Power*—the volume that Toni Morrison edited as a response to the Clarence Thomas hearings—is "Essays on Anita Hill, Clarence Thomas, and the Construction of Social Reality" (New York: Pantheon Books, 1992). "In addition to what was taking place," Morrison writes in her introduction, "something was happening . . . It became clear, finally, what took place: a black male nominee to the Supreme Court was confirmed amid a controversy that raised and buried issues of profound social significance" (x).

cultural commentators Melissa Fay Greene and David L. Kirp, John P. Dwyer, and Larry A. Rosenthal (discussed in chapter one), the popular novels of Tom Wolfe, Scott Turow, and Sara Paretsky (discussed in chapters two, three, and six, respectively), the television series *The People's Court* (discussed in chapter four), the more serious fiction of Margaret Atwood and William Gaddis (discussed in chapters seven and eight), the storytelling expositions of legal issues by law professors Derrick Bell and Patricia Williams (discussed in chapter five), or the treatments of law as literature by members of the legal academy (discussed in chapter nine), the faith in legal remedies, though sorely tried, even disappointed, is seen to continue.

American law may perhaps best be described as a Janus-like creature with two distinct, yet connected "faces." One of these is a rebellious and democratic one. It is the one we know the best and the one that comes to mind when we think and talk about American litigiousness and law-permeation. "I'll see you in court" and "it is my *right* to . . ." are phrases we associate with this face of the law. We hear them uttered over and over again by Americans who consider it their birthright as American citizens to have their day in court, and for whom the most effective path to fighting for a better life is the path of the law.

"Law begins where community ends," Jerold S. Auerbach once reminded us.[3] The success of nonlegal dispute settlement has always depended upon a coherent community vision. Once such community vision wanes—be it of a religious, political, or moral kind—close-knit communities, in which the adversarial framework of legal argumentation is seen as destructive to group solidarity, will allow conflicts to be settled legally. A pervasive legal culture often *increases* the likelihood of conflict and prohibits the kind of communication needed in a multicultural society. Within the adversarial framework of American law, a trial is looked upon as a struggle to be continued until there is a clear winner and loser. Conflicts are resolved in such a way that relationships will be destroyed rather than preserved. With its tendency toward a rhetoric of absolutism and exaggeration, moreover, American rights talk often results in unrealistic expectations that tend to heighten social

---

3. Jerold S. Auerbach, *Justice without Law? Resolving Disputes without Lawyers* (New York: Oxford University Press, 1983), 5.

conflict. When claims or positions are formulated as absolute rights, there is no common ground for negotiation and compromise.

The second face or level of American law is a more conservative, unity-seeking one. This face is the more interesting of the two and the one that has been discussed in this book. In this latter manifestation, the law operates at a more theoretical, even ideological level. Down through American history, it has provided a common bond among all the various subcultures, a common forum in which to raise and possibly resolve not only legal disputes, but also disputes of a moral and political kind. As one minority group after another has fought to be included in the American dream, to gain access to those rights and freedoms outlined in the Constitution, they have looked to law as a means by which change can be accomplished. This has made of the law less a matter of remote privilege and exclusion and more a part of daily affairs. Integration into American society and identity, national as well as personal, has come to be associated in the minds of most Americans with the law.

One individualistic and centrifugal, as it were, the other centripetal, working toward agreement and consensus, both levels of American law are of immediate importance in modern pluralistic America in catering to the diverse individual needs of its multiple (sub)cultures while simultaneously helping to provide a common bond. With its double appeal or attraction, in practice allowing the individual to fight for the right to live a good life while providing at a more theoretical-emotional level, as a civil religion, a secular version of truth and meaning, the law comes closer to satisfying the demands of contemporary Americans than any other currently available ideology or faith.

For the development of the law into a secular religion and of the United States into a law-permeated country, the common law—broadly conceived as a particular understanding of law, and a way of arguing legally, held by judges and citizens alike, that operates as much in constitutional cases as in areas like torts and contracts—has provided an ideal instrument. Focusing on concrete cases, emphasizing the practical wisdom of judges, understanding law to have a moral dimension, and perceiving law to spread upward from the bottom and not merely downward from the top, the common law has provided a vocabulary that recognizes people's hopes for rights and justice and a forum in which a common discussion may be conducted within a multicultural society. The semireligious overtones of much current law-talk, the attempt made by many to find in the law, as formerly in religion, explanations and answers to the "big" questions in life, are made possible by the common law's origin in and continued reliance on natural law. The kind of redemption sought and found in the common law is an individualistically centered one, one that talks less about responsibilities than about rights—and one that firmly bases American notions of community upon individual pursuits of happiness.

Works Cited or Referred To

Abel, Richard L. *American Lawyers.* New York: Oxford University Press, 1989.

Ackerman, Bruce. *We the People: Foundations.* Cambridge, Mass.: Harvard University Press, 1993.

Adams, Henry. *The Education of Henry Adams.* Boston: Houghton Mifflin Co., 1918; rpt. 1973.

Allen, Robert C. *Speaking of Soap Operas.* Chapel Hill: University of North Carolina Press, 1985.

Appleby, Joyce. "Recovering America's Historic Diversity: Beyond Exceptionalism." *Journal of American History* 79 (1992): 419–431.

Atwood, Margaret. *The Handmaid's Tale.* New York: Fawcett Crest, 1985.

——. *Surfacing.* New York: Fawcett Crest, 1972.

Auerbach, Jerold S. *Justice without Law? Resolving Disputes without Lawyers.* New York: Oxford University Press, 1983.

Baird, Robert M., and Stuart E. Rosenbaum, eds. *The Ethics of Abortion: Pro-Life v. Pro-Choice.* Buffalo: Prometheus Books, 1993.

Barron, Susan. "Lights! Camera! Justice!" *The Washingtonian,* July 1989.

Bartlett, Katharine T., and Rosanne Kennedy, eds. *Feminist Legal Theory.* Boulder, Colo.: Westview Press, 1991.

Belkin, Lisa. "Realism of the Courtroom Captivates TV-Audiences." *New York Times,* July 22, 1987.

Bell, Daniel. "The 'Hegelian Secret': Civil Society and American Exceptionalism." In *Is America Different? A New Look at American Exceptionalism,* ed. Byron E. Shafer. New York: Oxford University Press, 1991.

Bell, Derrick. *And We Are Not Saved: The Elusive Quest for Racial Justice.* New York: Basic Books, 1987.

———. *Faces at the Bottom of the Well: The Permanence of Racism.* New York: Basic Books, 1992.

———. *Gospel Choirs: Psalms of Survival in an Alien Land Called Home.* New York: Basic Books, 1996.

———. "Who's Afraid of Critical Race Theory?" *University of Illinois Law Review* 1995.4 (1995): 893–910.

Bercovitch, Sacvan. *The American Jeremiad.* Madison: University of Wisconsin Press, 1978.

Berman, Harold J. *Law and Revolution: The Formation of the Western Legal Tradition.* Cambridge, Mass.: Harvard University Press, 1983.

Binyon, T. J. *Murder Will Out: The Detective in Fiction.* Oxford: Oxford University Press, 1989.

Bollinger, Lee C. *The Tolerant Society.* New York: Oxford University Press, 1986.

Cawelti, John C. *Adventure, Mystery, and Romance: Formula Stories as Art and Popular Culture.* Chicago: University of Chicago Press, 1976.

Chrisman, Robert, and Robert C. Allen, eds. *Court of Appeal: The Black Community Speaks Out on the Racial and Sexual Politics of Clarence Thomas vs. Anita Hill.* New York: Ballantine Books, 1992.

Clark, Leroy D. "Critique of Professor Derrick Bell's Thesis of the Permanence of Racism and His Strategy of Confrontation." *Denver University Law Review* 73.1 (1995): 23–50.

Cornell, Drucilla. "The Double-Prized World: Myth, Allegory, and the Feminine." *Cornell Law Review* 75 (1990): 644–699.

Cowart, David. "Heritage and Deracination in Walker's 'Everyday Use.'" *Studies in Short Fiction,* 33.2 (1996): 171–184.

Cranny-Francis, Anne. *Feminist Fiction: Feminist Uses of Generic Fiction.* Cambridge: Polity Press, 1990.

Dahrendorf, Ralph. *Law and Order.* The Hamlyn Lectures. London: Stevens & Sons, 1985.

Darden, Christopher A., with Jess Walter. *In Contempt.* New York: Regan Books, 1996.

Davidson, Cathy N. "A Feminist '1984': Margaret Atwood Talks about Her Exciting New Novel." *MS.,* Feb. 1986.

Delgado, Richard. "The Ethereal Scholar: Does CLS Have What Minorities Want?" *Harvard Civil Rights–Civil Liberties Law Review* 22 (1987): 301–22.

Demers, Susan V. "The Failures of Litigation as a Tool for the Development of Social Welfare Policy." *Fordham Urban Law Journal* 22.4 (1995): 1009–1050.

Dershowitz, Alan. "The Verdict." *American Film,* Dec. 1987.

Douzinas, Costas, and Ronnie Warrington, with Shaun McVeigh. *Postmodern Jurisprudence: The Law of the Text in the Texts of Law.* London: Routledge, 1991.

DuBois, Ellen, Mary C. Dunlap, Carol J. Gilligan, Catharine A. MacKinnon, and Carrie J. Menkel-Meadow. "Feminist Discourse, Moral Values, and the Law: A Conversation." *Buffalo Law Review* 34 (1985): 11–87.

Dworkin, Ronald. "Hard Cases." *Harvard Law Review* 88.6 (1975): 1057–1109.

——. "Law as Interpretation." *Texas Law Review* 60.3 (1982): 527–50.

——. *Law's Empire.* Cambridge, Mass.: Belknap Press, 1986.

——. *Life's Dominion: An Argument about Abortion, Euthanasia, and Individual Freedom.* New York: Knopf, 1993.

Eagleton, Mary, ed. *Feminist Literary Criticism.* London: Longman, 1991.

Ehrenreich, Barbara. "Feminism's Phantoms." *The New Republic,* Mar. 17, 1986, 33–35.

Eisenberg, Melvin Aron. *The Nature of the Common Law.* Cambridge, Mass.: Harvard University Press, 1988.

Eliot, T. S. *Selected Essays.* London: Faber and Faber, 1951.

Erdrich, Louise. *Tracks.* London: Pan Books Ltd., 1989.

Ferguson, Robert A. *Law and Letters in American Culture.* Cambridge, Mass.: Harvard University Press, 1984.

——. " 'Mysterious Obligation': Jefferson's *Notes on the State of Virginia.*" *American Literature,* 52.3 (1980). Reprinted in Peter S. Onuf, ed., *The New American Nation, 1775–1820,* vol. 12, *American Culture 1776–1815.* New York & London: Garland Publishing, 1991.

Fish, Stanley. *Doing What Comes Naturally: Change, Rhetoric, and the Practice and Theory in Literary and Legal Studies.* Durham, N.C.: Duke University Press, 1989.

——. *There's No Such Thing as Free Speech: And It's a Good Thing Too.* New York: Oxford University Press, 1994.

Fleming, James E. "Securing Deliberative Autonomy." *Stanford Law Review* 48 (1995): 1–71.

Friedman, Lawrence M. *A History of American Law.* New York: Simon & Schuster, 1973.

Frug, Mary Joe. *Postmodern Legal Feminism.* New York: Routledge, 1992.

Hazard, Geoffrey C., and Michele Taruffo, *American Civil Procedure.* New Haven: Yale University Press, 1993.

Higgins, Tracy E. " 'By Reason of Their Sex': Feminist Theory, Postmodernism, and Justice." *Cornell Law Review* 80.6 (1995): 1536–1594.

Hixson, Richard F. *Privacy in a Public Society: Human Rights in Conflict.* New York: Oxford University Press, 1987.

Holquist, Michael. "Whodunit and Other Questions: Metaphysical Detective Stories in Post-War Fiction." *New Literary History* 3 (1971): 135–56.

Horwitz, Morton. "Rights." *Harvard Civil Rights–Civil Liberties Law Review* 23.2 (1988): 393–406.

——. *The Transformation of American Law, 1870–1960.* Cambridge, Mass.: Harvard University Press, 1991.

——. *The Transformation of American Law, 1700–1860.* Cambridge, Mass.: Harvard University Press, 1977.

Kahlenberg, Richard D. *Broken Contract: A Memoir of Harvard Law School.* New York: Hill and Wang, 1992.

Kammen, Michael. "The Problem of American Exceptionalism: A Reconsideration." *American Quarterly* 45.1 (1993): 1–43.

Karst, Kenneth L. *Belonging to America: Equal Citizenship and the Constitution.* New Haven, Conn.: Yale University Press, 1989.

——. *Law's Promise, Law's Expression: Visions of Power in the Politics of Race, Gender, and Religion.* New Haven, Conn.: Yale University Press, 1993.

——. "Myths of Identity: Individual and Group Portraits of Race and Sexual Orientation." *UCLA Law Review* 43.2 (1995): 263–369.

Kennedy, Duncan. *A Critique of Adjudication (fin de siècle).* Cambridge, Mass.: Harvard University Press, 1997.

——. *Legal Education and the Reproduction of Hierarchy: A Polemic against the System.* Cambridge, Mass.: AFAR, 1983.

——. *Sexy Dressing, Etc.: Essays on the Power and Politics of Cultural Identity.* Cambridge, Mass.: Harvard University Press, 1993.

Kennedy, Randall L. "Derrick Bell's Apologia for Minister Farrakhan: An Intellectual and Moral Disaster." *Reconstruction* 2.1 (1992): 92–96.

——. "Racial Critiques of Legal Academia." *Harvard Law Review* 102 (1989): 1745–1819.

Kirp, David L., John P. Dwyer, and Larry A. Rosenthal. *Our Town: Race, Housing, and the Soul of Suburbia.* New Brunswick, N.J.: Rutgers University Press, 1995.

Kluger, Richard J. *Simple Justice: The History of Brown v. Board of Education and Black America's Struggle for Equality.* New York: Knopf, 1976.

Kronman, Anthony T. *The Lost Lawyer: Failing Ideals of the Legal Profession.* Cambridge, Mass.: Harvard University Press, 1993.

Lazarus, Edward. *Black Hills/White Justice. The Sioux Nation Versus the United States, 1775 to the Present.* New York: Harper Collins, 1991.

Leader, Zachary. "Jarndyce U.S.A." *Times Literary Supplement* No. 4757, June 3, 1994.

Levinson, Sanford. *Constitutional Faith.* Princeton, N.J.: Princeton University Press, 1988.

Li, Victor H. *Law without Lawyers: A Comparative View of Law in China and the U.S.* Stanford, Calif.: The Portable Stanford, 1977.

Lieberman, Jethro K. *The Litigious Society.* New York: Basic Books, 1981.

Lind, Douglas. "A Matter of Utility: Dworkin on Morality, Integrity, and Making Law the Best It Can Be." *Constitutional Law Journal* 6.2 (1996): 631–81.

Lovibond, Sabina. "Feminism and Postmodernism." *New Left Review* 178 (1989): 5–28.

Luker, Kristin. *Abortion and the Politics of Motherhood*. Berkeley: University of California Press, 1984.

Macauley, Stewart, Lawrence M. Friedman, and John Stookey. *Law and Society: Readings on the Social Study of Law*. New York: Norton & Co., 1995.

MacKinnon, Catharine. *Sexual Harassment of Working Women*. New Haven, Conn.: Yale University Press, 1979.

——. "Feminism, Marxism, Method, and the State: Toward a Feminist Jurisprudence." *Signs* 8.4 (1983): 635–58.

——. *Feminism Unmodified: Discourses on Life and Law*. Cambridge, Mass.: Harvard University Press, 1987.

——. *Only Words*. Cambridge, Mass.: Harvard University Press, 1993.

Matsuda, Mari J. "Looking to the Bottom: Critical Legal Studies and Reparations." *Harvard Civil Rights–Civil Liberties Law Review* 22 (1987): 323–99.

McCombs, Judith, ed. *Critical Essays on Margaret Atwood*. Boston: G. K. Hall & Co., 1988.

Menkel-Meadow, Carrie. "Feminist Legal Theory, Critical Legal Studies, and Legal Education or 'The Fem-Crits Go to Law School.'" *Journal of Legal Education* 38 (1985): 61–85.

Minow, Martha. *Making All the Difference: Inclusion, Exclusion, and American Law*. Ithaca, N.Y.: Cornell University Press, 1990.

Moll, Richard W. *The Lure of Law: Why People Become Lawyers, and What the Profession Does to Them*. New York: Penguin Books, 1990.

Morrison, Toni. *Playing in the Dark: Whiteness and the Literary Imagination*. Cambridge, Mass.: Harvard University Press, 1992.

——, ed. *Race-ing, Justice, En-gendering Power: Essays on Anita Hill, Clarence Thomas, and the Construction of Social Reality*. New York: Pantheon Books, 1992.

Morrison, Toni, and Claudia Brodsky Lacour, eds. *Birth of a Nation 'hood: Gaze, Script, and Spectacle in the O. J. Simpson Case*. New York: Pantheon Books, 1997.

Mullen, R. D., and Darko Suvin, eds. *Science Fiction Studies: Selected Articles on Science Fiction, 1973–75*. Boston: Gregg Press, 1976.

Nicholson, Colin, ed. *Margaret Atwood: Writing and Subjectivity*. London: St. Martin's Press, 1994.

Olson, Walter K. *The Litigation Explosion: What Happened When America Unleashed the Lawsuit*. New York: Dutton, 1991.

Papke, David Ray. "Law in American Culture: An Overview." *Journal of American Culture* 15.1 (1992): 3–14.

Paretsky, Sara. *Bitter Medicine.* New York: Penguin Books, [1987], 1988.

———. *Blood Shot.* New York: Dell Publishing, 1988.

———. *Burn Marks.* New York: Dell Publishing, 1990.

———. *Deadlock.* New York: Dell Publishing, 1984.

———. *Ghost Country.* New York: Delacorte Press, 1998.

———. *Guardian Angel.* New York: Dell Publishing, 1992.

———. *Indemnity Only.* New York: Dell Publishing, 1982.

———. *Killing Orders.* New York: Ballantine Books, 1985.

———. *Tunnel Vision.* London: Hamish Hamilton, 1993.

———. *Windy City Blues.* New York: Delacorte Press, 1995.

Parker, Richard D. *"Here the People Rule": A Constitutional Populist Manifesto.* Cambridge, Mass.: Harvard University Press, 1994.

Parrinder, Patrick, ed. *Science Fiction: A Critical Guide.* London: Longman, 1979.

Petchesky, Rosalind Pollack. *Abortion and Women's Choice: The State, Sexuality and Reproductive Freedom.* Boston: Northeastern University Press, 1984.

Posner, Richard A. *Law and Literature: A Misunderstood Relation.* Cambridge, Mass.: Harvard University Press, 1988.

———. *The Problems of Jurisprudence.* Cambridge, Mass.: Harvard University Press, 1990.

———. *Overcoming Law.* Cambridge, Mass.: Harvard University Press, 1995.

Prendergast, Christopher. *Balzac: Fiction and Melodrama.* London: Edward Arnold, Ltd., 1978.

Raban, Jonathan. "At Home in Babel." *New York Review of Books,* Feb. 17, 1994.

Radway, Janice. *Reading the Romance.* Chapel Hill: University of North Carolina Press, 1984.

Rembar, Charles. *The Law of the Land: The Evolution of Our Legal System.* New York: Harper & Row, 1989.

Rigney, Barbara Hill. *Margaret Atwood.* London: Macmillan, 1987.

Rosenberg, Gerald. *The Hollow Hope.* Chicago: University of Chicago Press, 1991.

Sartori, Giovanni. *The Theory of Democracy Revisited: Vol. II.* Chatham, N.J.: Chatham House Publishers, 1987.

Schleier, Curt. " 'People's Court' Endured Long Trial before Verdict." *Advertising Age,* Jan. 10, 1985.

Sherry, Suzanna. "Civic Virtue and the Feminine Voice in Constitutional Adjudication." *Virginia Law Review* 72 (1986): 543–616.

Showalter, Elaine. *A Literature of Their Own: British Women Novelists from Brontë to Lessing.* Princeton, N.J.: Princeton University Press, 1977.

Slade, Margot. " 'The People's Court': The Case for and against It." *New York Times* (The Law), May 5, 1989.

Speiser, Stuart M. *Lawyers and the American Dream.* New York: M. Evans & Co., 1993.

Suvin, Darko. *Metamorphoses of Science Fiction: On the Poetics and History of a Literary Genre.* New Haven, Conn.: Yale University Press, 1979.

Tanner, Tony. *City of Words: A Study of American Fiction in the Mid-Twentieth Century.* London: Jonathan Cape Ltd., 1971.

Tocqueville, Alexis de. *Democracy in America.* New York: Doubleday & Co., [1835 and 1840], 1969.

Tribe, Laurence H. *Abortion: The Clash of Absolutes.* New York: Norton, 1992.

Tribe, Laurence H., and Michael C. Dorf. *On Reading the Constitution.* Cambridge, Mass.: Harvard University Press, 1991.

Turow, Scott. *The Burden of Proof.* New York: Farrar, Straus, Giroux, 1990.

——. *The Laws of Our Fathers.* New York: Warner Books, 1996.

——. *One L.* New York: Warner Books, 1977.

——. *Pleading Guilty.* New York: Viking, 1993.

——. *Presumed Innocent.* New York: Warner Books, 1987.

Tushnet, Mark. "An Essay on Rights." *Texas Law Review* 62.8 (1984): 1363–1403.

Unger, Roberto M. *The Critical Legal Studies Movement.* Cambridge, Mass.: Harvard University Press, 1986.

——. *What Should Legal Analysis Become?* London: Verso, 1996.

Wapner, Joseph A. *A View from the Bench.* New York: Penguin Books, 1987.

Ward, Cynthia. "The Radical Feminist Defense of Individualism." *Northwestern University Law Review* 89.3 (1995): 871–99.

Warren, Samuel D., and Louis D. Brandeis. "The Right to Privacy." *Harvard Law Review* 4.5 (1890): 193–220.

Weisberg, Robert. "The Law-Literature Enterprise." *Yale Journal of Law and the Humanities* 1.1 (1988): 1–67.

——. "Taking Law Seriously." *Yale Journal of Law and the Humanities* 7.2 (1995): 445–55.

Wellington, Harry H. *Interpreting the Constitution.* New Haven, Conn.: Yale University Press, 1990.

West, Robin. "Communities, Texts, and Law: Reflections on the Law and Literature Movement." *Yale Journal of Law and the Humanities* 1.1 (1988): 129–56.

Williams, Patricia. "Alchemical Notes: Reconstructing Ideals from Deconstructed Rights." *Harvard Civil Rights–Civil Liberties Law Review* 22 (1987): 401–432.

——. *The Alchemy of Race and Rights: Diary of a Law Professor.* Cambridge, Mass.: Harvard University Press, 1991.

——. "American Kabuki." See Morrison and Lacour.

——. *The Rooster's Egg: On the Persistence of Prejudice.* Cambridge, Mass.: Harvard University Press, 1995.

Wilson, William Julius. *The Truly Disadvantaged: The Inner City, the Underclass, and Public Policy.* Chicago: University of Chicago Press, 1990.

Wolfe, Tom. *The Bonfire of the Vanities.* New York: Bantam Books, 1987.

Wood, Gordon S. "The Origins of Judicial Review." *Suffolk University Law Review* 22 (1988): 1293–1307.

Index

Abel, Richard L., 3
abortion, 163–92; as intra-feminist
    polemic, 180–87; religion and, 182,
    187–89
Ackerman, Bruce, 22
Adams, Henry, 61
Africanism, 129
Allen, Robert C., 100
American exceptionalism, 13; law and,
    14–15
Amis, Kingsley, 189–90
Appleby, Joyce, 13–14, 24
Atwood, Margaret, 167–68, 175–80, 221
Auerbach, Jerold S.: and law as cultural
    force, 2; and patterns being more
    important than particulars, 12; and
    American urges to sue, 44; and plural-
    ism, 50; and justice without law, 58;
    and nonlegal dispute settlement in
    colonial society, 179–80; and law and
    community, 252

Babbitt, Irving, 219
Bell, Daniel, 16–17
Bell, Derrick: and criticism of liberal

rights discourse, 110–19; and creation
    of a new legal-literary genre, 126–27
Bercovitch, Sacvan, 179
Berman, Harold J., 24
Binyon, T. J., 148
Black Hills claim, 108–9
Bollinger, Lee C., 89–90
Bork, Robert, 174
Bracamonte, Jose A., 119
Brown v. Board of Education of Topeka, 4,
    20

case method, of instruction, 72–74. *See
    also* Kronman, Anthony
Cawelti, John C., 148, 150
Chandler, Raymond, 149
civic-mindedness, lawyers and, 21. *See also*
    Kronman, Anthony
civil religion, law as, 2
civil rights, fight for, 25–31
civil society, 16–17
Cixous, Hélène, 135, 139
common law, 6; history of, 21–24, 42–43;
    inclusiveness of, 35–37; dualist nature
    of, 23–24, 146–48; as instrument of